GRIM
SHADOWS
FALLING

GRIM
SHADOWS
FALLING

HAUNTING TALES FROM

TERRIFYING PLACES

BENJAMIN S. JEFFRIES

Schiffer Publishing Ltd

4880 Lower Valley Road • Atglen, PA 19310

ACKNOWLEDGMENTS

Pete Schiffer and Schiffer Publishing for giving me a chance;

My fearless and ever-amazing editors, Tina Libby and Dinah Roseberry;

The Jeffries / Yuill Clans: Arliss and Linda (Ma and Pa), Dan and Megan, Tyler and Josie, Becky and Damon, Anthony and Eric, Chuck and Aunt Susie Wynn, Uncle Wes and Aunt Sheryl;

My 765 Paranormal family: Denny, Justin, Ryan, Zach, Chelsie, Lauren, Travis, Megan, Amanda, Samantha, and Rich;

Traci Emerson and her daughter Hope;

Rob and Vicky Graves, for being such gracious hosts in their home, Fox Hollow Farm;

Jim Harold and The Paranormal Podcast;

Peggy at Barnes & Noble – Lafayette;

Marla Brooks at Stirring The Cauldron;

Reverend Tim Shaw from The Black Cat Lounge;

Ryleigh Black and Amy Lynn at Club Para;

Vonda McDaniel at The Haunted Harvest Moon;

Daniel Bautz of The Grand Dark Conspiracy;

Lauren Sedam from the Lafayette Journal and Courier;

Debe Branning from Examiner.com;

My label mate and the mayor of Saucerville, Jordan Hofer;

Polly Gear and Mountaineer Paranormal;

Cory Stolberg and Nexus Paranormal;

Stephen Black and Black Cross Paranormal;

Robert Eastes and Jeffrey Morgan of Original Paranormal Paparazzi;

Darrell, Theresa, and Jay at Poasttown Elementary;

The Eastes Family of Greenfield, Indiana, for their blessings and help with "Black Moon Manor";

Dan Guthrie and The Haunted Entertainment Awards;

Bishop James Long, Jeff Mudgett, Ursula Bielski, Duane Datzman;

Dan T. Hall, Sharon Coyle-Farley and Rolling Hills Asylum, Carolyn Bonney Peterson;

Danielle Pitcher-Garrison, Joe and Linda Moczan, Kimberly Walters, Troy Taylor, Jack, Crystal, and Belle Brant, Mark and Kari Beeler, Stacey Toeppe, Mike Bennett, Rob Elliot, Robin Rossitter, Brandi Diley, John and Kristie Graves, Jennifer Clawson Murray, Valerie Mahan, Heather Marshall Letizia, JR McLaughlin, David Stoker, Deb Miller, Rod Dimmick, Jim and Barb Hess, Scot Lawyer, Gena Silverstorm Jones, Darlene Harrison, Angel Sells of Eerie Voices Paranormal, and Brenda Mudrack.

And last, but certainly not least, all of my readers, fans, friends, and fiends, both old and new, for trying out Lost In The Darkness and sticking with me for this one.

"Schiffer," "Schiffer Publishing, Ltd. & Design," and the "Design of pen and inkwell" are registered trademarks of Schiffer Publishing, Ltd.

Type set in Max Rhodes, Poliet Paper & Adobe Caslon

"Man in a dark Fantasy Forest" © ando6. Image from BigStockPhoto.com

ISBN: 978-0-7643-4708-5
Printed in China

Schiffer Books are available at special discounts for bulk purchases for sales promotions or premiums. Special editions, including personalized covers, corporate imprints, and excerpts can be created in large quantities for special needs. For more information contact the publisher:

Published by Schiffer Publishing, Ltd.
4880 Lower Valley Road
Atglen, PA 19310
Phone: (610) 593-1777; Fax: (610) 593-2002
E-mail: Info@schifferbooks.com

For the largest selection of fine reference books on this and related subjects, please visit our website at **www.schifferbooks.com.**

We are always looking for people to write books on new and related subjects. If you have an idea for a book, please contact us at proposals@schifferbooks.com.

This book may be purchased from the publisher. Please try your bookstore first.
You may write for a free catalog.

CONTENTS

The Lion strode through the Halls of Hell;
Across his path grim shadows fell
Of many a mowing, nameless shape
Monsters with dripping jaws agape.
The darkness shuddered with scream and yell
When the Lion stalked through the Halls of Hell.
–Robert E. Howard, "The Scarlet Citadel" (1933)

AUTHOR'S NOTE

I want to take this opportunity to thank you all for coming back to the darkness with me. I lit a few candles, so it won't be too dark on our journey. Did you dress warmly? Good, you'll be glad later on.

What you're about to read could possibly horrify you. It is a book about bad things that happen to good people and the stains their horror left on the world. It is about tragedy, desecration, the loneliness of being forgotten. It is about the pain of loss and the terror that comes swinging in the night. I wanted to make sure you knew that going in. Then again, when it comes to ghost stories, I've never enjoyed happy endings much. In the words of the great Algernon Blackwood, "whoever heard of someone being haunted by a good deed?"

Murder was the most common tragedy to befall these once harmless places, yet it was not the only linking factor. In some cases, the monster that killed the girl was a disease or an accidental drowning. Sometimes, the death of a man is the result of a misunderstanding. Other times, it was the gross mistreatment of the dead that caused the spirits to rise up in anger. Tragedy knows no boundaries and never does it blink. It doesn't care who's suffered too much and who hasn't suffered enough. Tragedy pulls your card blindly and creates a scar on you, your family, and the things you love, making it difficult to look on them in the same way. Case in point: the small farmhouse in Villisca, Iowa. I envy those who haven't a clue what went on there, for they are able to see what the Moore family saw at one time: a cozy, warm house with limitless possibilities. They do not see the ghosts of children lying dead in their beds, the victims of an axe-wielding maniac. They do not see the sprays of blood that the wood floors and ceilings have soaked up. They won't hear the weeping of the children as they die. All they will see is hope for the future. But not many who go into the house at Villisca are unaware of its tragic past. It's hard to look past the huge sign in the front yard that reads "The Villisca Ax Murder House" and NOT get an idea of what happened there.

I found myself staring into the eyes of both victims and killers, lives and deaths, and the tragedies that affected them both. I discovered that these places hold onto their pasts like a sponge, but the real tragedy is how the most horrifying moments of their lives seem to get replayed over and over again. Like the moon rising every night, these specters watch their own grim shadows fall and realize that it is starting all over again in a repeating nightmare that haunts not only them, but us as well.

So then.

Are you ready?

Bundle up, friends and stay close to the light.

Here we go.

–BSJ
12/1/2013

Please be forewarned that this book *contains graphic descriptions of assault, torture, and murder that might disturb younger and more sensitive readers.*

THE VILLISCA AX MURDER HOUSE

VILLISCA, IA

Every murderer is probably
somebody's old friend.
–Agatha Christie

In the Sioux and Fox Indian languages, it is said that Villisca means "a place of evil spirits." This was a term used to describe the land where insane members of their tribe were separated from the others because they feared the evil spirits within. To them, the insane were evil and had no place amongst the cherished. It comes as no surprise that none of those tribes ever chose to settle anywhere near it. They knew the land was sour and evil. It wasn't until the white men came and saw it as a good stop on the burgeoning railroad system that the town sprang up and the new settlers, oblivious to its meaning, carried on calling it Villisca.

JUNE 10, 1912

It wasn't uncommon for the entire town to be awake and ready to take on the day by five in the morning. So when Mary Peckham was hanging her wash on the line outside between 5 and 6 a.m., she immediately noticed how still the house next door was, especially since the man of the house had a John Deere dealership and hardware store to run, his wife was a notorious busy-body, and their four young children were all known to be hard at work with outside chores by this time. She had gone to bed at eight the night before and hadn't seen Josiah Moore or his family return home, but where could they be on a cloudy, humid Monday morning besides getting ready for the daily grind? Odd, suspicious, and unnerving.

Across town, Joseph and Sarah Stillinger were wondering what had become of their daughters, Lena Gertrude, 10, and Ina May, 8. The two girls had spent the night with their friend Katherine Moore following the big church social, and one of the conditions of staying over was that they be back in time to help with the chores. They hadn't spoken to Lena or Ina; their fourteen-year-old daughter Blanche had given them permission to stay over at the Moore's via a quick telephone call the afternoon before. Their warm and friendly glow was noticeably absent that morning at the Stillinger homestead.

When 7 a.m. came around and there was still no movement or sign of the Moores in their home, Mary Peckham grew worried and placed a call to Josiah Moore's brother, Ross, the local pharmacist

Farmhouse windows 1940 (Courtesy of the Library of Congress).

and owner of a Rexall Drug Store. As she was telling Ross that he needed to come and check on his brother's family, Mary noticed Ed Selley, an employee of Josiah Moore's, arrive and begin feeding the horses in the stables out back, much like he did everyday. But it wasn't until Ross Moore arrived that the horrifying reality sank in and plunged the town of Villisca into a nightmare of horrific murder that would haunt them forever.

Deathly silence met Ross Moore when he entered the house, followed by dim light from the drawn curtains on each and every window in the building. He cautiously walked through the house, footsteps tapping lightly on the wood floors. It wasn't long before he found two small bodies in the guest bedroom. That was as far as Ross got; the sight of large masses of blood on the bedspread and walls led him from the house, where he ordered Ed Selley to fetch the Sheriff, Henry Horton. It was only after the Sheriff had arrived and inspected the scene that Ross learned the whole gruesome truth.

"I found someone murdered in every bed," reported Sheriff Horton before sending one of his men after the county coroner, a Mr. Linquist from nearby Stanton, Iowa.

The coroner would find Josiah and his wife Sarah waiting for him in their upstairs bedroom, their heads crushed under the weight of an axe that had been repeatedly brought down on them. Gouges in the low lying ceiling bore silent witness to the actions of the axe wielded by a madman. A glass oil lamp had been placed at the foot of their bed, the tornado-like chimney removed. That chimney was later found under a chair in the kitchen, deliberately placed there by the only one who understood the random strangeness of it all.

In the children's bedroom next door, sons Herman, Boyd, and Paul, and daughter Katherine lay in their beds, the red blood aging into a disturbing brown lacquer, their skulls crushed in the same manner as their parents. Downstairs in the guest bedroom lay the bodies of 11-year-old Lena and 8-year-old Ina Stillinger, friends of the Moore's children who were spending the night. All of the victims were found with linens covering the carnage left of their faces. Blankets were found covering all of the mirrors and the front-door windows. Lena Stillinger's night dress had been pulled up over her head with her undergarments removed, splayed out vulgarly to the world. The murder weapon stood against the south wall of the guest bedroom where the Stillinger girls had been killed. In a bizarre twist, a four-pound slab of bacon wrapped in cloth lay next to the partially wiped down axe.

Outside the Moore house, a mob scene had developed as neighbors from all over town descended upon the tiny house on Second Street. They would be turned away from the front door, only to turn around and sneak in the back door. By the time the coroner arrived, well over a hundred people had trampled through the crime scene and gawked at the bodies of the dead. Evidence, if there was any, had effectively been destroyed and the once respected and renowned Josiah Moore and his family had been transformed into a sideshow act that the curious fought to see.

George Whitmore, the Page County sheriff, arrived to find the maddening crowd and immediately deputized a group of young men, who tossed out the curious and erected a barb wire fence around the property, finally stemming the flow of curious bystanders.

As the coroner went about trying to determine what had happened, the mob of Villiscans turned their attention to finding the killer. They enlisted a pack of bloodhounds owned and trained by a man named Elmer Noffsinger from Nebraska; they set out across the tiny town with the scent of blood from the axe in their noses. The mob was convinced that, given the severity of the murders, the killer himself had to have been covered in his victim's blood. But the chase went cold very quickly, ending down by the Nodaway River. The mob would retrace their steps two more times before finally realizing the futility. The killer was gone. Long gone.

By 6 p.m., the National Guard had arrived on the scene to quell the gathering and Villisca officially went into lockdown as martial law was declared. At almost the same time, reporters and newsmen from Council Bluffs, Stanton, and Des Moines roared into town to spread the news to the rest of the world.

The coroner's report placed the deaths as happening between midnight and five in the morning. Also of note was that the arc of the axe's swing indicated that the killer was left-handed. A more minute, yet telling, detail was the fact that, while everyone else in the house were bludgeoned with the blunt end of the axe, Josiah Moore's head had been cleaved with the sharp portion, and he most likely died instantly.

THE TANGLED WEBS OF FRANK JONES AND OTHER SUSPICIOUS FELLOWS

In the dark of that quiet little house, a horrifying series of appalling things happened to good people. Josiah Moore and his family had gone to bed that night never to awaken again. Two young girls, sleeping in a guest room downstairs, became part of the story when they decided to sleep over with their friends instead of walking back home from church in the dark. For between the hours of midnight and five, a madman slunk from his hiding place in the attic, the Moore's own long-handled axe in hand, and brutally took the lives of eight people, six of them children. To this day, it is said that not only do the children still haunt this quiet little house, they are joined by the spirit of their killer as well, who, on a nightly basis, reenacts the gruesome murders he committed over 100 years before.

The house was originally built in 1868 by George Loomis on what was then called Lot 310. Josiah and Sarah Moore purchased the house in 1903 from Loomis himself, hoping to set about making the home a fantastic place to raise their children. Josiah owned a John Deere dealership in town, selling much needed farming implements to area farmers. This provided Josiah with a sizable income for the time, which unfortunately created a few enemies who would eventually become suspects in their murders. But the overall consensus of the Moores was that they were very well liked, philanthropic, and dedicated to their church. As Presbyterians, they were among the most devout of all Christians, attending morning and evening services. Sarah Moore was a director of children's activities at the church and Josiah had made many donations to the church in the form of cash and properties. By the evening of June 9, 1912, it could be reasonably thought that Josiah Moore was as content a man as any man could be, with a lovely wife, handsome sons, and a beautiful daughter. His home was small, but filled with love. His business could not have been better. He

was truly living the dream. But as he watched his wife direct the Children's Service at church, and his children performed their parts with gusto and vigor, a deranged lunatic sat alone in the attic of Josiah's house, cradling an axe he'd found in the yard, smoking Chesterfields, and waiting patiently for the Moore family to return home.

As the community struggled to come to grips with the horror of the tragedy, the notion that a madman was still on the loose became as frightening and devastating to the people of Villisca as the initial murders had been. Information about clues and suspects literally came from everyone in town and investigators struggled to differentiate the valid suspects from the more lofty ones. Yet there were a few suspects who seemed to hold the interest of investigators longer than most. What spilt forth from the investigation of four of these men forever changed the way Josiah Moore was viewed and a larger conspiracy driven by greed, money, and revenge began to develop.

Frank Jones was an Iowa State Senator and Moore's greatest nemesis. The two hated each other with a passion, so much so that they would often cross the street in order to avoid passing each other on the sidewalk. The hatred between them began when Moore left the farming dealership he worked at with Frank Jones. When he left, he took the John Deere franchise with him, setting up shop down the street from his former co-workers and new rivals. This move nearly devastated the old business and left a sour note of bad blood between Moore and Jones. Aside from Moore's apparently cutthroat business tactics, it was a fairly common rumor in gossip circles that Josiah Moore was carrying on with Frank Jones' daughter-in-law of two years, Dona. It was speculated by a private investigator named J.N. Wilkerson that Frank Jones had paid an ex-con named William Mansfield and two other men to carry out the gruesome murders. The deaths of Josiah and his family would eliminate Jones' business rival, as well as practice revenge for Josiah's dalliances with Dona Jones. Several witnesses testified to seeing Frank Jones and the three suspected murderers meeting close to the Moore house on the night of the murders. Oddly enough, it was Frank Jones who suggested bringing in Elmer Noffsinger's trained bloodhounds to find the killer the morning the bodies were discovered. Albert Jones was also a pallbearer at the Moore funeral, carrying his father's murdered nemesis to his grave.

Incidentally, Jones lost his lawsuit against Wilkerson and a case was immediately built against Frank Jones and William Mansfield as the prime suspects in the murders. Witness testimonies wavered, their stories changed, and they immediately became unreliable on the stand. None of the allegations stood up against the lack of evidence and the case never made it to trial.

All hope seemed to be gone until 1917, when police arrested a deranged traveling preacher by the name of Reverend Lyn George Jaclyn Kelly, an Irish immigrant who spent much of his time evangelizing across the Midwest and panhandle areas, until finally settling down with his wife in nearby Macedonia, Iowa. He'd been invited to the Children's Day festivities in Villisca and was indeed present on June 9th, 1912. Mysteriously, though, he disappeared three hours before the Moore's bodies were discovered.

An elderly couple who had shared a train car with Reverend Kelly the morning after the murders testified that Kelly even talked about it with them before the deaths were announced to the public. And Kelly, like the Villisca murderer, was left-handed. After weeks of being hounded, Kelly finally confessed, telling a very detailed story of madness and murder, claiming he was being led to the Moore house by voices in his head, voices he believed belonged to God, urging him on to slaughter the occupants of the house. Kelly's lawyer, however, withdrew the confession, Kelly recanted, and the case went to trial.

Reverend Kelly squeaked through two trials for the murders of the Moores and the Stillinger girls before being acquitted of the crime completely. Wisely, Reverend Kelly faded into obscurity and disappeared for the rest of his life, living quietly and anonymously until his death in a Long Island mental hospital in the 1950s. He was the only person to ever be brought to trial for the murders and the case remains unsolved to this day.

Chillingly, it was thought that there may have been a prolific serial killer at large in the area, for over the course of a year, five families from surrounding communities had been butchered in their beds with an axe. A possible total of at least fourteen men, women, and children were killed in ways similar to that of the Moores and the Stillingers, with the last murder taking place just four days before Josiah and his family met their destinies. With the exception of one case, all of the murders involved the use of an axe, all of the shades had been drawn over the windows, and the faces of the victims had been covered. In one of the murders, a glass oil lamp had been placed at the foot of their bed, mirroring what would occur at the Moore residence four days later. The man most suspected of these murders was Henry Lee Moore (no relation to Josiah Moore), an ex-con who was convicted of murdering his grandmother and her friend with an axe. After he was locked up, the strange rash of axe murders in Iowa suddenly stopped.

What is astonishing is that the police knew about this pattern, yet dismissed it in favor of suspects such as Frank Jones and Reverend Kelly. In 1912, the term serial killer hadn't yet become part of the collective vernacular. The local and federal police had tossed a blanket over the serial killer idea so that the public would not go into a frenzied panic of fear. Sheriff Horton had seen what happened when the town discovered the Moores had been murdered; they'd formed a 2,000-man lynch mob. What would have happened if they knew a serial killer was on the loose and was responsible for over twenty murders across the state?

THE HAUNTINGS BEGIN

Almost immediately following the murders of the Moores and the Stillinger girls, stories began to circulate throughout the town of strange lights passing from window to window of the empty house, much like the light of a lamp being carried from room to room. Those morbid enough to sneak inside heard whispery voices and ominous creaks in the floorboards upstairs, emanating eerily from the killer's former hiding place, the attic. The house went through seven owners in its lifetime, with each owner stressing that there was a darkness to the house that made them uneasy, nervous, and frightened.

One of the first renters in the house was Homer Ritner and his pregnant wife. They were offered half a year of free rent simply because the house had sat empty for so long; its reputation made it difficult to find anyone willing to step inside, let alone live in it.

At first, Mrs. Ritner began to only hear things in the house. Gentle whispers here and there, and footsteps walking up and down the stairs. She awoke one night to find an axe-wielding shadow standing at the foot of their bed; her screams of terror woke Homer Ritner swiftly and he also was able to catch sight of the specter. Homer's wife's health began to deteriorate. She couldn't sleep well at night and she barely ate. Doctors warned the couple that any further night terrors or stress could harm their unborn child.

The Ritners moved out within a week. Once again, the killer had driven out a family using an axe and sheer terror as his weapons. For decades, the house again stood empty until sometime in 1962, when the Williamsons moved in.

Sisters Patty and Linda Williamson, themselves only 10 or so at the time, woke to hear spine-chilling whimpers coming from the darkness. They were mournful, pained cries that played like icy fingers on the backs of their necks.

"It sounded like a little girl's faint crying and then the room was really cold," says Patty. "Our mother just said it was our imagination running wild with us."

Sounds of footsteps and objects being thrown, the sharp cutting chill on a hot August day, and the faint whispers of children in the dark...imagination? Patty and Linda's mother would soon learn that a vivid imagination was no match for the murderous spirit of Villisca's Axe Murder House.

"All of us kids were downstairs and she'd taken the laundry upstairs," says Patty. "When she went up there, all of the clothes that she'd taken up there had been thrown out of the drawers. The drawers had been thrown open and they were scattered all over the room." Linda Williamson-Cook added: "The attic door was flinging back and forth. She ran down the stairs; she told my dad about it. Dad said it was *those kids* playing a joke on her. It terrified her, and she wouldn't talk about it after that."

Their father refused to believe in the activity, chalking it up to active imaginations and cruel, childish pranks. But Patty and Linda's mother believed, and she forbade them from going into the attic space. "She told us we needed to stay out of that attic; it was not a safe place to be," Patty says.

But their father would believe soon enough. As he was honing his pocket knife at the kitchen table one day, drawing the blade back and forth over a sharpening stone, he began to feel a slight pressure on his wrist and hand. "It just turned that knife and stabbed him right in the thumb. He literally could feel like someone had a hold of his hand and turning that knife around.

"I just remember Dad saying we weren't staying here," recalls Patty with a chuckle. "I felt evil in here and I wanted out."

The house, again, stood empty until it was finally bought and renovated to its original 1912 state by Darwin Lin in 1994. It was Darwin who capitalized on the Villisca axe murders by offering the house to renters and thrill seekers eager to test the legends. His actions weren't immediately lauded by the community. After all, it was a dark and abhorrent stain on Villisca's past, something the townspeople were reluctant to be remembered for. But when it was seen more as a memorial to the Moore's and the Stillingers, tensions seemed to ease. Besides, it was something that was bringing tourists and money to the small Iowa town. It couldn't be all bad. Perhaps even Josiah Moore would have applauded the move to capitalize.

But just because no one had the nerve to live in the house anymore doesn't mean the spirit of the killer would just relax and become complacent. John Houser lives next door to the old Moore house in Mary Peckham's old place and he's seen enough horror coming out of that house to chill your blood into eternity. "In the kids room once I felt something tug my shirt and I felt something grab my arm. Right then, the hairs, the goose bumps, the whole works. It was a pretty bad feeling."

But that's not all. One day he was looking out of his own window and saw a menacing face looking out the attic window of the empty house next door. Nick Eisenhower, a visitor to the house, claims he's also seen the dark shadow of the killer. "I was next door talking to some friends and we looked across and saw the image of this shade opening up," he says. "It looked like somebody was in the house. Seemed like somebody was looking out the window, watching us. It was pretty creepy because we knew for a fact that no one was in there."

Very soon after opening, the Villisca Axe Murder House became THE hot-spot for all investigators, one of those places that you had to investigate just once before you died. But many of the groups that investigate there take the legends too lightly and find themselves being corrected not only by the spirits of the Moore and Stillinger children, but also by the killer himself. In a bizarre twist of fate, Electronic Voice Phenomena (EVP)has been captured on tape of children whispering and talking. But audio has also been captured of a deep male voice that comes off threatening and hostile.

Midwest Paranormal out of Detroit Lakes, Minnesota, captured a male voice calling them a "moron" when the unseen entity was presented with photographs of the suspects in the murders. They were also lucky enough to capture another male voice saying, "Why would you do that to me?" leading many to believe that it wasn't the killer, but Josiah Moore himself, perhaps questioning whoever would listen about why he had to die.

Two of the most chilling EVPs I've heard recorded in the house were by Miller Paranormal Research out of Kansas City, Missouri, and by Zak Bagans' *Ghost Adventures* crew. In the first EVP from Miller Paranormal, as investigators mill about the room, asking questions, a whispery male voice is heard saying, "It's just like killing hogs," an obvious reference to the Moore and Stillinger murders, as well as cattle and pork slaughterhouse modes of operation of the early 1900s. In the case of the *Ghost Adventures* crew, Zak, Nick, and Aaron caught an EVP of a gruff male voice, proclaiming, "I killed...six kids." At the time, Zak felt that he'd caught the voice of the killer confessing his crime. But in listening to the EVP, you can clearly hear the voice rise at the end, as if he were asking a question, not stating a fact. "I killed...six kids?" Interpretation, as with any EVP, is in the ear of the beholder. Find it on YouTube or catch a re-run of that particular episode and you can judge for yourself.

Many groups, however, tragically capture the voices of children calling for their mother, as well as hearing the muffled conversations between children that obviously weren't physically in the house at the time. Toys and balls, used by investigators to draw the child spirits closer to them, have been found in places other than where they were left. Balls have been known to roll away quickly in a straight line direction, ruling out random wind gusts that might have pushed them in a general, often staggered, direction.

Psychic Deborah Brockman claims to have connected with the spirit of the killer at the Villisca house. His spooky motives unnerved her. "There was something about him that thrilled him to kill children. He actually stood there and told me, kind of getting my goat, telling me he loved killing the children the most," she says. "His motivation was money originally...whoever approached him knew he would do it, but after thinking about it and waiting so long, his motivation was just to kill." This chilling impression leads us back to Josiah Moore's business rival, Frank Jones, and the alleged plot to hire William Mansfield to wipe out Moore and his family. But his most haunting reason for staying behind at the scene of his most notorious crime? Deborah Brockman got the answer directly from the killer himself. "He just told me 'Let me put it into terms that you can understand: I...like it...here.'"

My own meditations on Villisca's most famous house revealed a horrifying set of circumstances. The residual energies of the children coexist with the intelligent spirit of their killer. Just as in life, the children are constantly unaware of the danger that lurks in their home. As they play in the yard and in their rooms, they are oblivious to the smirking ghost of the Villisca Ax Murderer. He watches them, grinning at them from his hiding place in the attic, and every night, when they go to sleep in their tiny beds, he gets to murder them all over again, forever haunting the scene of his greatest work.

Today, Patty and Linda are adamant about the house: they are uncomfortable being inside and feel scarred because of what they experienced there. It wasn't just about the mysterious happenings, but it was also how it made them feel on a regular basis. Feelings of being watched, stalked, perhaps even hunted, and the chill in the air that swirled around them as they tried to dismiss the creaks and groans in the floor as just the house settling. They weren't aware of what happened in the house before they moved in, but wish now that the Moore and Stillinger families can someday have closure on this horrific incident that haunts Iowa to this very day.

JUKAI AOKIGAHARA

MOUNT FUJI, JAPAN

He would say, "How funny it will all seem, all you've gone through,
when I'm not here anymore, when you no longer feel my arms around
your shoulders, nor my heart beneath you, nor this mouth on your
eyes, because I will have to go away someday, far away..."
And in that instant I could feel myself with him gone, dizzy with fear,
sinking down into the most horrible blackness: into death.

–Arthur Rimbaud

Fuji from Lake Motosu by Herbert George Ponting 1905. At the base of Mount Fuji lies the dark, nearly impenetrable Sea of Trees, Aokigahara Jukai. (Photo by Herbert George Ponting, courtesy of the Library of Congress.)

Each year, an army of volunteers and police officers walk into Jukai Aokigahara, also referred to as Aokigahara Forest. Their purpose is grim, yet crystal clear. And when they exit the forest, they will bring probably close to a hundred corpses with them. It is a forest known the world over by scholars, psychiatrists, and paranormal investigators alike. Its quiet, sinister paths contain the remnants of secret lives and dashed hopes, hanging from tree branches and wafting through the air like shredded fabric. Sound doesn't exist here, and even on the sunniest of days, the light inside the forest is dim, kept out by the thick growth of large trees and brush. Author Wataru Tsurumui called it "the perfect place to die" in his book, *The Complete Manual of Suicide*. Lying at the foot of the glorious and sacred Mount Fuji, Aokigahara Forest also goes by a different name: The Suicide Forest, and this act of finding and retrieving bodies from within is grimly known as "harvesting the forest."

Because it frames the base of Mount Fuji, Aokigahara is considered a sacred place by the Japanese, a distinction held by this mysterious forest for thousands of years. The forest has been known as hub of both conventional and unorthodox religious expression. The cult responsible for the Tokyo subway nerve gas bombings, Aum Shinri Kyo, built its central temple near the forest, and Mount Fuji itself is considered a towering deity of the Shinto religion. Many critics point to the 1960 book *Tower Of Waves* by Seicho Matsumoto as the impetus for the many suicides that occur there. In it, two young lovers enter Aokigahara and complete a suicide pact. A good way to picture the draw of Aokigahara is to imagine what it would be like if author Stephanie Meyer had written about characters Edward and Bella committing suicide in the forest of Aokigahara; massive waves of copycat suicides would undoubtedly follow the publication. But the long history of suicide in Aokigahara overshadows *Tower Of Waves*'s publication by hundreds of years; many believe that the forest has always been connected to death, and nothing but death. Indeed, the ancient practice of Ubasute is said to have been performed here for centuries. Ubasute is the act of abandoning an elderly loved one in the forest, leaving them to fend for themselves in the harsh and perilous wilderness. There is an ethereal, almost fairy tale-like atmosphere to Aokigahara, reminiscent of a Grimm's Fairy Tale or a Tim Burton film. But it is a deceptive atmosphere that is heavy with a dark, suffocating energy that draws you like a fly to a spider web.

But to many, it is not *Tower Of Waves* that brings the suicidal to Aokigahara, nor is it *The Complete Manual Of Suicide*. According to Kyomo Fukui, a Buddhist monk, the dark spirits that inhabit the trees of Aokigahara take on a more active role in recruiting others to join their ranks. "The spirits are calling people here to kill themselves," he explains. "The spirits of the people who have committed suicide before. The spirits draw the unhappy people here. Prayers bring them peace, and send them home rather than doing mischief." That is why, every year, Fukui and fifty of his fellow Buddhist monks arrive at Aokigahara and bless the forest with prayers and light, hoping it banishes the darker entities looking to lead the living down the darkest paths of their lives.

But the prayers might not be helping: Japanese officials have seen a spike in the numbers of bodies being pulled out of Aokigahara every year, despite encouraging words posted on signs outside the forest. The annual Harvest of Death, also called harvesting the forest, consists of hundreds of policemen and volunteers venturing into the forest in search of bodies. The year 2010 yielded over forty bodies alone.

Asuza Hayano is a Japanese geologist who volunteers his time patrolling the forest for bodies and the troubled souls still trying to determine which fate they will choose. "Walking through Aokigahara uncharted is dangerous. But nature is supposed to be like that. Harsh," he says. "Aokigahara is filled with untouched natural beauty. To sully it by committing suicide is a slap in the face of the natural environment."

Hayano speaks with a weary rasp in his voice, his eyes tinged with exhaustion. Over the course of 20 years, Hayano has discovered over 100 bodies and it is obvious that he has grown tired of the constant search. But it is a mission he takes seriously and continues to do, simply because of its importance not only to Japan, but helping the souls of the damned, as well as their anxious families, rest peacefully.

"One suicide makes the news and provides others with the idea that this is the place to take your own life," writes Jeff Belanger, a noted author and paranormal investigator. "As more come to do the same deed, the word spreads, the legend grows, and the woods are stained. The spirit of that place is now covered with the horrible sadness and desperation that can only come from suicide."

Aokigahara Jukai is a special, reverent place simply because of its location at the base of Mount Fuji, named after the goddess Fuji who came to Earth and bestowed knowledge to the people of Japan. It is also one of the only places on Earth where, according to legend, the earth meets the sky, creating a spiritual or heavenly gateway for those wishing to leave Earth for Heaven, and vice versa.

THE PURGATORY OF YUREI

Many of those who enter Aokigahara never walk back out, leaving behind not only their bodies and belongings, but their restless spirits, stalking the forest quietly, forever imprisoned in their final moments. These ghosts, called Yurei by Japanese folklorists, haunt the woods forever, clothed in white, their black hair hanging low across their faces. Their howls of frustration and pain can be heard wafting through the dense trees, chilling the living to their bones.

"Even in these haunted woods, regular humans still have a job to do," says Zack Davisson, a researcher for SeekJapan. "Forestry workers rotate in and out of shifts at a station building in Aokigahara, and occasionally they will come upon unfortunate bodies in various states of decomposition, usually hanging from trees or partially eaten by animals. The bodies are brought down to the station, where a spare room is kept especially for such occasions. In this room are two beds: one for the corpse and one for someone to sleep next to it. It is thought that if the corpse is left alone, the lonely and unsettled Yurei will scream the whole night through, and the body will move itself into the regular sleeping quarters."

Usually seen as pale and black eyed, the Yurei are often dressed in flowing white robes or gowns, representing the funeral garb these unfortunates would have been dressed in. Their hair is long and black, covering their eyes and much of their faces. Movies like *The Ring* and *The Grudge* have shown the Yurei in horrifying yet exemplary form.

Sightings of these spirits are fleeting and rare in Aokigahara, but it has been known to happen. Many times, those who see something strange in Aokigahara see fleeting Shadow People and, from time to time, pallid white faces staring at them from the darkness. Others report malfunctioning compasses and electronic equipment, but these claims can be easily dismissed by pointing out that the forest bed of Aokigahara is covered in a thick crust of magnetized iron and other minerals spewed forth from volcanic eruptions over the course of Japan's history.

These spirits, all born from pain and suffering, whether it be emotional or physical suffering, keep most locals from entering the forest at all, let alone at night. In Japanese folklore, not only can ghosts haunt you, they can also curse and bind themselves to you, so that no matter where you go, you will always be followed by the angry spirit who turns its eye on you. Locals are convinced that Aokigahara is a purgatory for Yurei, which is why you will often only see foreign tourists and the suicidal enter the forest.

EVIDENCE OF
THE PARANORMAL

Those who choose to hike through Aokigahara have been known to come across the bones of long dead victims of suicide, clothes still hanging to pristine white bones. Personal items such as car keys, shoes, wallets, and eyeglasses have also been found littering the landscape, things that most living persons cannot live without, but the dead have no use for.

Ghost stories and encounters in Aokigahra are certainly not uncommon given the circumstances of the forest, resulting in incredible tales and chilling fables that have transcended time. Some have even claimed to have been possessed by the Yurei; American tourists with no knowledge of the Japanese language have been reported as suddenly speaking perfect, fluent Japanese while in the forest. Even their faces have been known to change to more accurately match the face of the possessing spirit. This very thing happened to columnist Lisa Lee Harp Waugh, a self-professed necromancer and writer for HauntedAmericaTours.com.

In her column entitled "The Most Haunted Forest and Hot Spot in Asia," Waugh wrote that the spirit of a Japanese man took hold of her body and possessed her. Her facial features changed to match the dead man's face and she suddenly began speaking Japanese, the voice emanating from her telling the story of the dead man's fate during and after death. He had come to Aokigahara to die by his own hand when his wife took up with another man and left him, disgracing him and his entire family.

"The man inside me told them of how he had died and that his hanging was actually botched," wrote Waugh. "He died from starvation and lack of water over a five-day period, until someone came along deep in the woods and found his lifeless corpse."

The spirit would go on to say that he would commit suicide again if given the chance, but would choose a way that would prevent so much suffering. Most chilling of all, as the dying man hung from the tree, unable to save himself or hurry along his own death, he watched scores of real ghosts approach, watching him die, some in curiosity, others in excitable anticipation. Waugh found herself very weak as the spirit left her and she fell to the ground, shaken.

Not surprisingly, this is one of the few paranormal experiences at Aokigahara that I could uncover. I say that because it is no secret that the Japanese are a superstitious people. To even speak of an experience with a Yurei or any other kind of ghost would be inviting it into your lives, curse and all. So paranormal experiences are spoken of—or rather, boasted of—by Americans and Europeans, mostly. Visitors to Aokigahara come out with chilling reports of full-bodied apparitions, hearing haunting whispers that seem to come from nowhere, and the menacing feeling of being watched. Examinations of the trees have found startlingly realistic visages of human faces in the twisted bark, hideously wrought faces in the throes of agony. Whether it be an actual record of a dying man's final moments recorded by nature or a clever example of how our eyes and brains interpret the area is up for debate. It is, for lack of a better term, fairly chilling, but still pretty cool.

SyFy Channel's *Destination Truth* profiled Aokigahara in one of the shows more memorable—and creepy—episodes. Host Josh Gates and his crew were able to capture the infrared image of a black, human-like mass rising up from the forest floor, then disappearing from whence it came. But aside from the few bits of evidence they retrieved, all crew members agreed that the emotional toll from being in a place like the Suicide Forest was far greater than the physical toll.

In an interview with Dave Schrader on *Darkness Radio*, Gates remembered how the area struck him, and the most lasting impression wasn't a wholly paranormal one. "There's just places in the world that you go to that have a certain heaviness to them, and I'm not sure exactly what that is, but there's something residual that just feels heavy about some places, and certainly the Suicide Woods in Japan is a place like that," he says. While he concedes that it is a very beautiful forest, it just feels creepy. "It was a place that had us on edge from the beginning of the investigation. But I also had the feeling that we were going to come across somebody. I had it in my head that I was going to see something I really didn't want to see...There's a degree of shame about it; its not a place (the Japanese) are really proud of promoting...It was just a really sad spot."

Certainly, the Japanese would concur with Josh Gates. "We want people to forget Aokigahara for a little while," an anonymous local police officer once told an American journalist. "Every time it's mentioned, it starts off a chain reaction and we end up with more suicides. I've seen plenty of bodies that have been really badly decomposed, or been picked at by wild animals. There's nothing beautiful about dying in there."

THE SLOSS FURNACES

BIRMINGHAM, AL

The world is full of ghosts, and some of them are still people.
–Peter Straub

The foreman just sneered at the visitors, teeth grinding slightly as he watched them traipse about his steel mill. It was hard enough to get work done with the motley crew of iron workers he was forced to oversee. Tossing in some tourists who want to check out the most productive steel mill in the South was just adding insult to injury. For James Wormwood, this just would not do. The rage inside him began to simmer and build until finally he rushed at the visitors, attempting to grab at them. He wanted them the hell out of his mill and, like with the other tourists before, had no problem using force to get his point across. But the visitors didn't see James "Slag" Wormwood. All they saw was a pitch black shadow with piercing white eyes screaming toward them before dissipating into oblivion once more.

They'll get out now, thought Slag; *they'll get out and they'll tell the world how tight a ship James Wormwood runs at the Sloss...*

There are more ghosts in the South per capita than in most small countries, inhabiting every kind of location, from old sugar plantations to crumbling jails and hospitals, Revolutionary and Civil War battlefields, not to mention all of the locals who catch sight of my Indiana license plates and decide they want to welcome me personally to their own neck of the woods.

But one place in particular has those places beat. Its hallways are dark, gritty, and hot. The smell of burning steel still hangs in the air, and if you listen to the darkness, you can hear the murmuring whispers of those who lost their lives doing one of the hardest jobs imaginable. It is difficult to imagine good men working in what must have seemed like the bowels of Hell, stoking fires that would help boost the steel industry, feed their hungry families in a post Civil War landscape, and put the South back on the map as a force to be reckoned with.

The iconic Sloss Furnace water tower. Directly behind it are the enormous furnaces where the cruel James "Slag" Wormwood lost his life in a suspicious smelting accident. (Photo by Jack E. Boucher, 1977.)

WELCOME TO SLOSS FURNACES

Built in 1881 by Colonel James Withers Sloss, it was fully intended to take advantage of Birmingham's booming industrial business. The city itself was close to a huge deposit of coal, iron ore, and limestone, much of which was located in nearby Jones Valley. Sloss was a plantation owner and railroad magnate who saw the steel industry's potential; he used money made from his railroad interests to fund Sloss Furnaces, where he built two huge blast furnaces. While he outfitted his furnaces with mostly immigrants and former sharecroppers from the city, he used almost all convict labor from the prison in his coal mines, leasing them cheaply to do some of the most dangerous work possible. Coalburg Mine alone was known for its deplorable conditions, claiming almost a hundred lives by 1890 due to explosions, falls from dizzying heights, and massive cave-ins.

The low pay and the long hours were the least of the workers concerns, however. Sloss Furnaces was a virtual Candy Land™ of death, with extremely hazardous risks looming around every corner, whether it was from the molten steel, volatile steam pipes, or one of the infamous Wheels. The Wheel is a gigantic flywheel that was used to power the boilers, feeding into an intricate series of heavy gears. To stop the Wheel meant stopping production all over the plant. It simply wasn't done and, if it was, there'd better be a good excuse for it, as restarting the boilers and the furnaces would cost upwards of thousands of dollars of manpower. So when an unfortunate worker got too close to the rotating Wheel and found his clothing getting caught in it, all his coworkers could do was watch as he was quickly dragged into the gears, crushed to death and spread thin across the grease and iron.

Despite the hazards of the job, Sloss Furnaces lasted a good deal of time, finally closing its doors in 1971, after new environmental regulations and energy shortages all but made the old mill obsolete in the wake of newer, cleaner, and more efficient technology. But it did not stand empty and unused for long. By September of 1983, the steel mill was designated as a National Landmark, its new official name being Sloss Furnaces National Historic Landmark.

Reaping that type of distinction insured that the Furnaces would be kept up and the property maintained.

But it wasn't long before the rest of the world would discover what so many Sloss employees already knew. Sloss Furnace was haunted—no doubt about it. The conditions were intense and dangerous. Temperatures ran high and most jobs required climbing to incredible heights and working with iron ore that could vaporize a human in a matter of seconds. Poor visibility added to the danger, making it easy to miss a step on the catwalks outside the furnaces. It is believed that close to 200 men may have lost their lives during the years Sloss was operational. This was a job where death could claim you in an instant, leaving behind a wandering and confused soul that still has unfinished business with the living world.

One of these men who lost his life to the furnaces was Richard Jowers. Jowers was one of those guys who was proud of what he did, constantly bragging to his family and friends about his job at the furnaces. In truth, he couldn't have been a better employee. He never missed work, seemed to get along well with all of his co-workers, and was well liked by his employers. It was one of these same furnaces that took his life one day, as he fell headlong into one, tumbling from one of the catwalks where he most often did his work. Co-workers tried to rescue him, but there was little that could be done. The molten steel claimed much of Jower's body, and the Sloss Furnaces claimed his soul. Almost immediately, sightings of Jower's ghost began to circulate throughout the furnaces, usually appearing on the same catwalks he had fallen from to his death.

Mind you, Jowers wasn't the only one who lost his life to the mill. Hundreds of workers found their ends as the result of such intense, dangerous work. It is said that the ghostly appearances of workers at Sloss Furnaces are so frequent that visitors who tour the plant can readily and easily identify the ghosts they've seen from a photograph of the workers hanging in the museum area.

But one ghost you probably don't want to tangle with is the infamous and dangerous spirit of a man named James Wormwood. Nicknamed "Slag" by his employees, a less than complimentary term, as "slag" is essentially the scum that rises to the top of molten ore. It serves no purpose and must be scooped off the top and discarded. "Slag" Wormwood was a brutal and intense foreman on the mill's graveyard shift. He would beat and intimidate those

Steel Worker. (Photo by Stanley Kubrick, courtesy of the Library of Congress.)

furnace."

It was in October of 1906 when one of the most despicable and darkest souls in the realm of parapsychology was loosed upon the world. During the graveyard shift, Slag Wormwood was high atop the 200+ foot furnace known as "Big Alice." What he was doing up there is a mystery; he was never known to work on that particular furnace. Suddenly, he was enveloped by a billowing cloud of erupting carbon monoxide that had shot up from the furnace below. Apparently becoming dizzy, he lost his footing and fell from the top of "Big Alice" straight into the furnace, his body vaporized by 7800 degree ore. Immediately, it was quietly questioned whether or not he was thrown into the furnace by workers fed up with his treatment of them. Officially, it was an accident. Very soon after Slag's death, the graveyard shift was ended.

The death of Slag added a whole other dimension of terror to the furnaces. If Slag was dangerous to others when he was alive, he was far more dangerous in death. He took his philosophy of no breaks and no holidays with him after death. In 1926, twenty years after his death, a night watchman was pushed violently from behind as a tough, gravely voice barked at him: "Get back to work!" The watchman, terrified, turned to look at his attacker and found nothing. He spent the next four hours combing Sloss Furnaces, looking for the man who had pushed him without success.

In 1947, three of Sloss's supervisors were touring the steel mill when their guide turned to point something out to them. The guide was mystified to find all three of them were gone. A search found the three supervisors unconscious, locked in a boiler room. Upon waking, none of the men could remember how they had gotten there. But with chilling clarity, they all remembered a badly burned man yelling "Push some steel!" as the one who had put them there.

Perhaps the strangest and most horrifying encounter came in 1971, when night watchman Samuel Blumenthal found himself face to face with what he described as a kind of "half-man, half-demon" that tried to push him up a flight of stairs. When Blumenthal refused to budge, standing his ground, the monster began to beat on him with its fists, leaving several intense third-degree burns on the old man's skin. He died of his injuries before he could return to Sloss.

under his command, mostly poor men who needed the work and couldn't risk losing the only honest work they could find. Slag knew that he had control of those men and exploited that knowledge freely. He would force his workers to speed up production, a daunting task in and of itself, all because he wanted to look good in front of his bosses. During his tenure at Sloss, forty-seven workers lost their lives to accidents, mishaps, and an explosion in 1888 that killed four and left six workers blind. Slag's philosophy was simple: "There were no breaks, there were no holidays...there was only the

One of the last reported incidents came on October 4, 2003, when a Sloss employee suddenly and without warning caught fire. He was taken to the hospital with burns over a good portion of his body, where he also reported to authorities that he had seen a "strange shape" in front of him only moments before he combusted. To date, over 100 reports of suspected paranormal activity have been recorded there in Birmingham. Nearly all of them deal with an assault by a scary, overbearing man enveloped by flames—who wants to share them with you.

Independent, amateur, and professional paranormal investigators have all been approached and/or assaulted by Slag, reporting slaps, punches, and pushes coming from unseen hands. Those who aren't there to work risk raising the ire of the old foreman, and if you choose to have a seat, expect a hardy slap from Slag to get you back up on your feet. Michael Scoggins, a former skeptic and security guard at Sloss, had an experience with Slag that he will never forget. "I see this black entity...a good thirty feet away and all of a sudden that thing was right in front of me," Michael told Zak Bagans of Travel Channel's *Ghost Adventures*. "It reached right inside my body and squeezed both of my lungs until it took every breath of air I had in my body out of me. My whole body went white and I went cold. And whatever it was, it peered inside my mind and told me, 'Get out of here.' And it scared me half to death."

Members of Birmingham's Alabama Paranormal Research Society (A.P.R.S.) experienced yanks on their arms, pushes, and heard the faint murmuring of steel workers conversing and the phantom sounds of machinery firing up. They were also lucky enough to capture EVPs of those sounds, as well as one that sounded to me like "help me." During that same investigation, they were able to capture an extraordinary sight. It was during the daylight hours outside of the furnace near an old excavator that most likely had cultivated coal for the furnaces when it was in operation. They hadn't noticed while they were filming, yet when they played back the tape, they were all floored to see what looked like three male figures standing on the ridge near the bucket of the excavator. All members of A.P.R.S. were accounted for and no maintenance workers or staff were on the property during their lockdown and investigation.

Additionally, Tuscaloosa Paranormal also captured a variety of EVPs, mostly in the tunnel beneath the furnace, widely considered to be the most haunted part of the complex. It was in this tunnel that most investigators claim to have been accosted or attacked by Slag Wormwood. In the case of Tuscaloosa Paranormal, they captured EVPs that ranged from "I Want To Sleep," "I Kill You" and even the chilling sound of a little girl singing in the dark, dank hallway. This same little girl has been caught on tape asking the members of the group, "What's wrong with you?" as if she's questioning why they're searching out the dead. If you were to listen to these EVPs (available online at their website) you would hear not only the words, but also the rage that pushes them into our world for us to hear.

But by far, the most overwhelming, the most terrifying and unnerving experiences people have had at Sloss Furnaces aren't what they see, but what they cannot see. "The biggest employee complaint in terms of being spooked out simply would be the sense of danger, the sense of being endangered by something inexplicable," says Shawn Barnes, lead project manager at the Sloss Furnace museum. "Something that's watching, something that's waiting, lurking in the darkness here."

THE BELL WITCH OF TENNESSEE

ADAMS, TN

Life was like the magic spell
That guides a laughing stream
Sunbeams glimmering on her fell
Kissed by lunar's silvery gleam
But elfin phantoms cursed the dell
and sylvan witches all unseen
As our tale will truly tell
Wielded scepter o'er the queen.

–M.V. Ingram, *The Authenticated History of The Bell Witch*, 1894

When you approach the Bellwood Cemetery, the first thing you see is a huge, towering monument to one single family that endured a tumultuous four years with an entity that showed little mercy and was seemingly on a mission to destroy them. Some say it succeeded. By all accounts, what happened was a very strange but true account and very little of the core story is contested, even by skeptics. The story of the Bell Witch was one of the first documented hauntings in America, as well as being the first documented death officially blamed on a ghost.

I remember where I was when I first heard the story of "The Bell Witch." Fourth grade, Mr. Volkman's class. During library time, I'd found a book about American folktales and legends. There was the usual gamut of tales...the "Headless Horseman," the "Headless Roommate," the "Thing in the Jar," the "Thing Outside the Jar"—you know the type. Urban legends and scary stories to tell in the dark. And then there was chapter twelve.

"The Bell Witch."

My first thought was, "How could a witch live in a bell?" Kind of odd that that's what piqued my interest in the story, but I had to know why they called her the Bell Witch. When I got done reading the story? "Cool, they had their own ghost witch! Lucky!"

Those were the kind of thoughts that kept me out of the really good schools and made guidance counselors flag my file. As it turns out, she was referred to as the Bell Witch simply because any supernatural act was considered "witchery," whether it was born from a witch or not, and also because she singled out John Bell Sr. and his family as targets of her wrath. The story of her hauntings and exploits inspired films like *The Blair Witch Project*, *The Evil Dead*, and *An American Haunting*. She was the first of her kind, this woman's spirit from beyond, creating a newer, darker folklore for American readers, enthusiasts, and scaredy-cats.

The story of the Bell Witch starts in 1804, when John Bell and his wife Lucy emigrated from North Carolina to a rather large tract of land near the Red River in Tennessee. A pious, yet prosperous family, they found themselves settling in very well with the other citizens, routing and maintaining a sizable position in the community. In short, John Bell held a lot of sway over both the political and secular roots of the town in Robertson County, soon to be called Adams. It was this power that some believed would be the reason for his ultimate undoing.

In 1817, John Bell got into a dispute with the nearby Batts family over the sale of a slave. When the local magistrate ruled in John Bell's favor, many believed it was because of his standing and position with the church and local government that led to his victory, fueling many imaginations into overdrive. Stories began circulating that Benjamin Batt's distant and thoroughly eccentric cousin, Cate, had conjured a vengeful spirit to exact the Batts Family's Revenge. While there's no proof that she didn't, it's likely she just didn't care too much. She and Benjamin Batts were not close and she and her husband Frederick were not wealthy enough to own slaves. If anything, she might have coveted her cousin's life, imagining herself with enough money to own slaves.

It wasn't too much later, while John was inspecting his corn crops, that his life changed for the worse. Standing in one of the rows of corn was a large black animal. It had the head of a rabbit and the hulking body of a horrific black dog, the hair rising in anger along its spine. The animal snarled and bristled, and when John finally got his bearings enough to fire his rifle, the animal vanished. Taken aback by what he had seen, John returned home in a shaken daze.

Later that night, the family woke to the sounds of someone—or something—beating on the outside of their home. The noises continued nightly for some time, always culminating with John and his sons attempting to apprehend the culprit by rushing outside while the insistent knocks were being heard. But they never saw anything and always came back empty handed.

Soon, the noises gave way to the children being visited in the night. They complained of rats chewing on their bed posts and that someone kept yanking the blankets from their beds. The chilling, oddly feminine voice of the witch called herself "Cate" and vowed to destroy and haunt the Bell family until the end of time. Betsy and her father endured brutal beatings at the hands of the witch while horrified family members could do nothing but watch and pray that it ended soon.

It is difficult to say just how this affected John and his wife. Being incredibly religious, the phenomena must have frightened them to the point of wanting to contact their clergyman or pastor. But

The original Bell home was demolished in 1909, but this photograph of a plantation house from 1936 is actually very close to the style and look of the original Bell homestead. (Photo by E.H. Pickering, courtesy of the Library of Congress.)

their position in Robertson County would be jeopardized if people thought that perhaps John Bell was somehow being assailed by the Devil and his minions. This is most likely the reason why the Bell family kept the phenomena to themselves for a time, for it wasn't until three months after it had all began that John Bell finally told someone, his neighbor James Johnston, about his "family problems." Johnston agreed to sleep over at the Bell house and was wakened in the dead of night by repeated slaps to his face. Exasperated, he cried out, "In the name of the Lord, who are you and what do you want?!"

There was nothing but silence. The witch didn't bother him anymore that night.

The nature of the Bell Witch is somewhat shocking. In many ways, the disturbances match the classic poltergeist phenomena with the knockings, flying objects, and such. But on the flipside, the witch would engage visitors in religious debates, sing hymns and carols, and even recited a sermon word-for-word that was being spoken over thirteen miles away. More surprising is the fact that the entity spoke perfect English, something poltergeists generally do not do. Poltergeists and their other accompanying spirits almost always are reported to be speaking in tongues.

By that time, the goings on had increased and gotten worse. Betsy Bell, the youngest daughter, seemed to attract the attention of this entity the most, enduring slaps and beatings nightly by invisible hands. She had shown a requited interest in a schoolmate, Joshua Gardner, but the witch repeatedly ordered her to end it with him. The witch didn't find favor in Betsy's other suitor, Richard Powell, but she left him be and did not intervene when they met together. Powell had been Betsy and Joshua's school teacher and he'd shown quite an interest in marrying Betsy when she was old enough. But Betsy's heart belonged to Joshua and when they would go out alone, the witch would follow, tormenting them both endlessly until they would split and go their separate ways. When Betsy finally tired of raising the ire of the witch, she broke off her engagement with Joshua, leading the witch to shift her main focus to Betsy's father. It also allowed her other suitor, Richard Powell, to step up and ask for the young girl's hand in marriage. This twist in the story often raises eyebrows and causes people to begin pointing fingers at Richard Powell, speculating whether or not he had a hand in either summoning or concocting the Bell Witch himself.

Even American royalty paid a visit to the Bells in search of dispatching the witchery going on there. General Andrew Jackson supposedly visited the Bell homestead during the peak of activity. Two of John Bell's sons had served under Jackson in the army and he was stopping by to do battle with the witch under the guise of checking on the welfare of two of his men. Jackson's first encounter with the Bell Witch occurred on his carriage ride to the Bell house. When a companion began to speak ill of the witch, it is said that the carriage wheels locked, keeping the wagon from moving. Suddenly, as if to prove to the doubters aboard the carriage, the voice of the Bell Witch called out, saying, "Go on, old general."

The carriage wheels immediately began to turn once more and Jackson and his party continued their trek to the Bell house. Once there, General Jackson and his men were not spared any of the activity the Bells had since grown accustomed to. Jackson was pinched, slapped, and the covers were torn from his bed as he slept. In the morning, Jackson reportedly said, "I'd rather fight the British in New Orleans than to have to fight the Bell Witch."

THE WITCH'S CAVE

It was during the time of the haunting that Betsy Bell, while walking the grounds of her father's land, happened upon a large chasm, the opening of which led inside to a series of intricate and beautiful cave formations. While exploring the cave with friends, one of the smaller boys got caught in a small opening in the rocks that led further into the bowels of the cave. Stuck in the rock and beginning to panic, Betsy and her friends found that they couldn't get the young boy loose.

Then, all of a sudden, a familiar voice wafted loudly through the cave. "I'll get him out!" bellowed the voice of the Bell Witch. The young boy immediately felt cold hands on his feet and ankles as he was pushed and pulled to freedom and safety. Upon thankfully finding his freedom, The Bell Witch proceeded to give the youngsters a scolding lesson in careful cave exploration.

Interestingly enough, the history of the cave—and of caves in general—bring a slight ray of light to a dimly lit story like the Bell Witch. Ancient Indians revered and celebrated caves, believing them to not only be a protective shelter from the elements, but also an abundant source of powerful, natural, and positive energy that came straight from the earth and was untainted by the surroundings of the outside world.

While the Bell Witch never admitted that the cave was her home, it was immediately thought of as such by everyone who heard the story, leading most everyone to dub the caverns the Bell Witch Cave, a name that still stands to this day. It became a place of darkness, a place where the foolhardy feared to tread, for inside its granite walls lay a devilish spirit just waiting for its opportunity to strike out at the pious and the righteous.

While it may seem that Betsy Bell was a sort of magnet for the witch, make no mistake that it was always her father who was the primary focus of the witch's bane. Once her mission to separate Betsy and Joshua was complete, she seemed to channel all of her energies into making sure that John Bell died of her own accord. Indeed, it can be said that the Bell Witch attacked Betsy only because she was John's favorite daughter, his pride and joy—torturing that which John loved must have seemed like an awfully good plan.

On December 20, 1820, John Bell Sr. was found dead in his bed, one day after having slipped into a coma. A small vial of liquid was found at John's bedside which, when tested on the family's cat, was soon proven to be poison. The Bell Witch immediately announced that it was her that had killed John, saying "I gave Ol' Jack a big dose of that last night, which fixed him!" The funeral for John that followed was the biggest ever attended in Robertson County.

Even the Bell Witch attended.

Legend has it that the Bell Witch laughed and sang during the funeral and continued on until the very last person left the graveyard. From then on, the Bell Witch was a scarce personality in the Bell family home; she had accomplished her mission of destroying their patriarch. A year after John was buried, the witch visited his widow, Lucy, and promised her that she would return in seven years. True to her word, the witch returned in 1828, centering her visit around John Bell Jr., engaging him in talks of Christianity and spiritual awareness. It is also said that the witch accurately predicted the coming Civil War. Upon leaving, she promised to visit John Bell's next direct descendant in 107 years.

She never showed.

Betsy Bell married Richard Powell and settled in Mississippi, where she lived to a ripe old age of 82. The descendants of Betsy and Richard have said that, while the family knew the history of their wizened matriarch and her battles with the witch, no one spoke of it out of fear that it could summon her wrath once more. Fifty years after their battle with the witch, the wounds were still fresh, the memories still haunting.

PARANORMAL FINDINGS

Visitors to the Bell Witch Cave have reported a multitude of paranormal events, ranging from hearing voices in parts of the cave that are inaccessible to humans, while others have felt heavy, dark weights on their shoulders and backs that make them collapse to the ground. Strange lights and other anomalies have been seen darting through the cave as well as in the woods surrounding the cave.

"Perhaps most disturbingly," writes Caesar, a journalist who posts on the Unsolved Mysteries website, "many visitors have taken pictures and discovered that some of their guests have either not shown up in their photographs, or there have been extra figures or even creatures showing up that were not visible at the time the picture was taken."

According to Joseph Flammer and Diane Hill, two prominent paranormal investigators who go by the name the Paranormal Adventurers, the spirits in the cave were a little more direct with them. As they came across the empty stone casket that had once held the remains of the 12-year-old American Indian girl, Joseph decided to get a photograph. "I suddenly felt my arm pushed hard from behind as I was preparing to take a photograph of the tomb," he wrote on their website. "I was jolted. The setup I had carefully made of the camera shot I was about to take of the tomb was ruined! In reaction I turned quickly around to chastise Diane for pushing my arm so hard to get my attention. It was so unlike her to do that!"

When Joseph turned to complain to his partner, he found that she was standing quietly five feet away from him. "A chill shot up my spine when I realized it was not a human hand that had pushed my arm." The two were visiting the cave with renowned author and Bell Witch expert Pat Fitzhugh at the time, and when Flammer mentioned what had happened to him, Fitzhugh essentially shrugged his shoulders. "You were not supposed to take that picture," he said, inferring that perhaps the spirit in the cave didn't want Flammer to photograph the tomb.

"Oddly enough, Diane reported to me that although she had a camera while she was down in the cave, she could not bring herself to photograph the tomb. She didn't know why."

"I just could not photograph it," Diane explained.

WHO WAS THE BELL WITCH?

There are theories and stories everywhere that point to the identity of the mysterious spirit who called itself Cate. You can take or leave any of them and none of them will conclusively prove who, or what, the Bell Witch was or is. The list of suspects who may have conjured a vengeful spirit is long and anyone can connect the dots and create a storyline out of nowhere. No one will ever know who or what the Bell Witch was, and tales of spirits acting out their revenge are plentiful in the Appalachian regions. What is known about the Witch is that her legacy inspired a great number of those legends, from the Boo Hag all the way down to the Jersey Devil and Pumpkinhead.

But was the Bell Witch a demonic presence, as suggested by some scholars, conjured up to act out some sort of revenge? While the Bell Witch was not a demonic spirit, it did show traits of a dark spirit, something that sometimes gets confused with being a demonic entity. But make no mistake: dark spirits are NOT demons, nor are they demonic in nature. Most times, it simply is what it is: a ticked-off ghost using all of its energy to darken the minds and spirits of those who it sets its sights on. True demonic hauntings are rare and almost always require the aid of a priest or medium to dispel them permanently.

Poltergeist hauntings, by contrast, are born from living people and aided by the dead. It is usually begun by a woman or a child who has psychic abilities and has repressed them, creating a good amount of negative energy that built up like a pressure cooker. That negative energy, when pushed down enough, can take form as an entity and do the off-handed bidding of its maker. What is interesting is that most poltergeist hauntings center around a young girl or boy going through that agonizing phase of adolescence. Is it possible that Betsy had abilities she wasn't aware of? Absolutely. Would she have had repressed negative energies and feelings? Of course, what teenage girl doesn't? In this case, during the early 1800s, it could be so much more intense due to the strict social mores placed upon women at the time. Had Betsy come out and said she had visions or the gifts of a medium, she would most likely have been stoned to death or exiled from her family for practicing witchcraft.

If the Bell Witch was the offspring of Betsy's clairvoyant abilities, why was her father the most targeted? Were the thoughts she was repressing negative ones about John Bell Sr.? There are no reports or stories of John Bell abusing any of his daughters, but incest and child abuse are hardly the inventions of 20th century deviants. It is possible that John Bell carried with him a secret, one he would much rather die with than expose at any time, even at the expense of his own family. But again, while there is no proof that John abused any of his children, there is no proof that he didn't.

Chillingly, it wouldn't be until almost a hundred years later that archaeologists discovered that much of John Bell's homestead sat on an ancient burial ground, used thousands of years before white men even thought of coming to The New World. By the time the Bell's took possession of the land, all of the remaining Natives had moved on and the forest had reclaimed the burial ground. Even in the Bell Witch Cave an old grave was found, empty, looted by thieves from years before. It sounds like a bad movie, but there is no denying that there is an abundance of negative energy in places where the dead are not allowed to rest in peace.

Of course, this is all conjecture, hearsay, and hypotheses run wild. In a case as cold as this one, all one has left are wild ideas. No physical proof exists anymore, if it did at all, and we are left with nothing but exaggerated stories heard secondhand. Maybe the Bell Witch was just a spirit, plain and simple, who saw an opportunity and ran with it. Perhaps she was an earth spirit or fairy-like being who felt disgusted by John's use of the farm and felt an urge to teach the old man a lesson. I understand that some people need more of a reason for a haunting and that all of us look for drama where there is none. We need an explanation. Nothing happens without a reason, right? Well, sometimes it does and I truly think this is one of those times.

Even today, in present day Adams, Tennessee, the locals and tourists alike concede that there is an air of mysticism in their little town, one that you feel when you enter and notice its absence when you leave. Some have even claimed to have seen phantom lanterns crossing the field that was once John Bell's property. Unearthly fogs have appeared and dissipated at the drop of a hat. There are even stories of people who devalue the Bell Witch's existence and find that their car won't start until they acknowledge her existence. The spirit of the Bell Witch is overwhelming in Adams. She is treated with a cautionary reverence that everyone seems to take part in; she is the unspoken guardian of Adams, demanding respect from all who choose to cross her path and if you happen to deny her existence? Well, I warned you...

HANNAH HOUSE

INDIANAPOLIS, IN

**Hope in reality is the worst of all
evils because it prolongs
the torments of man.
–Friedrich Nietzsche**

The Hannah House of Indianapolis, home to Alexander Hannah and a well-known stop on the Underground Railroad. (Photo by the author.)

In the dark of the basement, they hid out, quietly looking toward tomorrow, their dreams of freedom illuminated by their passion and the single oil lamp that lit the dark passage. They had traveled so far in such a short amount of time and freedom from the chains and the whips was within their grasp. Only two more nights of travel on the Underground Railroad and they would be in Canada, free from the tyranny of evil men.

And in an instant, it was over. In a single moment of terrifying pain, heat, and suffocating horror, they were all gone, as were their dreams of freedom. And now, over a hundred years later, they still remain in this house, wandering the opulent halls in the dead of night, still looking for a way out, still looking for the end of their nightmare, only to find that it goes on and on. Here at Hannah House in Indianapolis, Indiana, the shadows are long and the hallways stretch for eternities and whoever walks there never walks alone.

Built in 1858 by Alexander Moore Hannah, the house was initially designed to house only himself and his servants. But when he married, a separate wing was added specifically for the servants and staff. Hannah was a staunch abolitionist, of this there was no doubt. He was very vocal in his disapproval of slavery, and it is this passion for freedom and equality for all that ultimately led to the house being so haunted.

The house was eventually sold by Hannah's heirs, in 1899, to a man named Roman Oehler, a wealthy immigrant new to the area. He must have liked living in the house and the city, for Oehler's descendants still own the Hannah House to this day.

But one thing the Hannahs and the Oehlers never really mentioned were all of the ghosts that seemed to drift through its halls and vast rooms. From the residual pride Hannah felt in his home, to the tragic deaths of numerous runaway slaves, it is little wonder that Hannah House is teeming with activity. The most horrific story comes from Hannah's own dedication to the abolitionist movement. To the citizens who ran the Underground Railroad, the Hannah House was a welcome sight for escaped slaves on the road to freedom in Canada. They received food, water, and shelter as they waited for the next leg of their journey to begin. Hannah did this without fear of reprisal, knowing full well that he would be looking at prison time or worse if he aided an escaping slave. Alexander Hannah was so certain that he was doing the right thing that what happened on one dark night obviously left a scar on his soul.

Escaped slaves were being held in the basement area, as usual, with only a small oil lamp to light the darkness. The door to the basement had been locked from the outside, the reasoning being that if marshals or lynch mobs came looking for the slaves, they would not be able to open the basement door very easily. Sometime during the night while men, women, and children slept, that oil lamp was knocked to the ground.

Flames erupted around the sleeping slaves, igniting their straw beds as the oil from the lamp continued to spread. Those who were not burned alive died of smoke inhalation. No one survived the tragedy.

When Hannah discovered what had happened, he ordered the bodies be buried in the dirt floor of the basement and covered over with fresh soil. Had the secret of the Hannah House being a stop on the Underground Railroad gotten out, it would have compromised each stop of the Railroad and all of the people associated with it. Alexander Hannah buried the truth, both literally and figuratively, in the earthen floor of his basement, and moved on.

But that wasn't the only tragedy hidden away in the house. Elizabeth Hannah had given birth to a still-born child in one of the second-floor bedrooms. Alexander and Elizabeth Hannah shared their plot of ground with the body of a child whose tombstone bore only the date of its birth on its stone face. Even though the child came into the world without sound, some say they have heard the wails of a newborn child at different times of the day echoing throughout the house.

It wasn't until the house came under the care of David Elder, in 1962, that much of the eerie goings on came to light. Elder took over the day-to-day duties of Hannah House, but did not live in the building itself. Still, Elder began to notice odd happenings in the house that he couldn't quite explain. David Elder's first experience came while he was working in the mansion and suddenly heard the loud crash of breaking glass coming from the basement. It sounded like several glass jars being broken all at once, a terrifying sound to be heard in a nearly silent house. Upon investigating the area, Elder found nothing out of place, but did notice several broken jars of preserved fruit being stored in the area where the slaves had supposedly been buried over a hundred years before.

Eventually, the activity increased, steadily and rapidly.

THE SECOND-FLOOR BEDROOM

All haunted places have a center of activity, a place where the haunting seems the strongest. A place where there seems to be a gateway to the other side. In the case of Hannah House, this gateway lies directly behind the door to the second-floor bedroom. This is the bedroom where Elizabeth Jackson Hannah gave birth to her tragically still-born child. Their loss was a devastating blow, but it also seemed to mark the room forever as a place of darkness. These days, the room is used to house brides staging their weddings on the grounds of Hannah House. But sometimes, just sometimes, it is seen as a room that is far from pure, elegant, and innocent.

David Elder found this out when he noticed the room had begun to emanate a powerful odor of rot and decay, an acrid smell of true death. No amount of washing and cleaning could remove the odor until it mysteriously disappeared and did not return. Eventually, the room was sealed up and used for storage, but not before earning Hannah House the nickname "the house that reeks of death." But, by the same token, people have reported smelling the sweet scent of fresh-cut roses in the room as well, possibly signifying the presence of Mrs. Hannah as she manifests in the room that brought her so much pain.

Even though the room had been locked up and sealed away, it didn't stop the spirits from opening and closing the door repeatedly, swinging it open and closed at will. Those still living in the house began to hear strange noises, footsteps, the tell-tale mumblings of chatter and conversing voices, and felt the icy chill of cold drafts in rooms so securely insulated that there was no way a draft could have even snuck into the room. Doors and windows opened and closed at will. Eventually, the stories began to seep out of Hannah House and into the public conscience.

The house passed into the hands of the O'Brien family, and as the title changed hands, the activity increased even more. The O'Brien's had a long history of doing business in the Hannah House, and saw an opportunity to own what could possibly be the perfect home for them and their burgeoning business ventures as antique dealers.

Mrs. O'Brien had hired a painter to refurbish some of the more faded walls in Hannah House. The painter had heard all of those stories but blew them off as rumor and gross exaggerations from weak minds. But when he himself was confronted not only by swinging doors and falling picture frames, but also by flying silverware, the painter dropped his brush and fled.

Mrs. O'Brien's son picked up where the painter left off, attempting to finish the job, but he noticed right away the uncomfortable feeling of being watched by unseen eyes. On his second night of painting, he brought along his wife and two small daughters to keep him company. As he, his wife, and oldest daughter were working in one room, his youngest daughter could be heard having a conversation with someone on the stairs just outside the room. Going to investigate, she told her mother and father that she had been talking to an old man who reminded her of a grandpa-type of person, someone that only she could see. She felt no fear when she talked to this old man and, as they watched, she continued to carry on this conversation with the invisible old man.

Sometime between the Elders and the O'Briens taking control of the house, an antique shop had been opened in a portion of the downstairs area of Hannah House. It was in this area that Mrs. O'Brien looked up toward the second-floor staircase and caught sight of a man in a black suit walking across the floor of the upstairs hallway. When she went to investigate and make sure that the man found his way back to the first floor, Mrs. O'Brien found that the man had disappeared. He was nowhere to be found. Of course, this wasn't the only time Mrs. O'Brien had seen the man in the suit. She had also seen the old man in the suit standing in an archway on the stairs. He was semi-transparent with the same old fashioned black suit and mutton-chop sideburns. As Mrs. O'Brien tried to reach for him, his form fizzled and faded away.

Mr. O'Brien, in turn, also had dealings with the spirits of Hannah House, but was far less patient with them. After watching the attic door open and close by itself and listening to footsteps walking up and down the carpeted floors, he finally lost his cool while watching television in one of the upstairs bedrooms. He began to hear loud groans of torment and suffering traveling up and down the second floor hallways. Mr. O'Brien yelled out to the spirits, telling them to "Stop your bellyaching and leave us in peace!"

The second-floor hallway of Hannah House, where an antiques dealer recalled seeing the well-dressed specter Alexander Hannah walking about the floors before disappearing into one of the rooms. (Photo by the author.)

That seemed to do the trick. By 1972, the paranormal activity had come to a halt. But with new faces and new directions come the same old tricks, as the spirits got riled up again when the Indianapolis Jaycees used Hannah House to stage their annual haunted house from 1980 to 1982. Mysterious scratching was heard on the inside of the staircases, a new manifestation and one that couldn't be explained away when it was investigated more closely. Even spookier was the way the eerie haunted house sound effects coming from a sound system kept shutting off. When it was turned back on, something again turned it off. This happened over and over again until finally they just left it alone, figuring one of the spirits was tired of hearing all of the fake haunted house sounds, though it is entirely possible that faulty electronic equipment could have been the culprit.

In October of 1981, a local television station had gone to Hannah House to film a segment about the Jaycees' Haunted House for broadcast on the news that evening. While standing in the dining room doorway, a cameraman commented that it would be unsettling if the chandelier began to swing. Almost as if on cue, the chandelier began to swing back and forth in a six-inch arc. Dumbfounded and awestruck, the TV crew investigated the swinging chandelier, only to deduce that there was no possible way the chandelier could have started swinging on its own. Furthermore, this same TV crew was privy to another eerie happening just before they wrapped for the night. As they filmed the reporter doing his piece about the house, a picture frame fell from the wall with a loud crash. The nail that had held it up to the wall was still bent in its original upward direction, leading those who witnessed it to believe that the picture frame had been pushed up and out by unseen hands, a deliberate act by trickster ghosts intent on letting everyone know they were still there.

THE ATTIC

It always used to be a mystery to me why attic spaces tended to be the ideal hiding places for spirits until I realized that most attic spaces are 1) rarely visited, and 2) mostly used to store away family heirlooms and memories. If I was a spirit, an attic or basement would be the ideal place to be left alone until I wanted to interact with the living. And to be close to the family memories that would invariably help keep me shackled to Earth? That's another good reason.

Legend has it that a young boy was killed in the attic and that his body was burned in order to destroy the evidence. I've found no published accounts of the death—not surprising, as it was a murder covered up to avoid detection. But there is a lot of evidence to suggest that not only does a small boy haunt the attic, but it's

possible his killer does as well. So it really comes as no surprise that the attic space of Hannah House, like the basement, is a favorite spot for spirits. But in this case, the attic of Hannah House is adrift in creepy, scary activity that keep most people from walking through the door. In fact, most people go out of their way to avoid the attic at Hannah House.

Not Lorri and Caitlin Sankowsky.

Caitlin was sixteen at the time her mother, Lorri, was conducting a paranormal investigation of Hannah House with her Indiana Ghost Trackers colleagues. When the investigation had wrapped and the equipment was packed back into the trucks, Caitlin asked her mom to take her on a tour of the attic, one place that they hadn't gotten to during the course of the ghost hunt.

Lorri agreed to take Caitlin and some of her friends up to the attic where they would stage an impromptu investigation. What they got was far more memorable than any EVP they might have collected, and much more terrifying than either of them was expecting.

When they'd gotten up to the attic room, both Lorri and Caitlin noticed how heavy and oppressive the atmosphere felt. Paranoia gripped the both of them and they were convinced that someone—or something—was watching them. After a few tense moments, Caitlin and her friends had decided they'd had enough. They turned to leave, only to have the door slam shut in their faces. Panicking, they tried in vain to budge the door, but couldn't. It wasn't locked and it didn't feel stuck. It just wouldn't open.

Terrified, Lorri and the girls pulled on the door repeatedly until, finally, it swung open on its own. Not wanting to test fate any more than they already had, the group of women walked quickly out the attic door and down the stairs. They didn't look back. Perhaps they were afraid of seeing something watching them leave.

Their story of what happened in the attic isn't at all uncommon. In fact, it's tame compared to some stories that have come from Hannah House's uppermost floor. Members of the Indy Ghost Hunters group had an experience that one of them in particular will remember for the rest of her life. An investigator named Stacey was conducting an EVP session when she was touched on the arm by small, unseen hands. Later, EVPs were captured of a whispery, sharp voice saying, "Leave the house!" and "Get out!"

The dank and cool basement, where an untold number of runaway slaves burned to death in an accidental fire set off by a broken oil lantern. Their bodies supposedly lie beneath the concrete floor. (Photo by the author.)

THE BASEMENT

But while the house seems to be teeming with playful paranormal activity on the first and second floors, the scariest of it seems to be centered around the basement area and with good reason. This was the place where an untold number of escaped slaves perished in a tragic fire, only to have their bodies buried secretly in the earthen floor.

Visitors to the house have seen the shadowy apparitions of slaves darting about the basement. Some have even caught sight of a group of slaves huddled together in the darkness. Strange sounds such as knocks, mournful groans, deafening screams, and the sound of bare feet slapping against the stone have frightened many a visitor and ghost hunter at the Hannah House. The smell of human body odor, followed by the familiar scent of burning wood has also been known to traverse the basement area, as have the tell-tale cold spots of a spirit's presence.

Chillingly, some visitors to the Hannah House have reported hearing AND feeling banging on the floors beneath them, as if the dying slaves are trying to escape their deaths by any means necessary, even if it means punching a hole through the floors above them.

According to Lorri Sankowsky and Keri Young, authors of *The Ghost Hunter's Guide To Indianapolis* and former members of the Indiana Ghost Trackers (IGT), the basement also contains the tortured spirit of a slave, one who has no shame in telling people what it wants.

"Lorri and I started doing EVP around the perimeter of the basement," wrote Young. "We asked questions such as 'What year is it?' 'How did you die?' and 'Did you have any children?' After the investigation, Lorri and I played back the tape, and in one spot of the basement, the eerie, cryptic words 'Find me' were spoken loudly and clearly over the conversation we were having. We were alone in that corner of the basement when this was recorded."

Six months later, IGT members Chris and Amy Garrison were investigating the basement area and, to their utter shock and surprise, found that the same voice saying "Find me" could be heard over their conversation as well.

Keri Young summed it up well in her book, writing: "Someone not of this earth wants to be found in the Hannah House basement."

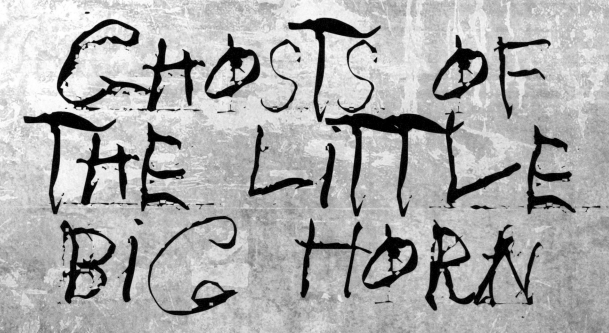

GHOSTS OF THE LITTLE BIG HORN

CROW AGENCY, MT

They made us many promises, more than I can
remember, but they never kept but one:
they promised to take our land, and they took it.
– Red Cloud, Chief of the Lakota Sioux

At this bend in the Little Big Horn river, hundreds of teepees held thousands of Cheyenne and Sioux warriors, who greeted Custer's troops eagerly. (Photo by Edward Curtis, courtesy of the Library of Congress.)

The corpses of 268 cavalrymen and over 100 Native Americans lay scattered across the land close to the Little Big Horn river, the ground, grass, and waters stained with blood. In time, the tribesmen would return to claim their dead and give them proper burial. But the bodies of the cavalrymen, most of them mutilated, destroyed, and stripped of valuable clothing by the attacking Cheyenne and

Sioux warriors, would spend more time on the field before their men would stumble upon the massacre and try to make sense of just what had happened on those bloody few days in June of 1876.

Both famous and infamous names such as George Armstrong Custer, Sitting Bull, and Crazy Horse all fought here at this lonely little section of plains crouched near the Little Big Horn river. It would be the only true, bona fide Native victory in the history of the plains Indians, and would ultimately turn the tide of the Great Indian War against the Natives forever.

In 1868, the Treaty of Fort Laramie was signed, which essentially granted the Black Hills area to the Sioux nation and ended Oglala Sioux Chief Red Cloud's war against the white men. But rumors of gold being discovered in the early 1870s caused white miners to start sneaking into the Black Hills reservation and poaching gold illegally from the Indians. The United States Government, in its infinite wisdom, decided to send a geological team, led by General George Armstrong Custer, into the reservation to examine the land and decide if the rumors were true.

Yes, reported Custer. Gold was amongst the other minerals of the land.

The onslaught of greedy white men was overwhelming, and the Black Hills War had begun as American Indians targeted the invaders of their land—land agreed upon by both the Indian nations and the U.S. Government.

The Indians were understandably and rightfully angry. This was yet another promise broken by white men, and it was the last straw. In 1875, Chief Sitting Bull of the Lakota Sioux created the Sun Dance Alliance between the Lakota, the Cheyenne, and a large number of "Agency Indians" who had slipped away from their reservations to join them. It was this enormous faction of Agency Indians that brought the U.S. Military to Montana. They were sent to force the Lakota and Cheyenne back to their reservations and, in doing so, completely underestimated the will and the intelligence of their opponents.

The Battle of the Little Big Horn began on June 25th, 1876, as Custer and his men slipped into Sioux territory and, against the advice of his Native scouts, attacked an enormous village along the Little Big Horn river. Custer was convinced that the Indians would scatter when attacked and one can only imagine his surprise when

they didn't. Rather, they banded together and, soon, Custer found himself surrounded by more and more Indian warriors, numbering well over a thousand men. Led by Red Cloud of the Oglala Sioux and Crazy Horse of the Lakota Sioux, and using a plan devised by Chief Sitting Bull himself, the Natives had anticipated Custer's arrival and surrounded the U.S. cavalrymen on all sides. With just a little over 700 soldiers of his own, General George Armstrong Custer knew that he'd made a mistake. Less than an hour into the first day of battle, Custer lay dead on the hill just beyond the Big Horn River. A Lakota Sioux warrior named Big Nose had delivered a fatal shot to Custer's chest from his Winchester rifle. A postmortem gunshot was also delivered to Custer's head.

The members of the Sun Dance Alliance engaged the remaining soldiers fiercely for two straight days. When they chose to finally retreat, they were chased down and slaughtered in large groups by the victorious Native Americans. Over 250 soldiers never returned home after the Battle of the Little Big Horn. The rest either escaped the slaughter by fleeing, or they deserted their posts early on in the fracas.

While the surviving tribesmen gathered up their dead and buried them, they took the time to mutilate and desecrate the bodies of several of the white cavalrymen. Some were stripped naked and disemboweled. Souvenirs of scalps, genitals, ears, and noses were claimed as well. Only Custer's body lay untouched, as if the victorious Indians were showing respect for his courage, but most scholars believe that, because he was wearing buckskin clothing rather than an officer's uniform, it might have confused the surviving Indians into thinking he was one of their own and left him be. The bodies of the dead cavalrymen lay on the field for days, decaying and rotting in the open summer sun. When reinforcements finally arrived, the scene was almost too much to take. The stench of death could be smelled long before they arrived at the actual scene and it is said that the men worked quickly to bury the dead where they lay.

In essence, the Battle of the Little Big Horn was the Indian's last hurrah. After the battle, the Alliance broke up. Crazy Horse and Sitting Bull fled, scattering in different directions. Crazy Horse eventually turned himself in at Fort Robinson, while Sitting Bull fled to Canada. But hunger and the extreme cold forced Sitting

You have to understand that this battle at the Little Big Horn was an important movement for the American Indians. For hundreds of years, they had been put under the thumb of invading hordes of Caucasian barbarians, forced to learn English, forced to convert to Christianity. They were forced from the lands they called home and moved onto spiritually and ecologically dead reservations that the white men either didn't want or couldn't farm. Entire villages were wiped out by disease due to tainted supplies given to them by the government. Their livelihoods were stolen from them with each passing moment. The men were killed indiscriminately, the women and children enslaved or sent off to finishing schools where all traces of their Native heritage could be forced out of them. And when gold was found on the reservations they were given? The white men took it back, stealing all of the wealth that the American Indians were entitled to by poaching it illegally. All of this rage, all of this oppression, all of this frustration came out during the Battle of the Little Big Horn, and it painted the landscape not only with the blood of the white and Indian men, but also with the supercharged energy of a passionate rebellion.

Using Sitting Bull's uncanny strategic planning, Chief Red Cloud of the Oglala Sioux executed the incredibly successful defense of his people against the invading Custer and his Cavalry. (Photo courtesy of the Library of Congress.)

Bull and his family to return to the U.S., where he surrendered to officers at Fort Buford.

And the Black Hills reservation? It was taken back by the U.S. Government in 1878. A hundred years later, the Sioux Nation sued the American government and won, but rejected the money offered as a settlement. They only wanted their land, sacred and rightfully theirs, back in Sioux hands and under Sioux control. The government refused.

WOUNDS NOT YET HEALED

The site of Custer's Last Stand near the Little Big Horn river is one of those places that is just alive with activity. While researching this chapter, I found literally thousands of stories detailing real-life experiences with both ghostly cavalrymen and Indian warriors alike. These weren't all stories from psychics, mediums, and clairvoyants. These were also stories collected from regular, normal people like park rangers, blue collar tourists, and a lot of skeptics. If only some of the stories were true, then the site of Custer's Last Stand must go down in history as the most haunted place in the country.

The Crow Indians are said to have been particularly superstitious about the Little Big Horn battlefield. "They called the superintendent 'ghost herder,'" writes historian Bob Reece, "because he lowered the flag at dusk, which the Crow believed allowed the spirits to rise from their graves and walk amongst the living. When the flag was raised, in the morning, the dead came back to rest."

According to Reece, the ideas and stories of ghosts at the Little Big Horn didn't start coming into the public conscience until the mid 1940s when author Charles Kuhlman claimed he had been visited by the spirit of General Custer once while he was visiting Last Stand Hill alone. He had gone there in hopes of contacting the dead, and according to Reece, that's exactly what he did. Kuhlman went on to write a graphic, very well detailed novel about Custer's Last Stand, one that he claims came straight from Custer's mouth. "It could explain Kuhlman's fantastic interpretation of the battle," theorized Reece. Stories of the sounds of Indian warriors charging on horseback through the cemetery soon followed. People who walked through the cemetery at night spoke of cold spots that seemed to come from nowhere and the disturbing shadows of men on horseback in the darkness of night.

More interesting are the stories of cavalrymen and Indians continuing to fight the battle to this very day. A cab driver, visiting from Minneapolis, stumbled into the visitor's center, his body shaking, and skin pale and ashen. He claimed to have witnessed soldiers and Indians viciously fighting each other on the plains near the battlefield. Obviously, it was quite a while before he had been able to calm down and tell the others what it was he had seen.

In August 1976, a National Park Service police officer visited Last Stand Hill and was shocked to feel a sudden drop in temperature that seemed to shoot through his body. As he was trying to process this sudden shock of cold rifling through him on a hot August night, he heard the slight murmurs of voices all around him, as if they were having a conversation. Sadly, he couldn't make out what they were saying; he didn't stick around long enough to properly eavesdrop.

GHOST WARRIORS

In August of 1987, the battlefield was visited by a psychic medium. Being from Colorado, she knew little to nothing of the battle, yet she described the action of the skirmish in stunning detail. As she stood by the Monument to the 7th Cavalry and the graveyard, she insisted that she felt the presence of spirits, restless ghosts belonging to Custer's lost army.

Upon visiting the cemetery, she watched as the ghost of a Lakota Sioux warrior charged toward a park employee who was resting near the Cemetery Ridge, his eyes closed. The warrior rode his pony up to the sleeping man, extended his war club and tapped him on the forehead before riding off, disappearing into oblivion. While the park employee saw nothing, when the Sioux warrior touched his head with his war club, the sleeping man woke and looked around, startled. "What was that?" he'd asked, clearly indicating that he'd felt something touch him.

It wasn't until much later, after the psychic had recounted the story, that she was told that the Sioux warrior had "counted coup" on the sleeping man. "Counting coup" refers to the practice of touching an enemy warrior with something held in one's hand during battle. For instance, a warrior would tap the top of a man's head with his war club, or perhaps press a knife against his cheek. It was like petting a cobra and surviving. A true test of bravery and strength. To the Sioux, it was far more praiseworthy to count coup on an enemy than it was to kill him.

Another park ranger, Mardell Plainfeather, was a member of the Crow tribe and worked at the battlefield during the 1980s. She was a devout Crow, still clinging to the rituals and ways of old. While on their way to make sure the fire at the sweat lodge had been properly extinguished, Mardell and her daughter saw something that changed their lives forever.

Two American Indian spirits, astride their horses, sat on the crest of the bluffs overlooking the battlefield. The moon cast them slightly as silhouettes, but Mardell could still see that they were dressed for war, complete with painted faces. One had long flowing hair, the other, braids. They carried shields, but only one carried a bow and arrow. A chill went up her spine when she saw one of the Indians lift himself from the saddle to peer intently down at her as she drove on toward the sweat lodge. Then, the two spirits faded into the dark night. Returning the next morning, Mardell found no evidence of horses or people on the hilltop. No tracks, no broken twigs or displaced brush, no clumps of waste dropped by the horses. To anyone else, it looked as if no horse had touched the ground up on the hilltop for months. But to Mardell, it only served to send

Last Stand Hill, where General Custer was shot down by a Cheyenne warrior named Big Nose an hour into the battle. Soldiers and Native warriors alike are said to still battle on these plains nightly, especially near the anniversary of the epic massacre. (Photo by H.R. Locke, courtesy of the Library of Congress.)

a chill up her spine and gave her a story to tell her children and grandchildren for years to come.

Christine Hope, another employee of the park service, was sleeping in the building known as the Stone House when she woke late one night and saw a man sitting at her kitchen table. He wore a pained look on his face and a distinctive handlebar mustache. It wasn't until some time later that Christine came across a picture of Lieutenant Benjamin Hodgson and immediately recognized him as the man that had been sitting in her kitchen. Hodgson had been a member of the B Company of cavalrymen and obviously had been killed in battle. Since that night, Hodgson's ghost has been a regular guest at the house known as The Stone House.

I literally could go on for page after page after page relating stories of haunted encounters at the Little Big Horn. The energy of the past is still alive in the present and the spirits of the battle will continue to try to reach out to the living. In truth, very few walk away from the battlefield without feeling that energy.

FOX HOLLOW FARM

WESTFIELD, IN

He fit all the components of a serial killer, among them
the ability to keep his crimes in control and silent under
an everyday nonchalance. He was a business owner whose
store many townspeople frequented. My own office was
only a mile and a half away from his place. I never met
him, but from what I understand, he wasn't the type of
guy you'd at first suspect of being a sexual psychopath.
–Virgil Vandagriff, on Herbert Baumeister

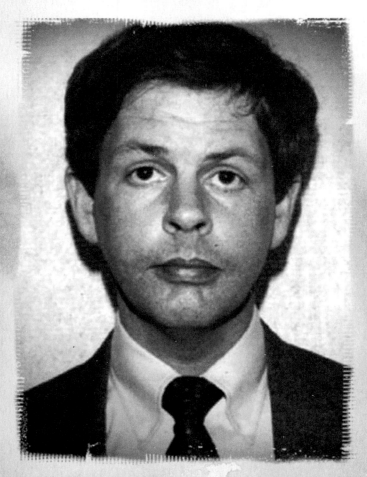

Suspected sexual serial killer and Indianapolis businessman Herbert Baumeister. (Source unknown.)

Tucked away in the rural countryside of Westfield, Indiana, about half an hour outside of Indianapolis, is a lonely estate surrounded by woods and shrouded by a darkening cloud from its past. At one time, it was a happy, joyous place, where a man's wife and children played and strolled along its many trails and scenic overlooks. But it was what the man did while his wife was away that cast a dark pall over the estate known as Fox Hollow Farm.

Herbert Baumeister was the oldest of four children, born to prominent Indianapolis doctor Herbert E. and his wife Elizabeth, and many remember his childhood as being quite normal. But something happened when he hit puberty that changed everything. He had begun to show aberrant and anti-social behaviors. Friends speaking with police and news agencies later on would remember how he tended to play with the corpses of animals and even urinated on his schoolteacher's desk. Doctors eventually diagnosed him as being a paranoid schizophrenic, but surprisingly, did not treat him for it. It is possible that, as the son of a well-thought-of physician, he was remanded to the care of his father, who tried to keep young Herbert's condition as quiet as possible. But as he grew older, Herbert grew stranger and more bizarre, alienating many of the few friends he was able to make with his outlandish and off-putting behavior. He attended North Central High School in Indianapolis, but became known as a nerdy, bookish type who always kept to himself. He began to attend Indiana University in Bloomington after graduation, where he was to meet the woman of his dreams. Herb Baumeister, never being the social type, eventually collected himself and was able to pass himself off as normal enough to court young Julie Saiter. Julie was taken by Herb's boyish good looks, but also by his affiliation with the Young Republican's group. Not only that, but they both yearned to have their own business one day. They seemed to click so well together that no one was surprised when the two agreed to get married in 1971.

Herb passed through a series of jobs, not keeping them at all, but working hard at them while he was there. The one place Herb flourished the most was at the Bureau of Motor Vehicles, yet his bizarre behavior, like high school and college, managed to alienate nearly every one of his colleagues. One Christmas, he sent his co-workers a photo of himself and another man dressed in drag. But his can-do attitude made his superiors look the other way, choosing to see Baumeister as a man who got things done, rather than focus on his eccentricities. When someone urinated on the boss's desk, everyone at the BMV knew it had been Herb, but the boss looked the other way. It wasn't until Baumeister urinated on a letter sent by the Governor that he was officially let go from the BMV. Herb immediately spiraled into a depression, one so severe that his father stepped in and had his son committed to Central State Hospital, an Indianapolis-based psychiatric hospital. It was a decision that was met with support from Julie, who obviously had noticed her new husband's crippling depression.

When Herb was released from Central State, he borrowed $4,000 from his mother to kick start a new business, a thrift store he would call Sav-A-Lot. Running Sav-A-Lot from a business space on 146th Street, Herb ran the business in collaboration with a reputable children's charity called the Children's Bureau of Indianapolis. His gamble paid off: his new store made $50,000 that year and paved the way for a second location to be opened.

But while professional and financial windfalls made life easier, the personal lives of Herb and Julie Baumeister were hardly stable. They had moved into the prestigious estate Fox Hollow Farm in nearby Westfield, which they were buying on contract. But Julie was beginning to see a different side to her husband. He was controlling to a fault, all but cutting her out of the decision-making process altogether. They spent a lot of time apart, with Julie staying at her mother's house with the children. The house became a shamble, rooms were cluttered and ignored, and the grounds became overgrown and unkempt. It was during this time that the true nature of Herb's spirit made itself known, but not to his family. Indeed, Herbert Baumeister was working feverishly to construct a facade of normalcy to mask his true, twisted personality. To maintain the facade, he would need to maintain absolute control over every aspect of his life, especially those times spent with Julie and his children.

Meanwhile, the police had begun an investigation into the disappearance of several young men who had last been seen leaving the 501 Tavern with a man known only as Brian Smart. Some who had been to Brian Smart's home had mentioned the lavish pool in the basement and a cadre of white, featureless mannequins set up as party guests around the pool's lounge areas. Smart enjoyed auto-erotic asphyxiation, a practice he and the informant had enjoyed together. Intrigued by this, their only lead, the police had a sketch made up of Smart which was posted in nearly every gay bar in the city.

Tony Harris, a regular at the 501 Tavern, had watched one of his friends leave with this Brian Smart, only to disappear into infinity. Harris had all but given up hope in ever seeing this character ever again. He knew Smart was responsible for his friend's disappearance, but lacked any kind of proof. So imagine Tony's elation when he looked up from his drink one night and saw Brian Smart enter the bar. Composing himself, he calmly chatted up the man and managed to write down his license plate number as he drove off at the end of the night.

Turning the license plate number over to authorities, Indianapolis police discovered that Brian Smart was, in fact, Herb Baumeister of Westfield. He lived at an estate called Fox Hollow Farm with his wife and three children. Chillingly, the home boasted a luxurious swimming pool in the basement.

According to police, while his wife and he were separated, Baumeister began cruising the local gay bars, most notably the 501 Tavern in downtown Indianapolis. It was there that he began to pick up gay men, take them back to his home, and kill them in the basement swimming pool, enticing them with the idea of auto-erotic asphyxiation. Baumeister's double life went unnoticed by his wife, largely in part because Herb was so controlling and she tried not to upset him. Julie Baumeister was, essentially, a wreck. She was living in fear from a man she thought she'd known, their marriage had become loveless and sexless, and their businesses were in a sharp decline.

The police didn't have enough proof to obtain a search warrant, and both Herb and Julie Baumeister refused to allow the police onto their property to search for evidence without one. But as Julie and Herb finally began to go through divorce proceedings, Julie began to feel less and less loyal to her husband, who by this time had become angrier, more controlling, and just plain weirder as time went on.

When Herb took his son Erich on a fishing trip to Lake Wawasee in nearby Syracuse, Indiana, Julie and her remaining children found what appeared to be a human leg-bone in the forests surrounding Fox Hollow Farm. Finally, Julie relented and allowed the police to search the house and grounds. Investigators found the remains of 11 young men, their charred bones found scattered across the forest floor. Of that number, only four were positively identified: Roger

Goodlet, 33, Steven Hale, 26, and Richard Hamilton, 20, all of Indianapolis, and Manuel Resendez, 31, of Lafayette, Indiana.

Julie chillingly recalled the time two years earlier when their son Erich had discovered a skeleton in the woods. When confronted, Herb Baumeister claimed it was only one of his late father's old dissecting skeletons, discarded in the woods while he was cleaning out the storage areas in the barn and house. She'd believed him at the time. Honestly, she had no reason to doubt him. That mistake of taking his word for it no doubt haunts her to this day, for if she had reported the skeleton two years earlier, how many lives could she have saved since then?

During the course of the investigation, one thing that became a particular interest was a concealed video camera in the pool area which investigators believed may have been the only witness to Baumeister's killing spree. "Where were the tapes?" was the question everyone seemed to have, but the house yielded no answers.

Herb Baumeister still had no clue that police had found the remains of his victims and with their son Erich with him, Julie was afraid for the boy's safety. Her lawyers and police drafted up an emergency warrant for the removal of Erich from his father's home, which they executed quickly. Herb had seen it coming and thought it was merely a ploy on Julie's part to complicate the coming divorce proceedings. Not letting on about the body recovery at his house, the police took Erich back to his mother and continued their investigation, allowing Baumeister to sit and wait, ignorant of what was about to happen to him.

This was what police had wanted: to keep Baumeister in a known location, unaware of their intentions, until he could be arrested and charged with murder. But Baumeister must have known something was up, for he left Lake Wawasee and disappeared. A Canadian Mountie reported seeing Baumeister's 1989 Buick along one of the highways, and he told her that he was just resting for a moment, that he'd had a long drive and was tired. The Mountie didn't think much of it, but was intrigued by the huge stockpile of VHS videotapes in Baumeister's back seat. Some time later, Baumeister's body was found lying next to his Buick near the Port Huron shoreline, with a self-inflicted gunshot wound to the head. The videotapes were nowhere to be found and their location remains a mystery to this day. In a short manner of time, the sheriff's department closed the case, stating that Herbert Baumeister was in fact the killer of eleven men and that he was dead. It has been speculated that Baumeister, who took frequent business trips to Ohio, could have been responsible for multiple disappearances in the central Ohio region, but I'm not sure I can agree with that. A serial killer like Baumeister would need his home court advantage in order to feel comfortable enough to commit murder and get away with it. He would need the upper hand and that included his house. His empty home at Fox Hollow Farm was remote enough to conceal any foul play, and with Julie away so often with the kids during any of their numerous separations, it made the home an ideal base of operations for Baumeister's twisted intentions.

But just because Herbert Baumeister chose to kill himself doesn't mean the story ends there.

THE HAUNTINGS OF FOX HOLLOW FARM

Fox Hollow Farm sat empty for nearly ten years before being bought in 2006 by Rob and Vicki Graves. They were impressed with the architecture, the remoteness of the estate, and were blown away by an indoor pool in the basement. An apartment had been added above the barn that could be rented out for added income. It was a perfect dream home for two people looking to get away from the hustle of city life. It would also be perfect for their two teenage sons.

But at half the price that it was worth, Rob and Vicki began to ask themselves why an estate worth millions was being undersold. It was during the initial walkthrough that Rob remembered where he had seen this place. It had been on the news some time ago. He knew it was Herb Baumeister's old house and he knew what had gone on there.

"Rob and I had talked about the impact of living in a home that had once been owned by a serial killer," Vicki said later. "People have lived in homes where people have passed away in it and they may not even have known it. At least we knew going into it."

Once Rob and Vicki decided that they could live in a place where

The entrance to the loft apartment above the garage, where Joe LeBlanc experienced a terrifying encounter with the spirit of one of Baumeister's victims. (Photo by author.)

multiple murders had occurred, they were happy to finally move into the house. But the eerie goings-on began when Vicki began to clean up the pool area. While vacuuming up some gravel along the poolside, someone or something repeatedly began to unplug the vacuum from the extension cord. When the extension cord shorted out, Vicki was besieged by a rash of cold chills and the feeling of being watched. "I just felt like somebody didn't want me there," she said.

Joe Le Blanc worked with Rob at the same car dealership and had been looking for an apartment that was closer to work; the hour-long commute he was pulling now was taxing his energy and his wallet. Rob immediately thought of the spare apartment above

Baumeister used the lure of his indoor pool to entice his victims to return to Fox Hollow Farm. It is believed that close to twenty young men had their last breaths in this pool. Afterward, he would drag their bodies through the exit to the right and then to the woods beyond.

the barn and he offered it to Joe, who accepted readily, again, despite knowing that it had been Herb Baumeister's house.

Around this time, Vicki began to see someone, a young man in a red shirt walking into the woods lining the perimeter of their property. "He had his back to me and he was slowly walking away," recalls Vicki, "and then I realized that I couldn't see his legs. Then he just disappeared into the trees." They went to the spot where she had seen the young man, but found nothing.

While Vicki had her share of experiences, it was Joe the renter who seemed to attract much of the attention from the spirits roaming about the property. Invisible hands would constantly bang on his door at night until he would open it to find no one there. He would hear footsteps in the gravel outside following him, but no one would be there. The knob to the front door would twist and turn eerily before the door would blow open on its own to reveal absolutely no one standing there. But by far, the most unnerving experience Joe Le Blanc had in the apartment was when he was scared out of his mind by the sudden appearance of a soaking wet, terrified, screaming young man. There was a desperate look on the young man's face, as if he were battling to escape his own death. "I honestly think that I saw one of Herb Baumeister's victims running for his life," Joe said later. "I think I see the victims because they're seeking closure, they're seeking our assistance."

Joe, meanwhile, was being beset by odd dreams of running away from something in the woods, as well as being plagued by someone banging on his front door at all hours of the night. He and his dog Fred began to feel the familiar gaze of something watching them from the darkness of the forest, of the barn, and from inside his own apartment. One night, while walking his dog, the animal caught sight of the young man in the red shirt. Fred took off after the figure in red, chasing down the man as he disappeared into the forest. Joe found his dog, but couldn't find the man in the red shirt. Instead, Joe found a human leg bone, a femur, lying on the ground, partially covered by foliage. To say this freaked him out is an understatement, but it also pulled him into a mystery he was feeling compelled to help solve.

Joe, Vicki, and Rob got in touch with the police detective who had been in charge of the case and he agreed to return to Fox Hollow Farm and give them a once over of Baumeister's actions on the property. Generally, Baumeister would go cruising the gay bars of Indianapolis until he found a mark who agreed to come home with him. From there, it was speculated that Baumeister would ply them with drinks and get them into the swimming pool. After a little coaxing, and perhaps a Xanax or other muscle relaxer, Baumeister would convince his victims to try auto-erotic asphyxiation—only Baumeister wouldn't stop. He would continue to strangle his victims even as they thrashed about the water and choked out pleas for their lives. Following the murder, Baumeister would burn the corpse and bury them in a shallow grave in the woods surrounding the property. This he did at least eleven times—police believed that close to 20 men or more may have been killed there, but only 11 were positively identified.

While reviewing video footage obtained from local news station WTHR, Joe excitedly proclaimed, "That's him!" Joe LeBlanc had pointed out Steven Hale as the man he'd seen in the apartment that night, dripping wet and screaming for help before disappearing completely.

Joe grew so obsessed with helping the spectral victims of Herbert Baumeister that he even resorted to conducting an EVP session in his apartment living room. All seemed to go well, but when Joe Le Blanc asked, "Which one are you?" the response on the tape was downright unsettling.

"The married one," a deep voice calmly responded. Being that Herb Baumeister's victims were all gay and unmarried, it only stands to reason that the spirit who responded was in fact the spirit of Herb Baumeister. Is it also possible that the man in the red shirt, seen by both Vicky and Joe near the outline of the forest, was Herb Baumeister?

Since then, Fox Hollow Farm has hosted a few paranormal events, and investigative teams from all over the country have come to the small Indiana town in an attempt to communicate not only with Baumeister's victims, but also with Baumeister himself. Champaign/Chicago Paranormal Society (C.H.I.P.S.) led an investigation of Fox Hollow Farm in November 2012 and almost immediately began to turn up EVP evidence. The spirits were hungry to talk apparently, and while the EVPs obtained by C.H.I.P.S. range from the murky to not so murky, all are decipherable and can be understood.

While investigating the rim of the woods near the house, they were able to communicate intelligently with both victim and killer, recording EVPs such as "Get out," "Help me," "Hurry up, he's coming," "They will get me," "They could find us," and "I'm stuck here." Lead investigator Marcia Mack heard many of these through the use of headphones, allowing her to hear the EVPs in real time, so imagine her surprise when she heard a voice say, "I'll yell, Marcia." When one of Marcia's colleagues tells the spirits that they are free to move on into the light beyond, a deep voice is caught saying, chillingly, "I want you to stay." Could that have been the spirit of

Current owner Robert Graves leads a tour through the woods behind the house, pausing at the infamous site of the former Burn Pile, where a mass grave of incinerated bones was uncovered shortly after Baumeister's suicide in 1996.

Herb Baumeister, controlling his victims even now, forcing them into remaining at Fox Hollow Farm for his own enjoyment? Like all EVPs, it's open to interpretation, but it is compelling nonetheless.

In June of 2014, I had the extreme pleasure of experiencing Fox Hollow Farm for myself, as I joined twenty or so other curious paranormal investigators at a paid open house that lasted most of the evening. Representatives of paranormal groups from all over Indiana, Illinois, and Ohio had descended upon Fox Hollow Farm that night. Rob and Vicky were gracious hosts, leading the entire group on a tour of the grounds, including the section of the surrounding woods known as The Burn Pile where Baumeister had

cremated a majority of the skeletonized bodies he'd left scattered around the woods. But the Pool Room was by far the most popular stop on the introductory tour, the one spot everyone was clamoring to see. This was, after all, the exact spot where most of Baumeister's victims had their last breaths.

Usually in an investigation, females tend to elicit the most responses from resident spirits. In the case of Fox Hollow Farm, only males seemed to garner any attention, which is reasonable considering who was haunting the darkened woods and halls of this amazing, luxurious mansion. Organized by psychic medium Darlene Harrison, the event was ripe for the curious, but sheer hell for those seeking a true paranormal investigation. With nearly twenty people attending the gathering and milling about unfettered throughout the mansion, capturing uncontaminated audio and video evidence would prove to be impossible. However, as many of you know, it is the personal experience that I value above all others, and I was privy to an experience that I can neither explain, nor can I deny.

One of the prevailing truths about investigating at Fox Hollow Farm is the fact that men elicit the most responses. Women investigating alone walk away empty handed, while men, with good reason, seem to grab Herb Baumeister's attention first and foremost.

That being said, I found myself teamed up with medium and paranormal investigator Angel Sells of Eerie Voices Paranormal and investigator Brenda Mudrack of Paranormal Researchers out of Fort Wayne. While investigating Joe LeBlanc's old apartment, timid shadow figures and caustic footsteps on the hardwood portions of the floor seemed to resonate throughout the darkened apartment. But nothing could prepare me for Herb Baumeister's old bathroom.

For most of the people who knew Herb, it was a well-known fact that he was meticulous about his appearance. Besides the pool, it was said that Herb's master bath was his favorite spot in the house. Even Rob Graves had mentioned that the bathroom seemed particularly packed with an unreal amount of energy.

Of course, this was one of the first places Angel, Brenda, and I went. We crowded into the bathroom, standing in the dark as Brenda looked about with her night vision goggles and snapped infrared photographs. Angel Sells, however, seemed to begin channeling Herb Baumeister himself. According to Angel, Herb was barking at Brenda to stop taking pictures. "He kept saying, 'Stop it, bitch,'" Angel recalled later in the evening, referring to Brenda's near-constantly flickering flash on her digital camera. "He didn't like that at all. He didn't want us there."

I'm not sure what prompted me to do so, but I felt the need to step inside the shower and close the door. Once inside, I held my digital voice recorder out in the palm of my hand, being careful not to grip it with my fingers; doing so would create unnecessary scratching sounds on the audio file, which I hate hearing during evidence review.

After a few moments of inviting Herb to join me in the shower, Brenda and one of her colleagues found that they had to leave the room. I found out later that they had become besieged by pounding headaches, sickening one of them to the point of vomiting. All of this was unbeknownst to me, as I was lost in the feeling of my digital voice recorder slowly starting to rock back and forth in the palm of my hand. It was almost as if someone or something was trying to flip it over or knock it from my hand completely. Had Herb driven the women out of the bathroom so he could be alone with me in the shower? Reviewing the audio later revealed no EVPs, but the suffocating energy in that bathroom was proof enough that something heavy was hanging around in there.

The activity at Fox Hollow Farm continues to this day but it is important to note one thing. Although they have hosted paranormal events in the past, Fox Hollow Farm is a privately owned residence. It is sad to think that Rob and Vicky, two incredibly nice and warm people, have had to set up security cameras and motion detectors to curb the curious from trespassing onto their property, but those who do see the inside of a jail cell, not Fox Hollow Farm. It is important that everyone respect this family and maintain a safe distance from this lovely home with an unfortunate past.

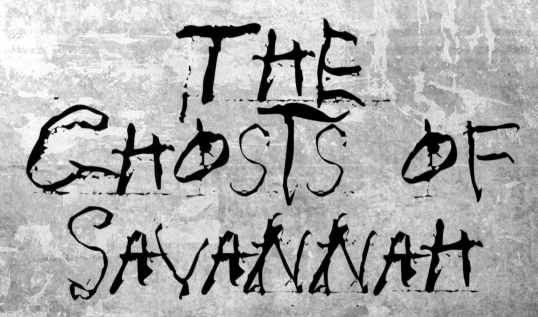

THE GHOSTS OF SAVANNAH

SAVANNAH, GEORGIA

A beautiful woman with a dirty face.
—Lady Astor of England,
when asked to describe Savannah, Georgia, in 1946

Initially, this chapter was supposed to be exclusively about the Moon River Brewery, Savannah's most haunted brew pub. But with all deep-seeking research missions, I turned up more haunted places that seemed to be worthy of recognition as well. It ranks at the top of the list with Charleston, South Carolina, as one of the most haunted cities in America and those who live there honestly claim that every inch of their fair city is haunted, crawling with spirits of the dead.

Having played a key role in the ending of the American Civil War, as well as being a wellspring for the founding of the American nation, Savannah, Georgia, has seen a lot of tragedy, drama, outbreaks of disease, famines, and blood in anger and defiance. And while profiling every building in Savannah would encompass an entire book, here at least are three of the most fascinating and compelling locations in that ghostly city where spirits linger on every street corner, building, and park bench; where ghosts of every age and century sway in the breeze and watch the living now with either longing or pity.

THE MOON RIVER BREWERY

The Moon River Brewery has not only seen blood and death, but recorded it into its walls and stairs, stone and brick, playing it over and over again for those of us lucky enough to bear witness to it. The building began its life in 1821, when Elazer Early of Charleston, South Carolina, built the City Hotel. Over the years, the building opened and closed as a bank and a post office as well. In 1851, Peter Wiltberger bought the building and reopened it as the City Hotel. Wiltberger, a graduate from P.T. Barnum's school of advertising, placed a live lion and lioness on display in the lobby just to try and drum up business. It worked for a while, at least. His tenure at the building was good for about thirteen years, as the hotel closed down in 1864, just as General Tecumseh Sherman arrived.

When word of Sherman's march into Savannah got around the city, most all of the residents fled, which, in retrospect, was a great idea. With the town near empty, Sherman didn't feel a need to burn any or all of the buildings. They could be easily used for Union needs, such as places to sleep, strategize, and recuperate. Being so close to the ports, Savannah was a wonderful place to put down Union roots as they infiltrated Southern ships and were able to re-route their own ships to these safer ports. Sherman's arrival in Savannah came at the end of his famous March to the Sea, a campaign he promised would "make Georgia howl." Before he'd arrived, it was said that he and his troops had caused nearly $100,000,000 in damages to properties from Atlanta to Savannah. Understandable why people would flee such a character.

The City Hotel building went through a number of incarnations, such as a lumber and coal storehouse and, as coal consumption dropped off, as a general storage space. It was essentially one of those old buildings that a lot of people just didn't know what it was really used for—it was just there. In the 1960s, it housed an office supply store. The onslaught of Hurricane David in 1979 forced the store to close when its roof was blown off. Sixteen years later, the building was turned into the Moon River Brewing Company, as massive renovations transformed the dilapidated, old building into a vital, viable business once more as a local brew pub.

It was during these renovations that the very first inklings of a haunting began to seep into the legend of the newly minted Moon River Brewery and the once forgotten tragedies that occurred there began to again show themselves. In fact, the paranormal activity got so bad that it put a temporary halt to the renovation process. Workers found themselves being shoved and tools would disappear in one room only to re-appear in another. The darting shadows of spirits, accompanied by the familiar blasts of cold air, plagued the workers and scared off many of the workers who felt uncomfortable in that sort of environment. But it was when something happened to the wife of the construction foreman that all work stopped. She had come to visit her husband on the job and when she turned to leave, walking down the stairs from the third floor, something pushed her violently from behind. The Foreman gave his resignation that same day, having had enough of the paranormal activity that was now targeting his own family. To this day, the third and fourth floors remain in a constant state of damage and urban decay. But with the basement, first, and second floors already restored, the owners of Moon River Brewery decided to open anyway. It was around that time that local historians finally clued the new owners in as to what might be going on in their new brew pub and restaurant.

First off, in 1832, a prominent local doctor named Phillip Minis got into an argument with a local man by the name of James Stark. Minis shot Stark in the back as he was headed down the stairs of what was, at the time, the City Hotel. Stark fell the rest of the way down the stairs, dying from his wounds. Minis later claimed during his trial that Stark had drawn his weapon first, but it would have made little difference what Minis's defense was; Stark was an undesirable, foul-mouthed and quick tempered. The jury almost immediately acquitted Minis of the crime of murder, sending the good doctor back to his job as the town physician. To this day, visitors and investigators still claim to see James Stark's ghost walking down those same stairs, still stepping into the present from the past to meet his destiny.

Then, in 1860, a Northerner from New York named James Sinclair checked into the City Hotel. On the cusp of the coming Civil War, it comes as no surprise that his arrival was not entirely welcomed in the Southern town. A lynch mob showed up at the hotel, dragged Sinclair out into the streets and very nearly beat him to death. Although Sinclair never succumbed to his injuries, this incident was indicative of how volatile the entire region seemed to be; lynchings and beatings were not reserved exclusively for Northerners. Slaves accused of rape, thievery, murder, or trying to escape were generally dispatched in much the same way, almost always resulting in death.

Bottles, both full and empty, have been tossed from shelves by unseen hands and shadows have been seen darting about the basement. The sounds of children playing where there are none has also crept into the air in Moon River Brewery. A ghost by the name of Toby appears in the basement and has been known to push and shove people out of his way. He's also touched them on the arms and on the backs of their necks as they enjoy their drinks at the bar. Two of the most famous ghosts that call the Moon River Brewery home would be the Woman in White, an icy specter that has been seen meandering on the third floor, and an extremely belligerent male spirit who guards the second floor staircase. He seems to get irked very quickly when visitors try to pass by him.

He's been known to push people, threaten them with violence, and try like the devil to scare the poop out of people by coming off as fearsome as possible.

432 ABERCORN STREET

One thing I know about Savannah, Georgia, is that you don't really need to make up a ghost story or two to sell a place as being haunted. The city and its buildings are certainly old enough and steeped enough in turbulent history to ensure that each building has at least one family ghost. That being said, the house at 432 Abercorn Street is known to be not only Savannah's most haunted house, but also its most controversial.

Several urban legends have popped up over the years, most of them perpetrated by those lovely as all get-out tour guide operators who make a pretty penny off of their haunted city. One story that's been circulating for some time, but has no truthful merit to it whatsoever, concerns the murders of three young women in the 1960s, whose bodies were placed into a triangle, feet to head. Another story is that of a college student who stayed at 432 Abercorn Street while attending the Savannah College of Art and Design. He just seemed to disappear into the house, becoming lost in some weird vortex or alternate dimension.

The house was built in 1868 by Benjamin J. Wilson. Some claim he was a Civil War General, but I wasn't able to find any evidence of a general by that name having served in any of the Civil War armies. After moving in, however, it is said that Wilson's wife succumbed to Yellow Fever, leaving Wilson to raise his daughter alone. Suffice it to say, men couldn't handle raising a child on their own back then as well as they can now, and Wilson's parenting skills would be taken under serious consideration in this day and age.

Massey School is right across the street from the Wilson's house and the Wilson's daughter Rebecca, being an only child, found it difficult to not go out and play with the other children on the playground. The school was a public one, full of children of lower income and poverty stricken parents, while Rebecca herself was high class and private schooled. She knew her father disapproved of her socializing with these children, but Rebecca would continue to sneak out and go play with her friends across the street.

When her father found out, he punished Rebecca by sitting her in her chair in the attic room, looking out over the schoolyard, watching her friends play without her. He even tied her to the chair in which she sat, leaving her there for two days before returning to check on her. But during the hot summer months in a house without air conditioning, he discovered that his daughter had suffered heat stroke and dehydration, dying in the chair. Wilson was so distraught over what he had done to his daughter that he himself sat in her chair in a fit of depression until he expired as well.

To this day, visitors, tourists, and general passersby claim to see the apparition of a little girl and an older man in some of the windows of the house. Bluish orbs of light have been captured inside as well as outside the house.

Those really are unsubstantiated stories, birthed from urban legends and folktales woven by tour guides wanting to earn a dollar and a cent from a good ghost story. Truthfully, the only factual story to come from the house is the fact that it was built on the site of an old slave cemetery originally in Calhoun Square. While most historians and researchers agree that the bodies of the former slaves were most likely removed prior to construction of the house, it is highly likely that it was done in a less than respectful manner, prompting the restless dead to begin spreading their negative energy.

THE PIRATE'S HOUSE

The Pirate's House restaurant sits on the eastern side of Savannah's historic district in the oldest building in Savannah. At 250 years old, its hard to dispute that for 100 of those years ghost stories have been told about the building that now houses the restaurant—legends told around its quarter-century old fireplace as spectral energy swirls about the room like tobacco smoke from an old pipe.

Perhaps the single greatest attraction about this place lies beneath the building. An old tunnel, now sealed, leads away from the structure and empties out into the harbor a few miles away. The exact purpose of this tunnel is unclear, but most historians agree that it was most likely a "Shanghai" tunnel, possibly built around the late 18th century. Men would drink themselves into a stupor, pass out cold, and wake up the next morning on a ship headed to Africa, the Caribbean, or England, forced to work the chores necessary to keep the ship seaworthy. Before the tunnels were closed and sealed, it was reported that people would hear the sounds of moaning and the voices of men coming from within.

Most harbor or portside cities had tunnels like these beneath some of their bars. As Shanghaiing was illegal, it was important to smuggle out the kidnapped men in secret. Oftentimes, the men would wake as they were being dragged through the tunnels and their captors would resort to murdering the men in order to keep the practice of Shanghaiing secret. Instead of unloading the men into a waiting ship, the captors would dump the bodies of those who woke too soon into the waters of the Atlantic. But it wasn't only men who were subjected to forced labor on a ship. Women, too, were kidnapped and often sold into lives of prostitution. Like the Shanghai tunnels in Portland, Oregon, it is also quite possible that the tunnels underneath Savannah became popular with drug addicts who had discovered opium dens in the Far East and found the practice literally going underground when they returned to the U.S. Opium overdoses, prostitution, armed robberies—all of these practices could have led to any number of deaths in the tunnels. Just how many is anyone's guess.

The Pirate's House Pub and Inn, circa 1939. (Photo by Frances Benjamin Johnson, courtesy of the Library of Congress.)

All over the building, staff, visitors, and investigators have reported seeing the translucent ghosts of sailors and yeomen as they walk through the building. But the most fascinating room in the building, hands down, seems to be the captain's room. It is said that a man by the name of Flint died in that room, and many believe that he still haunts his old room, his heavy boot heels resounding loudly on the old wooden floors. Interestingly enough, this Captain Flint was said to be the inspiration for the pirate of the same name in Robert Lewis Stevenson's classic novel, *Treasure Island*. Staff members have seen things fly off of shelves, shadowy figures moving about the rooms on the first and second floors, and eerie sounds of music and talking coming from all over the building. Self-arranging furniture also seems to be in abundance at the Pirates' House, as staff members have come to work to find table and chairs in places where they weren't before. Laughter and the sounds of a drunken party have also been heard in the dead of night, as if the spirits of the Pirate's House are still boozing it up to this day, enjoying the scant hours they have on dry land before shipping out to sea once more.

BORLEY RECTORY

VILLAGE OF BORLEY, ESSEX, UNITED KINGDOM

Everyone was open-minded about this.
–Harry Price

On July 28, 1900, the young sisters of presiding priest Reverend Harry Bull had just finished their chores inside the rectory owned by the village of Borley. As they frolicked and escaped into the acreage of field, wood, and stream, they were stunned to see something that just shouldn't have been there. It was Ethel Bull, the eldest, who saw her first, walking quietly across the fields of their father's home. Her head was drawn down as if in prayer and she walked with purpose through the trees and tall grass as if they weren't even there, her delicate footsteps barely causing any disturbance in the rippling waters of the stream where she walked.

The nun had materialized from the thin air, appearing before the girls slowly from nearly forty yards away. She walked with an ethereal gait, as if her feet weren't even touching the ground. The preternatural sight made the girls recoil a bit at the sight of this ghostly nun, but it was the youngest sister, watching her siblings react to this vision from inside the rectory, who chose to approach her. The young Bull daughter had run from the house and sprinted past her sisters to approach the nun bravely, arm tentatively outstretched for the ethereal woman. But she stopped suddenly when the nun abruptly faded from view without ever acknowledging the young girls.

Although it was the youngest daughter who showed the most enthusiasm for the spirit, it was Ethel who seemed to attract her, for after that initial sighting of the nun in the fields, the sleeping spirits of Borley Rectory seemed to awaken and the legend of Britain's most haunted house quickly began to proliferate.

The story of Borley Rectory began in the 13th century as a troupe of monks sought out land to build a monastery close to the neighboring convent. The isolated land near the border of Sussex seemed perfect and construction of the monastery began. Once finished, the building housed the monks and all seemed well for over six centuries. But as the 19th century began, the monastery suddenly closed its doors; the building was sold as a private residence. It wasn't until the mid 1850s when the Reverend Henry Dawson Ellis Bull saw the potential of the land. He was the newly commissioned rector at the Borley Village church, and sought to build his residence near the old monastery. This residence, called a rectory because it would be used to house the rector and his family, came under suspicion almost immediately after he had

bought the land, for the locals were convinced that the land was haunted—cursed even.

One story involved a 14th century monk who fell in love with a new nun at a convent in Bures. They carried on for some time until the affair was discovered, whereupon the monk was hanged and the nun found her fate bricked up in a wall in the basement of the Cistercian monastery. Three centuries passed before another nun, Marie Lairre, left her convent in Le Havre, France. She arrived in England and had even stayed at the same nunnery in Bures. Eventually, she met and married Henry Waldengrave, the owner of the manor home and former monastery where Borley Rectory would soon be built. But Waldengrave was a jealous and spiteful man. According to some of his servants, a worker from a neighboring farm appeared at the house engaging Marie in conversation. While most likely innocent in nature, it was looked on by the rest of the servants as an insult to Waldengrave, who ratted her out almost immediately. Enraged, Waldengrave strangled Marie and buried her in the basement, probably not far from where the nun had been bricked up in the wall 300 years before.

Ever since those events transpired, local villagers had seen strange lights on the grounds, visitors heard footsteps in the empty hallways, and strange figures would often show themselves in the windows and in the fields surrounding the house.

But Reverend Bull paid the stories no mind. In fact, he almost seemed to relish the idea of living in a haunted location. If nothing else, the stories the locals had told him made him speed up construction of the house. He even built the rectory over the old foundations of the former monastery and the house was soon finished and ready to inhabit. From the very beginning, and over the years they lived there, the Bull family endured the sounds of spectral knocks, mysterious footsteps in empty halls, and the rather startling appearances of the nun and sudden, new appearance of what has been called the Tall Man ghost. He had been seen standing by the children's bedsides, wearing a top hat, with darkened eyes that stared down at the girls as they slept.

While the daughters of Reverend Bull were mortified by these events, the Reverend himself, and particularly his son Harry, found the goings on to be highly entertaining. The two even built a summerhouse near the rectory where they could enjoy post-dinner

A photograph of Borley Rectory from 1892, depicting Reverend Harry Bull, his wife, and one of his daughters on the lawn.

brandies and cigars as they awaited the appearance of the nun, whose ghostly visage roamed the fields. The appearance of the nun was so famous that even the local villagers had called the path she takes through the fields the "nun's walk." It is still there to this day, a small pathway hewn through the grass where the nun supposedly made her nightly jaunts.

Inside the house, however, it was a different story. The daughters all reported hearing servant bells being rung at all hours of the day and night, as well as the sounds of loud smacks on their bedroom doors. When they would rise to see who was knocking, they would open the door to find no one there.

Reverend Bull passed away in 1892, his son Harry succeeding him as rector of the Borley church. Harry moved out of the rectory and into Borley Place across the street when he married in 1911, leaving his sisters alone in the house. For all intents and purposes, the sisters endured the haunting rather well. They grew accustomed to the noises, the creaks, the phantom whispers. They even began to almost ignore the spirits when they manifested, having seen this happen dozens and dozens of times. Eventually, the Bull sisters married and moved away from the rectory, and when Reverend Harry Bull died in 1927, the house sat empty for more than a year.

The new rector, Guy Smith, took up residence in the rectory in late 1928, and it is during this time that the tales of Borley's ghosts become more fanciful, extravagant, and terrifying. In an odd twist, Guy Smith's wife discovered an old skull in one of the cabinets in the kitchen, wrapped in brown paper. As odd and terrifying as that was, it was nothing compared to the terrifying vision of a phantom coach and driver, the driver whipping at his spectral horses as it roared up the path toward the rectory before dissipating from view entirely. Mr. and Mrs. Edward Cooper, who lived in a cottage near the rectory, also witnessed a phantom coach and horses.

This last incident prompted the Smiths to contact the *Daily Mirror*, one of England's more prominent newspapers. Journalist and paranormal researcher Harry Price was dispatched to investigate. Price was taken with the house immediately, and a fascination with Borley Rectory began that would almost certainly become obsessive. He was also witness to much of the phenomena, including stones and household objects being thrown at him by invisible hands. The Smiths endured as much phantom trauma as they could, but when their young daughter was found locked in a room without a key, they quickly made up their minds. It had only been a year and they were ready to move out.

Reverend Smith requested a transfer to another parish. He got his wish and moved out of the rectory on July 14th, 1930. But

Reverend Bull, a few years prior to his death.

Harry Price had made Borley Rectory a priority in his personal and professional life. He would often host parties at the rectory with fellow reporters and big wigs in the burgeoning field, such as Lord Charles Hope and Price's loyal secretary, Miss Kaye. Price kept a detailed journal of events that transpired at the hands of the spirits of Borley and, within a month, there were already over 2,000 logged entries of unexplained happenings. Because of his fantastical tales told of the house in the *Daily Mirror*, Borley Rectory was quickly gaining that fearsome reputation of being "the world's most haunted house." Newspaper articles were soon eclipsed by BBC Radio broadcasts about Borley, and soon much of the civilized world was aware of the haunted house in England that seemed to delight in terrorizing anyone foolhardy enough to step across its threshold.

Finally securing a new rector, the village of Borley installed Reverend Lionel Foyster. He, his wife Marianne, and two-year-old daughter Adelaide, moved into the house in October 1930. Their presence reigned in the rectory's most terrifying, and controversial, era. New, different kinds of manifestations began to occur with the onset of séances performed by Marianne. Formerly harmless spirit manifestations became mean and violent. Marianne would wake in the dead of night, as she was thrown from her bed with such violent force that it left bruising. She was hit, slapped, and had to routinely dodge thrown objects. Reverend Foyster performed an exorcism of the house as well, but it didn't seem to take. In fact, it seems that the rite of exorcism only succeeded in making the spirits angrier.

Almost immediately, Price and his colleagues began to suspect that Foyster's wife, Marianne, may just have been responsible for a good number of the incidents that occurred, noting that the phenomena seemed to center around her and no one else in the house. Not only that, but the fact was that the hauntings were now so much more violent compared to the relatively benign phenomena experienced by the Bull sisters.

One such controversy involved the questionable use of automatic writing, a practice used by a psychic, medium, or other sensitive. The medium will open their self to the spirits, asking questions of them as their hands hover over sheets of paper holding a pencil or pen. The spirit will take control of the pencil and write out the answers to the medium's questions. In this case, the Foysters alleged that the writing just appeared on the walls of the house, calling out Marianne by name and begging for prayers and spiritual help. Painting over it didn't help; the writing bled through every single time.

Harry Price, never one to be skeptical, found himself questioning the Foyster's honesty. The spirits had always shown their power to everyone in the house. But now, Price was hearing of things happening while he was out of the room or the house completely. For this reason, as misguided as it sounds, Harry Price confronted the Foysters with his suspicions. He was immediately asked to leave and never to return. But Harry Price knew something was there. He was drawn to it beyond anything he had ever been drawn to before. To Harry Price, Borley Rectory represented the possible culmination of his life's passion and work. It could be said that Harry Price was aware that his beloved Borley Rectory was quickly becoming a sideshow, that the phenomena he had discovered was being bastardized into nothing more than a series of parlor tricks with well-practiced hoaxes taking the place of the real thing. He once told a colleague that, "Five years ago the place was literally alive with…something." Harry Price was aching to return, knowing his work with the true spirits of Borley Rectory was far from over. But he also knew the Foysters would never allow him to return under any circumstance. He could do nothing but bide his time and wait for them to leave. After all, no one stayed at Borley for long.

The Foysters lasted five years in the house, abandoning Borley Rectory in October 1935. Harry Price finally had the chance he'd been hoping for: an empty haunted house that could serve as the perfect basis for an uncontaminated paranormal investigation. He jumped at the chance to rent Borley Rectory for himself and quickly set about to prove the hauntings were real and not the act of a dubious woman. He organized séances and Ouija™ board sessions. Nearly fifty volunteer researchers plowed into Borley Rectory, intent on recording and deciphering any and all forms of paranormal activity, no matter how mundane they were. One Ouija board session revealed the spirit of a woman who came forward with the name Marie Lairre. She explained that she would be in constant limbo and torment as long as her bones lay undiscovered in unconsecrated soil.

Another spirit, calling itself Sunex Amures, told Price and his cohorts that he was going to burn down the rectory and that the bones of the dead would be exposed once and for all. Harry Price made note of Sunex Amures threat and, following the end of his official probe into Borley Rectory, left the house alone and in peace.

Eleven months later, a monstrous chill went up Harry Price's back when he received a call from one of his colleagues, who informed him that Borley Rectory had been gutted by a massive fire. Racing to the scene, Price found that the news was, sadly, correct. In the midst of unpacking, the new tenant at Borley Rectory had knocked over a lit oil lamp. The fire spread quickly throughout the house, eating everything it came into contact with, leaving behind only brick walls and buried secrets. But Harry Price wasn't finished with the house just yet. He seized on the opportunity to search for the mysterious remains of Marie Lairre in the rubble of the burned-out home.

Price was not disappointed.

Deep within the debris and soil of the basement, Harry Price unearthed a nearly intact human skeleton. His findings were certified by the local pathologist, who confirmed the sex and age of the bones as being that of a young woman. In accordance with the spirit's wishes, he had the bones laid to rest in a cemetery in Liston in 1943. Immediately, sightings of the nun ceased and the trail known as the nun's walk was forgotten. The next year saw the final destruction of Borley Rectory as all traces of the ruined house were demolished and removed, leaving a glaring bald spot. Harry Price himself wrote three books on the house, investigating the Borley Rectory phenomena up until his death on March 29th, 1948. At the time of his death, he was certain that the spirits were not gone from the earth, but had instead gone across the street to Borley Church, where he claims they still reside to this day.

But following Price's death, a number of skeptics came out of the woodwork, calling him a con artist fluent in the language of hoaxing. Marianne Foyster even made a statement to the press in her defense, saying that she believed Borley Rectory wasn't haunted at all, that it was her own husband working with Harry Price who concocted all of the "ghost nonsense." Even Mrs. Smith, who had discovered the skull in her kitchen cabinet and had fallen victim to much of the antics perpetrated by the spirits, recanted her story and claimed no such haunting occurred. Is it possible that they recanted their tales because they saw a backlash coming that would make them look like charlatans or fools?

Borley Rectory has been gone for almost eighty years, yet the debate over whether it was really haunted hasn't died down at all and most likely never will. At issue are the statements made by the participants, as well as the shady backgrounds of those closest to the case. It is a well known fact that Harry Price was not only an expert in the art of magic, but he was also known to be a huckster in some circles of his professional life.

"By every account, Harry Price was a practiced hoaxster and very much of the P. T. Barnum mold," writes Brian Dunning of Skeptoid. com. "Harry Price did not investigate Borley Rectory for his own health. He achieved a great deal of notoriety from it, including the publication of three books, *The Most Haunted House in England*, *Poltergeist Over England*, and *The End of Borley Rectory*." Harry Price profited from Borley Rectory's haunts, yet his obsession is one that can only be understood by those who have walked in his shoes—namely, the paranormal community, people brought together by personal experiences with the other side in an attempt to unravel the mysteries of spirits and hauntings. It becomes obsessive. For me personally, Central State Hospital was my Borley Rectory; the first time I visited that old hospital, I felt bound to it, drawn to it, compelled to listen to each and every voice that wanted to be heard. So yeah, I understand Harry Price's obsession all too well, I think.

Speaking honestly, if one were to pile up the inconsistencies of everyone's stories, you would get a very disjointed and downright confusing account of the Borley hauntings. Sorting out the truth from the fiction is a subjective task; in my opinion, I believe that Borley Rectory was haunted, but to what degree is certainly unclear. In a case as outlandish and landmark as this one is, the facts often tend to get twisted and exaggerations can become part of that. Right now, Borley Rectory's story teeters carefully upon the line between fact and fiction, capturing perfectly the transition from true event into ghostly legend. In this line of work, no matter how many photos you take, its still not going to be enough to convince everyone. What changes minds are the personal experiences, those interactions with spirits that make it undeniable that a ghost is communicating with you. It changes you. The truth is, we weren't at Borley Rectory. We don't have those personal experiences of interacting with Borley Rectory's ghosts. But one thing is certain: it all makes for one helluva story.

THE OLD EASTES FAMILY HOUSE

(BLACK MOON MANOR)

GREENFIELD, IN

We'll be remembered more for what we destroy than what we create.
–Chuck Palahniuk, *Invisible Monsters*

In the small township of Buck Creek in Hancock County, located just outside the bustling metropolis of Indianapolis, Indiana, there sits an old dark house that, for all intent and purposes, shouldn't be there. It is a solitary home, surrounded by nothing but farmland, seclusion, and nature. The small town of Greenfield once knew the house as the Old Eastes House. For a time, it was called "Black Moon Manor," and now, following a turbulent misappropriation of facts, the house is no more. Like Borley Rectory before it, The Old Eastes House found its fate in its destruction and mercifully ended a dark chapter in the Eastes family history. The house was constructed in 1862 by John C. Eastes, who built it for his family. Surrounded by woods and acres of cornfields on each side, the house enjoyed a modest privacy away from the main roads, serving as the perfect home for the farmer and his family. It remained in the family for more than 150 years, first as the Eastes family home, and then, in the 1980s, as a rental property to various tenants. By the time 2009 came around, the house was almost uninhabitable. Work was needed to restore the property and, for the most part, it was good only for storage.

The first nail in the house's coffin was hammered in when Matt Speck, an aspiring showman with a hungry taste in his mouth to profit from a haunted attraction, happened to drive past the old place. He barely saw it from the road, but once he was able to take it all in, he marveled at the opportunity laid out before him. This old, rundown plantation house would become "Black Moon Manor, "a house haunted by hundreds of spirits. It would be a place paranormal investigators would flock to, a place where the cash of thrill-seekers would magically reappear in his bank account.

So that's what he did. Matt Speck sat down and concocted the chilling back story of what he hoped would become the most famous haunted house in the world, Black Moon Manor.

What he came up with, much of the world believed. Taking a page from Waverly Hills Sanatorium, one of the more reputable and legitimately haunted buildings in the world, Matt Speck began crafting a tale of sickness, suicide, torture, and death that would rival the plots of most horror films, using the Eastes family's name to his advantage in a slanderous—and ponderous—account of the "haunted history" of Black Moon Manor. This story would be told to those who came to investigate and was also the backbone of his

website that promoted and touted Black Moon Manor. The supposed incident there was recounted by Speck himself on his MySpace Page in a June 6, 2009 blog entry entitled "The House Reacts!" This was the first entry he made on that blog, causing excitement Did it really happen this way, or was it just another ploy to get people inside? It's hard to say, but given Speck's reputation for distorting truths, his account must be taken with a grain of salt.

Hello everyone! Just thought I would throw this exciting and kind of freaky info. at you. It seems that Black Moon Manor might really be haunted after all! The other day I started construction inside the house knocking some holes in some of the walls and creating some entry ways for our soon to be guests, and I think I have awoken the house! Some say when you make drastic changes in an old house it can disturb the energies left inside them! This house has had plenty of energies left inside it being that it was used to show the dead! Two days after I started my construction, we were there to work again and Jenny my girlfriend was standing on the front porch while I had left to gather supplies. When I returned She [was] standing at the end of the long drive just shaking like she was scared to death. When I asked what was wrong she said she heard a voice inside the house that said "I can't!" and that it was a young girl's voice. I asked her if she was seriouse [sic] and assured me she was! So now I am trying to hear it myself! I will keep you updated!
–Black Moon Manor MySpace blog entry
(Presumably by Matt Speck)
June 6, 2009

And he did keep people updated: by posting his number and the going rates for investigations into "his" house. But this inciting blog entry was just the beginning. What you are about to read is, essentially, what Speck came up with, and became the *raison d'être* for all the hauntings at the house.

I've highlighted the story in italics simply because I don't want anyone who reads this to confuse it with fact. While they are my own words and it looks like I'm quoting a source, I am not. I merely want to make certain that the "story" doesn't get confused with the "history." Enjoy...

The old Eastes house, named "Black Moon Manor" by Matt Speck, used to sit between the old willow tree and the sycamore to the right. The site still commands your attention, with or without a dwelling. (Photo by author.)

In 1892, a small pox outbreak struck Buck Creek Township, resulting in hundreds of infected men, women, and children. With only one doctor in the small town, the outbreak soon began to prove too tough for one small doctor's office to handle. A doctor by the name of James Harvey had married into the Eastes family and became owner of the house. Dr. Harvey opened this home to the sick residents of the Township, a place where all patients could be housed and he could maintain a watchful eye over all of them at the same time. But the constant influx of patients kept Dr. Harvey from administering proper medical care and a great many of his patients began to die. It is also speculated that Dr. Harvey intentionally infected people with smallpox to both grow his medical practice and give him access to bodies with which to experiment.

To avoid the spread of the smallpox disease, Dr. Harvey had the dead buried in the backyard. It was this rash of deaths that supposedly led to the building of the house in 1895, its purpose being to serve as a funeral home of sorts with a body preparation room, a room for wakes and funerals, and even a cold storage unit in the basement. The backyard swallowed up over 200 bodies before the spread of small pox lessened.

An Eastes family descendant named Georgia had told Matt that a woman had committed suicide by jumping into an open water well in the basement. This occurred sometime in the 1930s, and the distraught woman is said to wander the basement aimlessly, searching for something she'll never find.

The house went back to being a home to the Eastes family descendants until the infamous blizzard that struck Indiana in the winter of 1978. Fifteen-foot-tall snow dunes made travel impossible and the last living Eastes family member found herself trapped in her own home. An elderly woman, she died from hypothermia after the electricity went out. She too was supposedly buried on the property.

Matt Speck drove by one day decades later and the old Eastes house caught his eye. Speck had recently begun looking for a house or building that seemed suitable to renovate into a profitable haunted attraction. The old Eastes house seemed perfect for what he was looking for, though he had no idea who had owned it or what its story was.

Speck renamed the old house Black Moon Manor and set about to create the ultimate Halloween thrill. But from the very first time he stepped into the house, the ghostly residents began to make themselves known, proving that you didn't need fog machines and strobe lights when you had the real thing.

Looking closely at the tale, one can pick out elements of actual history that Speck seems to have pulled from other places. The smallpox hospital idea seems nearly identical to that of Waverly Hills Sanatorium in Louisville, while the idea of the "mad doctor" is an old staple in many books, films, and ghost stories. But the facts always overrule the back-story, no matter how fantastic or believable it may seem.

First and foremost, it should be understood from the beginning that Matt Speck, while telling everyone that he owned it, never held the deed to the house at all. Furthermore, while he was telling people that the last Eastes family member died in 1978, he was busy RENTING the house from Walter Eastes, who presumably had no idea that their name was being used by Speck to sell a lie and make money. The Eastes name is far from dead, the lineage far from over, for the Eastes descendants still hold a prominent place in the Greenfield and Indianapolis communities.

Dr. James Harvey was, in actuality, Dr. Obadiah Harvey, who worked his way into the legend by marrying Permelia Eastes. While Dr. Harvey was a preeminent physician in Greenfield, his work with small pox patients was, in actuality, very limited. Records on file with Hancock County have proven that only three adults and two children ever died in his care due to small pox and it's unclear that they even died in the house itself. There have also been no records found to indicate that the Old Eastes Family House also served as a make-shift hospital. And finally, in no way have up to 200 deaths been recorded or placed on file due to small pox. It just didn't happen. So it should come as little surprise that no such person named Georgia ever lived in the Eastes family house, and certainly no one in the family would have told him the lies this "Georgia" told him.

On the October 12, 2012 episode of *Ghost Adventures*, Zak Bagans and his crew investigated Black Moon Manor and were a bit shocked to be presented with a doctor's bag full of patient records of those people that supposedly died in the house or, at the very least, were patients staying in the house. Speck claimed to have found it in the attic, the solitary item on a dusty floor. A convenient artifact to be sure, and one corroborated by "Georgia." But as Zak looked into the supposed history of this house, Matt Speck's story began to fall apart right before millions of people watching on television. Surprisingly, Zak never called out Speck on the gross inaccuracies and fabrications of the property's history, instead turning away and refusing to address it outright, focusing his attention on the house and not on its proprietor.

While the *Ghost Adventures* episode brought portions of Speck's deception into a very public arena, it was the smaller, more tenacious paranormal group Ohio Gothic Paranormal (O.G.P.) that really seemed to call Speck out on the inconsistencies of his stories. They too researched the property's history and found the same glaring inaccuracies, to which Matt Speck refused to comment on. On their Facebook page, Ohio Gothic Paranormal had this to say:

Part of the old fence line and gate leading to the Eastes Family Cemetery are the only clues that a house ever stood on the property. (Photo by the author.)

He (the Renter) has constantly refused to answer any and all questions and has resorted to name calling. The reason the investigations have come to a halt and the threat of demolition is the result of years of neglect of the building and neglect and disrespect to the family.

Surprisingly, the Ohio Gothic Paranormal Group didn't receive a hero's welcome from a good portion of the paranormal community;

instead, roughly half of their colleagues dismissed O.G.P.'s claims that Speck was acting fraudulently, branding them as pariahs. It seems that while a lot of people seek out the truth, few are willing to accept it, and fewer still are willing to evangelize it. The most telling statements regarding Black Moon Manor's mission come from Matt Speck himself. On the Black Moon Manor website message boards, a user named

Sally wrote: *Sad spirits struggle; you should try to show them the light so they can move onto the other side.*

Matt Speck responded: *That would be bad for business Sally!*

This was allegedly the same response he would give to paranormal groups when asked why they couldn't perform cleansings and sagings, rituals designed to free the house of its spirits and send the unhappy ones off to their true destiny beyond. This man deliberately held these spirits hostage with no intention other than to profit from their tricks, which they performed like professionals, while being treated like circus animals. These despicable lies told at the expense of a very decent family, however, does not diminish the actual hauntings themselves.

When I tried to track Matt Speck down to get his input for this story, it was as if he had literally fallen off the face of the Earth. His trail was cold as of May 2013, his MySpace page hadn't been updated since 2010, and it would seem that all evidence of his involvement in the Eastes family house had been eradicated. Rumors persist that he moved away and is setting up a new haunted house attraction near Kentucky.

THE OLD HOUSE IS STILL HAUNTED

But what of the old house itself? Yes, The Old Eastes House was haunted. The varied experiences and occurrences there tell tales of classic ghostly activity. Numerous teams and visitors have recorded the same kinds of activity without having known about the others findings. There is little doubt about that. But if the facts on file at the County records office are to be believed, then there should be no reason why that house is so haunted.

So…WHY is it so actively haunted? The answers to that question are numerous and very open-ended, but my thoughts tend to drift to one or two very possible reasons. The first reason could deal with the ever popular notion of teenagers or occultists using the house to stage séances with—or without—a Ouija board. Séances performed with a Ouija board can be a very powerful tool in matters of the paranormal. To use it without taking the proper precautions can open a doorway from the spirit world to our own, allowing ANY spirit, demonic or otherwise, to step through and cause general mayhem. You can't control which spirits come through and an inexperienced Ouija board user will most likely not even think to close the portal once the séance is done. Only an experienced medium should dabble with Ouija boards, for they are the only ones who know how to properly open, then close, the portal and send away all who came through it. Playing with a Ouija board is kind of like leaving your back door open all night in a rough neighborhood: anybody can come in if they want and, once they do, you'll have a hell of a time trying to get rid of them.

The other side of that coin lies in a more philosophical realm. Take Matt Speck for example. He sought out a place to stage a haunted attraction. Already, he was looking for a darkness that perhaps even he didn't really think he had in him. That darkness can attract darkness. The need to be around spirits and want spirits in your life can attract them to you in spades. It's a lot like the Ouija board, except in this case YOU are the Ouija board that calls the spirits in from the cold. The sheer desire to be surrounded by ghosts is such a powerful magnet for spirits that those looking for dark things tend to find them fairly quickly.

Matt Gephart lived at the house from 1993 to 2004. Gephart was merely a teenager at the time and told Zak Bagans that weird things seemed to happen on a regular basis. "It was creepy," he said. "You could play in my mom's room and hear people walk across the floor all day long. All the time. She called my dad home from work to have him check it out, thinking someone was in the house." One night, Gephart and some friends were sitting around a fire, telling stories about the house when one of them jumped up and proclaimed that he didn't believe in ghosts and that house wasn't at all haunted. The boy was greeted by the spirits with a punch to the gut, silencing his skepticism forever.

One of the more interesting stories, and one backed up by historical records, is of the ghost of little Rachel Eastes, a five-year-old girl who died in 1842, probably from an illness such as typhus or yellow fever. Presumably one of two children that died on the property, she was the first to be buried in the Eastes Family cemetery. Some legends state that she visits the house on the day of her birth, but others claim that Rachel walks the house every night, still playing with her toys and trying to reach out to the living. Paranormal investigators have reported feeling small hands tug on their clothes as well as the pitter patter of little feet on the hardwood floors. Some even claim to have captured her playing with an old hobby horse in one of the upstairs rooms.

Quest Paranormal of Indiana performed a full scale investigation of The Old Eastes House, coming away with an incredible array of Electronic Voice Phenomena, including one of a child that may have been the mysterious Rachel. It is an EVP that proves these hauntings are intelligent in nature, in that the entity provides an intelligent response to a statement made by an investigator.

"This (next) EVP was also caught upstairs," writes one of the investigators on their website. "You hear Pamela say 'we're gonna head downstairs' with the hopes of the entity following them and after that you hear what sounds like a kid saying, 'ok.'"

THE OLD HOUSE TODAY

In the end, Walter Eastes decided to end the controversy once and for all. He had Speck evicted, then tore the house to the ground, a sad end to a 112-year-old landmark that could have become an honorable memorial to the past, but instead became a stained footnote in the science of parapsychology.

When I finally got to visit the site where Black Moon Manor had stood, I was quite taken aback. It literally looked as if nothing had ever stood there amongst the trees and vegetation. It was as if the surrounding woods and foliage had risen up and folded its arms over the old site, swallowing it whole. The only clue that the house had been there was a section of old fencing and an old metal gate that led off the property and to a trail that led to the Eastes Cemetery about half a mile away. As I walked the land where Black Moon Manor had sat, the same phrase repeated itself over and over in my head:

This is not for the living.
This is a place for the dead, and the dead alone.

It was at that moment that I realized: not only was destroying the house the right thing to do, it was what *needed* to happen, was *supposed* to happen, and *should have* happened all along. The land surrounding Black Moon Manor is rife with fertile ground that is used to grow thousands of tons of corn each year. It is land literally springing forth with life and constant rebirth.

But the land in the middle, shrouded by trees and dense vegetation? That land belongs to the dead, and nothing living should live there ever again.

The Eastes Cemetery, walking distance from the old house, contains many of the Eastes family members, including Dr. Harvey and Rachael, who was the first Eastes to be buried in this cemetery. (Photo by the author.)

SUMMERWIND MANSION

VILAS COUNTY, WI

What worth was a man who could not be haunted?
–Clive Barker, *In the Flesh*

It sits now amongst the dense forest, nature creeping up and reclaiming the spot once occupied by a grand old house that was visible from most areas of West Bay Lake in northeast Wisconsin. Like the Old Eastes House, at one time, it was a tall, proud, and warm home for a family that loved it very much. But now, all that remains are two forty-foot chimneys, a desolate foundation, and eerie, moss-covered steps leading up to a house that no longer exists. It was here that a spirit named Jonathon Carver made his plight known to the living and was met by horror and a few bullets.

Summerwind began life in 1916, built by a wealthy businessman by the name of Robert P. Lamont. It would initially serve as a summer home for his large family and he spared no expense when it came to their comfort. Dual forty-foot chimneys and their accompanying fireplaces ensured warmth on cold nights and its location next to the lake made swimming and boating excursions almost too easy. Eventually, Summerwind became Robert's safe haven when he became President Herbert Hoover's Secretary of Commerce, a retreat after the highly stressful days of working alongside politicians in Washington, D.C.

While good times were had by all at Summerwind, it was still not without its snags. After construction came to an end and the Lamont Family moved into their new home, the children would often report being wakened by the sound of boots walking across the wood floors. Strange noises would be heard coming from the cellar, as if someone were moving things about. Legend tells of one particularly famous incident at the mansion when Lamont, asleep with his wife in his bedroom, heard movement coming from the kitchen downstairs. Taking up his pistol, Lamont went to investigate. Slowly entering the kitchen, he gasped in horror at a tall, solid-looking man standing near the cellar door. Believing it to be an intruder who broke in and entered via the basement, Robert Lamont fired his pistol at the black shape. Flipping on the light, he was even more surprised to see that the figure had disappeared. There was no evidence of any blood, no body, and nothing was broken. In fact, it looked like nothing had been there at all. There was only Robert Lamont, his smoking gun, and a bullet hole in the cellar door that was directly behind the figure he'd shot at point blank. For some time afterward, through various owners and occupants,

the bullet riddled cellar door remained as it was, a grim testimony of what Summerwind Mansion was capable of.

Robert Lamont died in 1948 in Chicago, Illinois, and as a result, Summerwind was sold to another family. It changed hands numerous times over the course of the year, with little to no paranormal activity occurring in the house to any of the occupants. It stood empty and alone on its hill overlooking the lake until the summer of 1969. Arnold Hinshaw, his wife Ginger, and their four children moved into Summerwind that year and right from the start, it seemed as if the house was ready to once more show off its power.

It was Ginger who saw the house first, falling in love with the dilapidated mansion on the shores of West Bay Lake. She'd heard about the house from the people in town who commonly referred to it as the "Old Haunted House."

"I fell in love with it immediately," remembers Ginger today. "I had to have it. Absolutely wanted that house in the worst way. I felt sorry for the house. Really, really sorry. I thought it had great potential on a really beautiful site. But everyone kept telling me 'but that's the haunted house.' So I said, 'Fine, then I'm living in the haunted house.'"

Both Arnold and Ginger Hinshaw, as well as most of their four children, saw the potential of Summerwind. Arnold was a licensed contractor with his own construction business and therefore saw what could be done to rehabilitate the house. But it was nine-year-old April Hinshaw who wasn't so easily convinced.

"This place was huge," recalls April. "Dingy, no paint, decrepit. And I'm thinking, 'we're going to live here?' And immediately, being possessed of a feeling that I didn't want to be there."

Ginger and Arnold attempted to hire some workers to come to Summerwind and assist them in the renovation, but their offers were all rebuffed; no one wanted to set foot inside the "haunted house." In the end, the Hinshaws took on the task themselves, intent on finally bringing Summerwind back to life. In time, their hard work paid off. Fresh paint, lacquer, new trim and windows, and a meticulously landscaped yard seemed to breathe new life into the old mansion. But to Ginger, rehabilitating the house became dangerously obsessive. She found herself going through eleven different shades of paint in a desperate bid to find the correct

A home that resembles Summerwind in its prime. (Photo courtesy of the Library of Congress.)

color to match the original woodwork. To Ginger, it seemed as if someone—or something—was guiding her, making certain she restored it exactly as it had been during its heyday. But as they got comfortable in their new house, it was impossible to avoid all of the strange activity that would occur around them. "The chairs would move," says Ginger. "First they'd be there, then they'd be against the wall." April agrees with her mother, adding, "No matter what room, no matter what area of the house you were in, you were watched. I always felt that, and I think that all the kids felt this."

Feelings of paranoia and quiet dread were soon replaced by the very real appearance of shadowy figures darting to and fro in the darkened hallways. Mumbling, muffled voices would be heard in otherwise empty rooms, and various appliances and machinery would break down, only to begin working perfectly once repairmen were called. Windows and doors opened and closed on their own, leading Arnold Hinshaw to nail one of them closed when it refused to stay shut.

Up until that point, Ginger and Arnold were certain of the activity, but wondered if it centered around them at all, or if they were continually walking into the middle of it. One day, Ginger got her answer when, as she was walking up the stairs, she heard a voice call her out by name. "It was a male voice, a very deep, strong voice," she says. "There was nobody there, so I started up the stairs again." As she walked, the feeling of being watched intensified. When she again heard the voice call her name, she turned and found herself staring at the translucent figure of a spirit rushing toward her in a gust of icy cold air that chilled her blood. It would be days before Ginger would accept the fact that she had just seen a ghost and that it knew her name.

In the meantime, Arnold was becoming increasingly erratic, temperamental, and edgy. His attitude went from being mellow and unassuming to becoming a man full of rage. His temper would flare at the drop of a hat and his wife and kids began to walk cautiously around him, not wanting to raise his ire. In addition, he took up playing an old Hammond organ the couple had bought prior to moving in. He slept all day, stopped going in to work, and stayed up all night playing eerie and oftentimes unruly melodies on the organ. It creeped out the family so badly that they usually found themselves huddling together in one room while Arnold's creepy organ playing wafted through the house.

On one of the few occasions that Ginger was able to cajole Arnold into helping her around the house, he was sent to put a fresh coat of paint on the interior of one of the closets upstairs. Along the back wall, a shoe drawer had been installed. When Arnold pulled the drawer out to paint around the edges, he noticed quite a bit of open, dark space behind the closet. Reaching in with his hands and peering about with a flashlight, Arnold saw a collection of strange objects within the recesses of the shoe drawer cavity. Pulling out the objects, he and Ginger were horrified to find that they had just uncovered a human skull, an arm, and part of a human leg bone. Confused over what they should do, for whatever reason, Ginger and Arnold left the pieces of the body where they found it, replaced the drawer, and attempted to forget it was there.

But Summerwind would not let them forget.

While entertaining some friends at their home, Ginger had excused herself to the kitchen to retrieve some hors d'oeuvres. A bloodcurdling scream brought her back into the living room, only to find her friends running from the apparition of a spectral man who hovered and materialized before their disbelieving eyes. "I will never forget their faces," says Ginger. "I've never talked to them again. That's when I knew that it wasn't just me."

This, in addition to Arnold's deteriorating mental condition, was almost too much for Ginger to take. To April and the rest of the children, it was Summerwind that was to blame for the crises in their lives. "I knew she was struggling," says April. "And I knew my step dad hated us and hated her. He didn't before and he cared for us before. He didn't there."

Eventually, Arnold stopped speaking to everyone else in the house. He lost his construction business, utilities were being shut off due to unpaid bills, and as winter approached, Ginger and her children knew that their dreams of familial bliss were at an end. Ginger swallowed her pride and called upon her father, who arrived at Summerwind the next day with an RV to pick up Ginger and her children. "I remember my grandfather coming to the house and it was like a war was over," recalls April. "I don't have to deal with this anymore. Everybody just sighed."

Ginger and her children left Summerwind that day; it is said that Arnold left the next day. The two eventually divorced, and Ginger and the children never saw him again. Today, it is unclear whatever happened to the man, but one hopes that he was able to escape whatever was tormenting him at Summerwind during those hellish six months. Ginger herself remarried a good man by the name of George Olsen and settled into a peaceful life with her kids in nearby Granton, Wisconsin. All seemed perfect and the evil of Summerwind was behind them.

That is, until her father announced that he was going to buy Summerwind, with plans to convert it into a resort.

Ginger had never told her father, Raymond Bober, about what had happened to her and her family at Summerwind Mansion. To speak of it would be inviting it back into their lives. But had she told her parents everything about her experiences, chances are very good that Raymond Bober would have jumped on the purchase anyway. Once Ginger had told her father everything, he still went ahead with the purchase. Having spent some time at the house, Raymond Bober now claimed that he knew the identity of the spirit haunting Summerwind. Through séances, trances, and several Ouija board sessions, Bober discovered that the ghost was a man named Jonathon Carver, a British explorer who was haunting the house in order to search for an old deed given to him by local Sioux Indians, a deed that granted him ownership of much of Northern Wisconsin. Placed in a box, the deed had supposedly been sealed into the foundations of Summerwind.

There are several things wrong with Bober's story, most notable the claim of the deed sealed into the foundations. Summerwind was built almost 130 years after the death of Jonathon Carver, making it impossible for anyone to inter a box into the foundations. Moreover, after doing some homework, Raymond Bober was able to find a man who had helped pour the foundation for Summerwind back in 1916. This man swore up and down that no box was ever added to the concrete or sealed into Summerwind's foundations. Furthermore, it seems unlikely that a spirit seeking help from the living would treat them with such darkness and devilry, namely the oppression of Arnold Hinshaw and the terror tactics acted out upon Ginger and her children.

In an effort to get behind all of the madness and strange goings on, Ginger, her husband George, and her brother Karl agreed to help their parents rummage through the house, looking for anything that might point to the cause of the hauntings.

Robert P. Lamont, Summerwind's architect was the first to have a strange occurrence happen there that he couldn't explain. Things would get stranger as the years passed. (Photo courtesy of the Library of Congress.)

They had all gotten through the house and were about to leave empty handed when George spotted the upstairs closet and the mysterious shoe drawer where the secret compartment had been. Ginger remembered all too well what had been hidden there and she begged her husband to stop. He did not. To Ginger's surprise, confusion, and horror, George discovered that the secret compartment was empty. Gone was the skull, arm, and leg bone that she and

Arnold had discovered earlier that year. Where had the pieces gone? And more importantly, were they ever there to begin with?

Sometime later, Karl reported back to his family that once, while in the house, he'd heard a deep, rough male voice call him out by name. The experience terrified Karl and lent credence to Ginger's story of having heard her own name called out by a similar voice.

Eventually, the project to convert Summerwind into a resort was abandoned. Those workers that did bother to show up at the "haunted house" would leave mid-shift and not return, having experienced something terrifying or, in the very least, the frustrating occurrences when tools would mysteriously disappear at random. For Raymond Bober, though, finding the deed that Jonathon Carver was searching for became an obsession. He spent days, even weeks, digging in the basement, chipping away at the foundations, and exploring all the darkest corners of Summerwind trying to find the elusive document. In the end, all roads led to dead ends and Raymond Bober finally conceded defeat.

But the question still remains: was Summerwind haunted, and if so, by what? While most believe that it was the house that was haunted, many believe that it was the land itself that was sour and bad, that anything built on the land would play host to the malevolence that dwelled in the trees and soil and rocks. No murders had ever been reported at Summerwind, yet the spirits of the dead seemed to show themselves early on to Robert Lamont, the builder of Summerwind. Speculations have run wild, with theories involving Indian burial grounds and unkempt space-time portals. Writer Troy Taylor has researched the haunting of Summerwind thoroughly and believes that Summerwind may have been a place where the past continually replayed itself over and over again. "Perhaps the place wasn't haunted at all, but instead, was a mysterious site where time was distorted in ways that we cannot understand," he wrote on his website. "Perhaps the shadows and figures that were seen could have been people or images from the past (or the future) and perhaps the sound of someone calling Karl's name would happen in reality several months later. We will never know for sure now, but the idea is something worth considering."

In 1986, it is said that a trio of investors bought Summerwind with the hopes that they could make Summerwind into the resort Raymond Bober had wanted. Again, it was not to be. During a ferocious storm in June of 1988, Summerwind was struck by lightning and burned to the ground, leaving behind only a set of stone steps leading up to an enormous concrete cavity and two ghostly stone chimneys, monuments left behind in honor of what may have been one of the most haunted, and mysterious, houses in America.

BOBBY MACKEY'S MUSIC WORLD

WILDER, KY

Don't worry about the ghosts in here;
they're my friends.
– Carl Lawson
Upon meeting Bobby Mackey for the first time

There's rarely a time during business hours that it is quiet and dark. The halls are filled to the brim with the strains of banjos, steel guitars, and plaintive crooning. The energy that fills the air is electric and intoxicating. People go there to celebrate, ride the mechanical bull, and bask in the feel of a real-life honky-tonk, country and western bar.

But when the music stops and the lights go down, when the doors lock and the chairs are put up for the night, a different kind of energy comes out, oozing from the woodwork in thick rivulets that paints the shadows in darker shades of black. Here at Bobby Mackey's Music World, the building is just as populated when it is closed as when it is open.

Most paranormal investigators consider Bobby Mackey's to be ground zero for paranormal activity, showcasing full-bodied apparitions, phantom smells, physical assaults, even demonic possession and violent physical attacks. Bobby Mackey himself may downplay the activity now, but when he first bought the old music club, he, his wife, and his co-worker Carl Lawson experienced strange, unusual, and downright terrifying episodes of ghostly activity.

The building that now houses Bobby Mackey's Music World was originally a slaughterhouse, opening and operating during the latter half of the 1800s. In its time, literally millions of heads of cattle and hogs met their ends on the basement killing floor, their blood washed down an old well that led out to the Licking River. When the slaughterhouse was closed down, the abandoned building supposedly began to see use as a place for a covert group of Satanists to practice their religion, sacrificing animals and even children who were deemed mentally handicapped or crippled from birth. Two of the men from that group, Scott Jackson and Alonzo Walling, would soon use the old slaughterhouse to cover up a crime of their own. In 1896, it was reputed that Jackson had an illicit affair with the daughter of a wealthy businessman from Greencastle, Indiana—a woman by the name of Pearl Bryan. By all accounts, Pearl Bryan was a striking young woman of 22 years of age, with a svelte figure and lush, long blonde hair. The youngest of twelve children, Pearl was one of the most popular girls at Greencastle High School. Because of this, multitudes of suitors sought her hand in marriage. But her heart was lost forever when she laid eyes on Scott Jackson.

The lovely Pearl Bryan in her only known photograph. (Source unknown.)

The two had been introduced to each other by Pearl's cousin, William Wood, a medical student at DePauw University, who counted both of them as friends. At the time, Scott Jackson was a student at the Ohio College of Dentistry with a bright future in medicine ahead of him. However, the attraction he and Pearl felt for one another was too strong to resist and Pearl became pregnant with Scott's child. Pearl was elated, thinking Jackson would finally marry her. Jackson, on the other hand, was mortified and saw his professional and social life in medicine coming to a swift end because of this scandalous pregnancy.

Pearl left her parent's house on February 1, 1896, and told them she was going to meet with friends in Indianapolis. In reality, she was headed in the opposite direction, heading to Cincinnati to meet up with Scott and his roommate, Alonzo Walling. She was five months pregnant.

Scott had failed to make proper arrangements with a doctor to perform an abortion on Pearl, so he tried to induce the death of the baby himself by spiking her drink with massive amounts of cocaine, a drug that was legal at the time and would be found in her bloodstream during her autopsy.

But the drugs didn't work and Jackson and Walling had to think quickly. Using his dental equipment, Jackson attempted to perform the abortion himself, but mangled Pearl's insides with his inept medical skills. Bleeding massively and tremendously frightened, Pearl Bryan knew she'd made a mistake by going with Jackson. It would be impossible for her to not see the darkness that was coming.

Pearl, Scott, and Alonzo all left Cincinnati and crossed the Ohio River into Kentucky. Pearl was undoubtedly weak from blood loss and most likely fatigued from the incredible stress of the botched abortion performed on her by the inept dental student and blindly entrusted her care to her psychotic suitor. Unbeknownst to her, Jackson and Walling had already decided what must be done with the poor woman. In a secluded spot near Fort Thomas, Jackson and Walling dragged Pearl into the woods and, as Alonzo Walling held her down, Scott Jackson murdered poor Pearl Bryan as she weakly struggled underneath them. In a clean, fell swoop, he had beheaded the once beautiful mother of his unborn child.

Jackson and Walling devised a plan to dismember her corpse and drop each piece into a different sewer system, but in the end, they opted to dump her body near the Alexandria Turnpike, where authorities eventually found her headless body. Pearl's head was never found, though locks of her blonde hair were later found in a valise in Scott Jackson's room.

Most believe that Jackson and Walling took Pearl's head to the old slaughterhouse, now the site of their Satanic rituals, and offered the head to Satan as an offering. While this is all hearsay and conjecture, it's also as believable as any other explanation. Jackson and Walling were brought to trial to face murder charges in 1897 and were quickly found guilty. The crowds and the prosecuting attorney's clamored for their executions, but the presiding judge offered them life imprisonment instead if they revealed the whereabouts of Pearl Bryan's head.

Both men flatly refused and were hanged from the gallows outside the Campbell County courthouse in nearby Newport. Walling reportedly threatened to return to haunt Campbell County after his execution as the noose was being tightened around his neck.

The place stayed empty for a good twenty years before being torn down and replaced by a more modern roadhouse, servicing truck drivers, traveling salesmen, and other road-weary travelers looking to unwind. Prohibition turned the roadhouse into a not-so-secret speakeasy and gambling parlor. At the same time, a strikingly high number of murders were said to have been committed in the bar, leading suspicious locals to think that perhaps the Mob may have been involved.

In 1933, a man by the name of Buck Brady bought the building and renovated the old roadhouse into a bustling casino and bar called The Primrose. Having been a Mob-run bar in the past, Cincinnati mobsters had hoped to just walk in and muscle Brady out of his profits. When Brady refused to sell the Primrose, he found the tavern being vandalized and his customers beaten up. In a 1946 shootout, Brady was charged, but released, in the attempted murder of a small-time gangster by the name of Albert "Red" Masterson. Such violence was not Brady's way of life and he was appalled at how he had reacted in a such a violent way. He reluctantly sold out to the gangsters.

The building re-opened in 1953 as the Latin Quarter and it is during this period that the second legend of Bobby Mackey's began. Johanna, daughter of the club's owner, fell in love with one of the dapper singers who performed regularly at the club and became pregnant. Her dad was understandably upset and he used his influence in the organized crime racket to have the philandering singer killed. Despondent, Johanna attempted to poison her father before taking her own life. He survived. Sadly, Johanna did not. Like Pearl Bryan before her, she was five months pregnant at the time.

The bar hit some rough times after that, closing up and shutting down on numerous occasions, under numerous owners. It wasn't until May of 1978 that the bar found its stride with an up-and-coming country singer and his wife, a respected musician by the name of Bobby Mackey and his wife Janet. Opening a to-the-bone honky-tonk bar was Mackey's dream, a place where he would always have a place to perform and where he could get his heroes to perform as well. The old Latin Quarter bar was perfect, exactly what he had been looking for, like it had been waiting patiently for him to come along. Ironically, Janet was pregnant at the time, a fact that drew the attention of the spirits of the old bar almost immediately.

"Janet didn't want to come in here, she didn't feel right about it at all," recalls Bobby.

Janet Mackey agrees, explaining further that it "felt like somebody was in there, and there wasn't anything in there except him and I. I wanted to get out of there as soon as possible. I was afraid of it, but it was always his dream."

Bobby hired a local man named Carl Lawson to take care of the joint and even offered him the small apartment upstairs for him to stay in. Carl had worked at the club before when it was the Latin Quarter, but was out of a job when it closed down due to the number of unexplained murders that took place there. "I had seen more unexplained acts of violence in and around that building than you can shake a stick at. Any night club or bar is gonna have its share of brawls and fights, but on this scale here, it was abnormal. Something's going on with this place." He was convinced that something inside the club made people do violent and crazy things.

It was Carl who first began to tell people about the strange and crazy things he'd see in the bar after the lights had been turned out and the front doors locked. Most of his tales were met with a roll of the eyes, but Carl knew he wasn't crazy. Carl recalled the first inklings of strange activities to paranormal investigator Doug Hensley for his book, *Hells Gate*. "I'd double check at the end of the night and make sure that everything was turned off. Then I'd come back down hours later and the bar lights would be on. The front doors would be unlocked, when I knew that I'd locked them. The jukebox would be playing the "Anniversary Waltz" even though I'd unplugged it and the power was turned off."

He even remembered a time when he looked up from the bar and found a strange, ethereal woman standing in front of him. When Carl asked what she wanted, the woman replied, "I'm waiting for Robert Randel." Bobby Mackey's real name is Robert Randel, a fact that sent Janet Mackey into near hysterics, for only a few days later, Bobby and his wife bought the Latin Quarter club with intentions of making it into a bona fide honky-tonk.

While Bobby seemed immune to the spirits, Carl and Janet were not. Both were plagued by spirits who would attack and bully them. Carl had gotten used to the rough activity and even referred to the ghosts as "his friends," but Janet was never accepting of the abuse, especially as a woman carrying her husband's child. She constantly feared for the safety of her unborn baby, to which Bobby always seemed to take the hysteria lightly, chalking it up to nerves.

There was plenty of activity in the bar areas, but the darkest of activity seemed to emanate from the basement, more specifically, from the well area where the blood of slaughtered animals was washed out to the Licking River and where legend had it that Pearl Bryan's head had been discarded as an offering to Satan. Shadow figures and strange, demonic voices passed through this basement area. Over time, the activity increased so much that patrons of the bar began to notice the odd happenings. Bartenders and customers alike would report seeing glasses move about on their own and hear low, aggressive voices in the bathroom areas. Stories began to fly about town and Bobby got worried his business would be affected. "Carl starting telling stories and I told him to keep quiet about it. I didn't want it getting around, because I had everything I own stuck in this place. I had to make a success of it," he told Doug Hensley. Mackey didn't believe in ghosts and in that neck of the woods of Kentucky, nobody wanted to have anything to do with a place that had strange things going on like that.

It wasn't until Janet Mackey confessed all of the experiences she'd had to her husband that Bobby began to change his mind about the place, that Bobby Mackey's Music World, Kentucky's answer to Nashville's world famous Gilley's, was haunted beyond belief. She told him everything, including the most terrifying encounter she'd ever had at the bar. It was an encounter that, to this day, has kept her from stepping foot inside her husband's honky-tonk. While she was in the basement, Janet had smelled the scent of roses, a telltale sign that the spirit of Johanna was near. All of a sudden, she felt something begin to swirl around her, taking control of her movements. "Something grabbed me by the waist. It picked me up and threw me back down. I got away from it, and when I got to the top of the stairs there was pressure behind me, pushing me down the steps. I looked back up and a voice was screaming 'Get Out! Get Out!'" Janet was five months pregnant

The building, now known as Bobby Mackey's Music World, would mark the end of Pearl's life and the beginning of her legend. In a cruel twist, her spirit shares space not only with another tragic lady—the doomed showgirl Johanna—but also with Pearl's two killers, Scott Jackson and Alonzo Walling. (Photo by the author.)

at the time of her attack, the same time along as both Johanna and Pearl Bryan when they were killed.

Carl Lawson, meanwhile, found himself getting chummy with many of the spirits residing at Bobby Mackey's, even being laughed at by the other employees when he would confess to talking to the ghosts whenever he was caught seemingly talking to himself. But

the strong whiff of rose perfume would change nearly everyone's mind when it would waft past them, proving Carl's case almost irrefutably. In fact, Carl got so friendly with the spirits that he seemed to open himself up to them in a dangerous way; one of the spirits, a particularly nasty and spiteful ghost (perhaps that of Scott Jackson or Alonzo Walling) took possession of Carl Lawson's body and the poor caretaker who lived alone found himself relying on others to help him get rid of the demonic influence imprisoning his mind and soul. An exorcism succeeded in freeing Carl from the clutches of whatever had taken hold of him, and he began to think twice about being so open to their influence.

But Carl and Janet weren't the only ones to have to deal with these violent, dark entities. Investigators from around the world have converged on Bobby Mackey's for years, and while some walk away disappointed, others get more than they bargained for. This is a place where the spirits are so strong, so powerful, and so determined that they WILL follow you home.

A colleague of mine we'll call Timothy runs a small paranormal group in rural Kentucky, and was on his way to visit his grandmother who lived just down Route 9—the same road that runs past Bobby Mackey's. He was alone when he left nearby Newport, heading back into Wilder a few miles away. "As I was up on the bridge that goes over the train tracks, I don't know what came over me, but I said loudly in the car and to nobody 'I don't believe in ghosts or that Bobby Mackey's Music World is haunted!'"

As soon as Timothy had made that comment, he suddenly felt flush and his chest tightened. The air conditioning in the car was on, but he felt as if he were standing in front of a blast furnace. As he approached Bobby Mackey's, however, his blood began to chill and run cold.

Walking leisurely from the club's front doors was a solid, black figure that stepped from the building and moved toward the road. It stood in the fast lane of the highway, watching Timothy approach. "As I got down there to the bar," he says, "the figure looked male and sinisterly happy to see me come up on it. I kept driving and the figure disappeared into thin air, but it felt like I'd ran it over and it had gotten into my car."

Timothy felt extreme pressure in his chest as he felt someone or something trying to pull his heart out from behind his driver's seat. Waves of anger raged over him in an instant and all he wanted to do was go back home and pray. Flicking on a Christian radio station seemed to do the trick, as the pressure in his chest quickly subsided. But the feeling of having a dark entity near him persisted, like dark, disturbing eyes were on him the whole time he was in his car. A few nights after seeing the dark shadow man leaving Bobby Mackey's, Timothy caught sight of a dark shadow man in the rear view mirror, sitting there placidly, grinning.

"I think I finally got it to leave me alone when I said, 'In the name of the Father, Son, and Holy Ghost, I command you to leave me and my car alone and I am not interested in you or Bobby Mackey's Music World!'" Almost immediately, the oppressive feeling of the dark entity seemed to lift, replaced by a very welcome push of positive energy. "One thing that this whole situation has taught me is that there are definitely some evil entities out there that are not flesh and blood that can try to scare and seriously hurt a person if that person's not careful."

Bobby Mackey still doesn't believe in ghosts. He does, however, believe in opportunity, and for $600, you can investigate his club overnight. For $5, you can get a tour of the basement and see the well where Satan is believed to have risen from the blood of animals and Pearl Bryan's head. Yes, Bobby Mackey doesn't believe in ghosts, but he loves the people who do, and all are welcome at Bobby Mackey's Music World.

THE WHALEY HOUSE

SAN DIEGO, CA

Mad from life's history,
Swift to death's mystery;
Glad to be hurled,
Anywhere, anywhere, out of this world.
–Violet Whaley, 1885

The Whaley House, circa 1960. (Photo courtesy of the Library of Congress.)

Like Amityville, Lemp Mansion, Waverly Hills Sanatorium, or the Lizzie Borden house, the Whaley House is one place that investigators of the paranormal can all agree does not need much of an introduction. But for the benefit of our new readers and those who don't know of Thomas Whaley's former home, we'll give the house its due and its backstory. The Whaley House was not only Thomas Whaley's home, built for his family in 1857; it also happened to serve as the Whaley's general store and San Diego's courthouse. Portions of the Whaley House were built over land that once served as a town cemetery and at one time, executions by hanging were carried out when it was serving its purpose as a county courthouse.

Thomas and his wife Anna married in August of 1853 and returned to Thomas's home in San Diego. They lived in a small home near the center of town as their dream home was being built. On August 22, 1857, they officially moved into their new house and began to start a family. Together, they had six children: Francis, Anna, Thomas Jr., George, Violet, and Corrine Lillian.

Thomas Jr., however, was the first casualty of the house, succumbing to scarlet fever when he was just 18 months old. Added to that is the devastating fire that wiped out their general store next door to their home. After losing their child and their livelihood, Thomas and Anna left San Diego and moved north to San Francisco. While there, Anna gave birth to George in 1860, Violet in 1862, and Corrine Lillian in 1864. By 1868, Thomas Whaley had decided to return to San Diego and give it another go at their old home and general store.

With 1882 came another life changing experience, this time for 20-year-old Violet Whaley as she married George T. Bertolacci. But two weeks into their marriage, George disappeared and it was soon revealed that he was a major league con artist who had married Violet only to get his hands on the substantial dowry Thomas Whaley had offered his daughter's husband. Though he had been the wicked, horrible one, it was Violet who was publicly shunned and humiliated, left to endure snide comments by the so-called "polite society" belles. Such was the plight of women at this time of restrictive morals and standards. A year later, their divorce was finalized, but Violent never recovered from the betrayal and humiliation. She committed suicide on August 18, 1885, shooting herself in the chest with her father's pistol. Her suicide note, left behind on her hope chest, was only four lines long, but summed up nearly everything the poor woman had suffered through:

> Mad from life's history,
> Swift to death's mystery;
> Glad to be hurled,
> Anywhere, anywhere, out of this world.

The suicide even caused Corrine Lillian's fiancée to break off their engagement, as the scandal of Violet's divorce and suicide was just too much for him to bear. To Thomas Whaley, it must have seemed like his home, the place where so many hopes and dreams were possible, was cursed. Thomas Whaley saw the lives of two of his beloved children end so quickly that he and his wife found it difficult to remain there. They built a new home across town and abandoned the Whaley House, where it stood empty for more than twenty years. While the house was empty, it also saw the deaths of Thomas Whaley and his daughter, Anna Amelia.

In 1909, Thomas and Anna's oldest son, Francis, stepped in to revive, renovate, and rebuild the crumbling family home he had once lived in. By 1912, renovation was complete and he turned it into a popular tourist attraction. He was also successful in reuniting the surviving members of the Whaley family, including his mother Anna, sister Corrine Lillian, and brother George. All of them, Francis included, died in the house their father and husband had built for them and it is said that they have yet to move on.

THE HAUNTINGS OF WHALEY HOUSE

Although many deaths have plagued the house, most believe that the property was thoroughly haunted well before Thomas Whaley purchased the land and built his dream home. Like I said before, the property once housed the San Diego County Courthouse and its adjoining cemetery. Criminals who were judged and sentenced to be hanged in the Courthouse would generally find their next step would be to the gallows waiting outside, and then, to the graveyard beyond following that.

One spirit that seems to be a holdover from those days of ruthless justice is said to be the ghost of James Robinson, nicknamed "Yankee Jim." Robinson had been arrested and convicted for trying to steal a boat. During his arrest, it is said that he sustained some suspicious head injuries and wounds. During his subsequent jail time before his trial, Robinson's medical care was certainly lacking and those close to him claim he suffered infections and delirium as a result. Nonetheless, James Robinson was hanged in 1852, taking an agonizing forty-five minutes to strangle at the end of

In any case, even Thomas Whaley and his family thought that Yankee Jim was haunting their house, having heard footsteps on their wood floors at all hours of the day and night. Thomas even wrote in his journal that he believed it was Yankee Jim's footsteps in the upper hallways. Today, visitors and employees of the Whaley House Museum still report hearing these phantom footsteps on a regular basis.

A former employee has said that she remembers a little girl saying hi and waving to someone who wasn't there, then proceeded to describe James Robinson to a tee. The archway separating the music room from the living room of the Whaley House is said to be the precise location of the actual hanging of James Robinson, and witnesses have reported seeing oddly colored lights, mists, and even a shadow person radiating from this archway and reaching into both of the rooms it separates.

Visitors have also claimed to have seen the Lady of the House, Anna Whaley, as she tends to her old garden, takes in the coziness of one of the rooms downstairs, and has even appeared in the courtroom section of the Whaley House. Her demeanor is described as sad, yet somehow peaceful, as if she has endured a lot in her life, but has finally found some brand of peace in death. In a scenario that can only be described as thoroughly bizarre, renowned parapsychologist Dr. Hans Holzer and TV host Regis Philbin stayed overnight at the Whaley House as part of a television assignment. Both reported seeing Mrs. Whaley's spirit in the downstairs hallway, though Philbin scared her away when he couldn't resist shining a flashlight on her.

One of the more odd hauntings is said to be that of a two-year -old girl named Marion Reynolds. Marion was the great granddaughter of Thomas and Anna Whaley and, it is said that, while visiting the Whaley House in 1913, she accidentally ate ant poison while she was playing under the table in the dining room. She died on her way home just ten days shy of her third birthday. But people believe that she remains at Whaley House, tugging on the clothing of visitors and grabbing at their hands and legs. Marion's presence was first detected by trance medium Sybil Leek in 1963.

Perhaps most chilling is the phantom sound of a single gunshot emanating from Thomas Whaley's workshop, out behind the Whaley House. This shop was where Violet Whaley had taken her

The living room of the Whaley House, where Mrs. Whaley has been spotted, most notably by the thoroughly odd combination of parapsychologist Dr. Hans Holzer and TV personality Regis Philbin. (Photo courtesy of the Library of Congress.)

the rope. Pretty harsh for someone who only meant to steal a boat, but never actually got away with it.

own life and people have reported hearing a very clear, very precise gunshot coming from that workshop on numerous occasions. The disembodied cries of a baby, possibly Thomas Jr., have echoed throughout the house. Rocking chairs have been seen moving back and forth with no one in them. The odor of cigar smoke and fragrance of perfume have been smelled permeating the air of the downstairs parlor. Even the ghost of Thomas Whaley's dog has been seen trotting up and down the hallways, disappearing into one of the rooms or licking the fingers and ankles of visitors.

One distinction Whaley House has over all the other allegedly haunted houses in America? The California legislature has officially recognized it as being haunted.

NEW JERSEY'S CLINTON ROAD

WEST MILFORD, NJ

The boundaries which divide Life from Death are
at best shadowy and vague. Who shall say where
the one ends, and where the other begins?
–Edgar Allan Poe

Doty Road Bridge by Mark Drumlevitch, 1999. (Photo courtesy of the Library of Congress.)

It seems like most every town in the world has one road that most locals fear to travel down. Whether it be cursed, haunted, or horrifyingly difficult to navigate, these roads don't get a disturbing rap for nothing. Such is the case of New Jersey's Clinton Road, a desolate ten-mile stretch of two-lane blacktop, beginning at Route 23 near Newfoundland, cutting through the town of West Milford, and coming to an end at Upper Greenwood Lake. The road gets its name from a settlement named Clinton that literally died out and vanished around the turn of the century. This lonely stretch of road boasts little to no housing and runs mostly through undeveloped forest. It is the lack of people that supposedly drew the New Jersey and New York mobs to this place, finding it an ideal location to dispose of bodies.

But for the few people who DO live on Clinton Road, their lives are disrupted not by the hauntings, but by the people who come looking for ghosts and choose to be the rudest, loudest legend trippers in the known universe. The residents of Clinton Road live a very different kind of hell than the ghosts who stalk the highway. In all of my research on this mysterious road, I haven't come across anything to indicate the hauntings of a house on Clinton Road. The hauntings there are much scarier in that the ghosts aren't confined to a house. Their domain is the entire forest and asphalt of the road—unlimited possibilities for paranormal activity that spans for ten miles.

"Many people have had accidents here, some people have died here," says Mark Johnson of the New Jersey Paranormal Research Society. "There's a lot of strange activity going on here on Clinton Road."

Clinton Road gained much of its notoriety early on when it was speculated that Satanists, witches, and even the Ku Klux Klan held their meetings deep in the piney forests, spreading not only their incantations and rituals, but also their unbridled hatred. If that is true, and there's no evidence supporting either argument, then the atmosphere of racial hatred mingling with demonic rituals and incantations of white and black magic could very well create a literal cauldron of activity, opening portals all over the land. These portals, as we well know, allow any spirit or demon to just walk into our world and do as they please. They also can amplify or intensify hauntings that may already exist.

As you approach the Clinton Brook and the bridge that spans it, you might catch sight of a young boy sitting off to the side of the road. More specifically, drop a coin onto the yellow line at midnight and it will be returned to you by this boy who drowned while swimming in the brook that runs underneath Clinton Road. Others say that this ghost will push you into the water as well if you lean over the side too far.

Sounds like an urban legend, but the story of the drowned boy is actually true. The truth of the drowned boy, though, takes place not at the bridge, but at the lake near the end of the Clinton Road stretch. According to the *Newburgh Evening News*, on Tuesday, December 28th, 1965, two brothers drowned in Greenwood Lake. Fourteen-year-old Robert Neal and his nine-year-old brother, Dennis, fell through the ice while skating and drowned within minutes. Very soon after, stories of seeing two young boys near the lake's edge began to circulate quietly. Some told tales of being pushed into the water by two sets of small hands. Boys will be boys, I suppose.

While many teen drivers have lost their lives on Clinton Road, one teen in particular seems to remain at large on the poorly paved road. A young teenage girl, driving her brand new Camaro, supposedly crashed the car in 1988, dying instantly from her wounds. In recent years, people have reported seeing the Camaro pass them, a pretty young girl in the driver's seat. Once the pass is complete, the Camaro miraculously disappears in front of them. Again, we have the trappings of an urban legend, but it could possibly stem from truth. Clinton Road is notorious for claiming the lives of people not used to navigating the road, especially a precarious bend known locally as "dead man's curve," a sharp turn on a bridge that tends to sneak up on you as you drive. Drivers have been known to lose control of their cars and plummet off the side of the bridge. Those who do, generally do not live to talk about their experience. Hence the name and the reputation.

Generally, tales of the Jersey Devil are reserved almost exclusively for the Pine Barrens region of New Jersey, but the forests along Clinton Road have been a haven for this creature as well. Sightings of hellhounds, monkeys, and other unidentifiable animals have been spotted along the road at night. Some speculate that the animals were part of a jungle habitat attraction that closed down in 1976. Surviving in the wilds of the forest, these animals are thought to have crossbred with each other, making for some strange creatures to come across during a moonlit walk in the woods.

Near the reservoir, a man named Richard Cross built a castle for his wife and three children in 1905. The castle fell into ruin after it was abandoned and consumed by a fire. It is believed that occult and Satanic practitioners eventually claimed the castle as their own, staging their rituals of blood and fire in relative privacy. While visiting the old castle, people have reported going into violent convulsive seizures, and thick bruises of unknown origin have appeared on their bodies. Newark's Water Department destroyed the building in 1988, but its foundations remain, as do the trails leading to it, making it fairly easy to find.

But perhaps the creepiest secret the forest held for quite some time was the proven tale of the forests on Clinton Road being used as a body dump for the mafia. In May of 1983, a man was riding his bike down the old Clinton Road when he noticed a swarm of vultures crowding around a spot in the woods. Wise or not, the man investigated, finding a male human body at the center of their feast. An autopsy found that the man had been murdered, but found ice crystals in the blood vessels of his heart, indicating that whoever had killed him had frozen him very quickly after death and prior to dumping him in the woods. The dead man had been identified as a small time mafia hood from Rockland County, New York.

The trail of his death led to the 1986 arrest of Richard Kuklinski, a notorious New Jersey hit man who claims to have murdered over a hundred people for those willing to pay the price. Kuklinski's modus operandi? After killing his mark, he would hide their bodies in a freezer so that he could dispose of them later at a more opportune time. This was how he got the nickname the Iceman, not only because of how he treated the bodies, but by how coldly and callously he did his job. Kuklinski died in prison in March of 2006 while serving two life sentences. One has to wonder, though: how many more bodies are out there that haven't been found yet?

THE LIZZIE BORDEN HOUSE

FALL RIVER, MA

Go for Doctor Bowen as soon as you can.
I think Father is hurt.
–Lizzie Borden
To the Borden Family maid Bridget Sullivan

A hatchet similar to this one was used to crush the skulls of both Andrew and Abby Borden—a hatchet most believe was wielded by none other than Andrew's own daughter, Lizzie. (Photo by William Smock, courtesy of the Library of Congress.)

It was close to 100 degrees that day in Fall River, Massachusetts, so hot that Bridget Sullivan was glad to be outside washing the windows of 92 Second Street that day, rather than inside the hot and stuffy home of Andrew J. Borden. But what happened while Bridget was outside forever shook the little town of Fall River and threw a very bright light onto Andrew Borden's daughter, Elizabeth.

While his daughter Lizzie was in the barn looking for iron to use as sinkers for her fishing line, and while Bridget the maid was washing the outside windows, someone snuck into the house and brutally bludgeoned to death Andrew Borden and his wife Abby with what appeared to be a hatchet. Mr. Borden was found first, lying prone on the living room sofa, his head and face crushed by repeated blows from the weapon. His wife was found later in the upstairs bedroom, dead from a similar attack.

Almost immediately, suspects arose in the murders, from a mysterious salesman that Andrew Borden had cut out of a deal, to Bridget the maid, and finally, onto Lizzie herself, for it was Lizzie who didn't seem to have an airtight alibi. Moreover, there were smoldering clothes that belonged to Lizzie in the kitchen's wood burning stove, and the broken-off head of a hatchet found at the bottom of a water well in the basement. There were no signs of a break-in and it is possible that the Bordens knew their attacker; there was no sign of any forced entry and no defensive wounds suffered. Because Bridget seemed accounted for, and Lizzie's sister Emma had witnesses placing her out of town at the time, all eyes fell on Lizzie.

Axe murder was pretty hot in the late 19th to early 20th centuries. Forensic sciences, such as DNA evidence and fingerprinting, wouldn't come into usage until the mid 20th century, leaving the whole axe murder job openings relatively safe. Case in point? Both the Villisca axe murders and the Lizzie Borden murders—two tremendously brutal crimes that occurred only twenty years apart from each other, and no one was ever convicted of the crimes.

Lizzie Borden claimed that someone had broken into their palatial home and murdered not only her step mother Abby, but also her father. Her story was doubted from the start and bits of circumstantial evidence placed the blame directly on Lizzie's shoulders. But true, carved-in-stone evidence was not to be found and it led to Miss Lizzie being acquitted due to lack of evidence. In those days, if no one saw you do it, then it couldn't be proven that you had. Lizzie lived out the rest of her days with her sister Emma in a home across town, living essentially as a reclusive exile, shunned by the townspeople. Speculation ran rampant through the town as to why Lizzie had killed Abby and Andrew. Theories ranged from the classic (that Lizzie killed them to gain control of their money) to the scandalous (that Lizzie and Emma Borden planned the murder together because their father had sexually molested them) to the thoroughly bizarre (that Lizzie was actually a man who resented his/her father for raising him/her in the way he did). In all honesty, there have been murmurings of sexual abuse upon Lizzie at the hands of her father since the day he and his

Even when charged with a brutal double murder, Lizzie Borden still managed to come off as unrepentantly ladylike—one trait that many scholars believe may have helped lead to her acquittal. (Illustration courtesy of the Library of Congress.)

wife were killed. Medium Amy Allan is convinced that Lizzie killed her father because he was sexually abusing her, and murdered her step mother because she may have known it was going on and did nothing to stop it. Amy's theory has been backed up by many other psychics, including Chelsea Damali, a medium with the prestigious Paranormal Syndicate.

In the case of Lizzie Borden and her murdered parents, it was also one of the first and only times a woman was put on trial for what was—up until that point—a crime reserved for swarthy madmen wearing asylum bed sheets. The arrest, prosecution, acquittal, and eventual shunning of Lizzie changed the way people viewed crime. She was a woman of high regard, born to affluent and wealthy parents, a beacon of Fall River high society at the time. Though many believed that she did it, they probably did not want her death to lie upon their conscience.

Nowadays, its legend is what helps keep Fall River alive, as the house has become a very popular bed and breakfast. When I visited Fall River with my family in the mid 1980s, I found that most people weren't as willing to reveal the location of the Borden house, or they just didn't know of it. The stigma of the murders is used to the current owner's advantage: they get just as many paranormal teams renting out the house as they do weary travelers looking for a novel place to crash.

But they don't come to the Lizzie Borden house because the breakfast is so good. There is activity going on there that draws them like flies, and with each EVP session that comes along, the hope that the killer will reveal itself grows ever stronger.

One of the first instances of a paranormal occurrence in the house was recorded in the mid 1990s, just after it was converted into a bed and breakfast. A man and his wife checked into the Lizzie Borden B&B looking for a good nights sleep. As he took the luggage up the stairs and set it down in their room, he noticed the bed was perfectly made, the sheets crisp, clean, and pressed. He was alone in the room and began to unpack near the dresser, away from the bed. After a few moments of unpacking, his gaze turned to the bed and he was absolutely shocked by what he saw. The comforter and sheets were disrupted and rumpled, and the contours of the duvet had shifted so that it now looked like a human body—albeit an invisible one—was laying on the bed. Exasperated and clearly upset, the man retreated to the living room and sat down on the sofa, which is where his wife found him, pale and nervous. He told his wife what had happened, then took her upstairs to prove it to her. Again, the man was shocked by what he found. The sheets and comforter had been replaced and looked like new once more. The couple found out later that they were staying in the room where Abby Borden had been slain, which would turn out to be one of the more active locations in the entire house.

Other people claimed to have seen a woman in period clothing making the bed. Whether it was Abby Borden doing the daily cleaning or the residual haunt of the maid going on her rounds, we'll never know for sure. But sketches made up of the spirit tend to resemble Abby in likeness. Fair enough, considering Abby was cleaning up that particular room when she was murdered.

From all over the house, people have heard disembodied voices coming from empty rooms and along darkened hallways and staircases. Spectral footsteps have been heard coming from different spots in the house and the sounds of a sobbing woman have also been heard. Doors open and close often and muffled conversations can be heard coming from inside the otherwise vacant rooms.

Rie Sadler of the Eastern Paranormal Research Group out of Maryland investigated the house in February of 2007. Once inside Lizzie's bedroom, the team began to smell a sweet perfume, something classic and old timey. "The scent began to move around the room and we began to chase it, following it as it seemed to pace around the bed," she said. "I also caught some EVPs in this room, mainly to the tune of 'Get Out.'"

THE DYBBUK BOX

PORTLAND, OR AND ST. LOUIS, MO

In Jewish history, there
are no coincidences.
–Elie Wiesel

One of the scarier tales to come out of the United States recently is the story of the so-called Haunted Dybbuk Box, a story so unique and terrifying that its adventures in the States has inspired a film and numerous television reports from both paranormal and mainstream news agencies. It first came to the public's attention in 2003, when an antiques dealer named Kevin Mannis purchased the strange box at an estate sale. The original owner was 103 at the time of her death and the box had been a possession she kept close to her throughout her life, up until she peacefully passed.

A granddaughter of the woman told Kevin that her grandmother had been born in Poland and lived there peacefully before being sent to a concentration camp during World War II. Of her entire family, the woman was the only one to survive. She did this by escaping with other prisoners and making her way to Spain. "I was told that she acquired the small wine cabinet listed here in Spain and it was one of only three items that she brought with her when she immigrated to the United States," Kevin once wrote. "The other two items were a steamer trunk and a sewing box."

After purchasing the wine cabinet and a couple of other things, Kevin was approached by another of the woman's granddaughters. "I see you got the Dybbuk box," she'd said, motioning to the wine cabinet. Kevin was at a loss; he'd never heard the term before and he prodded the young woman for more information.

While she was growing up, her grandmother had always kept the box in her sewing room, always shut, and always out of reach. The grandmother always referred to it as the dybbuk box, for it was said to contain a dybbuk and a keselim. Neither Kevin, nor the granddaughter knew what a dybbuk or a keselim was, but her grandmother was always adamant: the cabinet was never to be opened under any circumstances. Though he didn't know it at the time, the Dybbuk Box had belonged to a Holocaust survivor, a Polish woman by the name of Havela, who had purposely sealed a dybbuk inside the box after it appeared to her and her friends during what must have been a very exciting Ouija board session.

Now Kevin was at a crossroads. He could sell the box at his store, but he also now realized how important a keepsake it was to the woman's grandmother. Kevin Mannis offered to let her keep the sentimental keepsake, but the woman became insistent, hardened. "No, no you bought it! You made a deal!"

Kevin was perplexed and tried to speak calmly to the woman, but she became more agitated, telling him, "We don't want it! Now please leave!" Ending their conversation, she walked back into the house.

When he returned the box to his antique store, he left it in the basement storage room until he could take a closer look at it properly. But later that night, his assistant at the store called him, frantically telling him that there was someone in the basement, throwing things and cursing at the top of his lungs. Furthermore, the electronic security gates had been locked, effectively trapping the hysterical young girl in the store. While Kevin told his assistant to call the police, he jumped into his car and raced toward the store.

By the time Kevin reached the antique store, the noise had stopped and there was an eerie stillness about the store. His assistant was thoroughly disturbed and refused to go near the basement storage door. Kevin himself stepped into the basement and realized that every light bulb in the room was burnt out. Later, upon closer inspection, Kevin would realize that they weren't burnt out, but shattered inside the socket. The whole place reeked of cat urine, though Kevin didn't own any cats. There was no sign of any intruder or otherwise in the entire basement, which was odd because there was only one way out of the basement and Kevin was standing directly in front of that doorway. No one would have been able to escape without him or his assistant knowing it. At the time, he didn't make the connection between the locked doors, the broken lights, and the strange box on his workbench. In time, that realization would hit, but not before it got worse. Much worse.

Kevin forgot about the episode and set about refinishing the wine box as a gift for his mother. While prepping the box, he managed to unlock it and open the doors. As he did, the mechanism inside pushed open the other door and a small drawer slid out. It resembled a flower budding in the sunlight, the petals opening freely on their own. In the drawer he found a seemingly random array of personal objects, including:

- Two pennies dated 1925 and 1928
- Two locks of hair—one blonde, one brown
- A small granite statue that had been gilded and marked with the Hebrew term of "Shalom"

An undated etching depicting the Dybbuk as an evil spirit who oppresses and commandeers the living for its own unfinished deeds. Artist unknown.

- A dried out rosebud
- A golden wine cup
- A strange cast iron candlestick holder with ornate "octopus" legs

Once he'd opened the box, Kevin opted not to refinish it, but clean it up with some lemon oil. He was still intrigued by the

103

Hebrew lettering on the back, but had no idea what it meant.

On October 31, 2001, Kevin's mother came by his shop to take her son out to lunch. Before leaving, he gave her the Dybbuk Box. While she looked over the odd contraption, Kevin returned to his office, intent on making a quick business call. "I hadn't been out of sight more than five minutes when one of my employees came running into my office saying that something was wrong with my mom," says Kevin. "When I went back to see what the matter was, I found my mom sitting in a chair beside the cabinet. Her face had no expression, but tears were streaming down her cheeks. No matter how I tried to get her to respond, she would not. She could not."

Kevin's mother had just suffered a massive stroke, and suffered from debilitating paralysis and the loss of her speech. "When I asked her the following day how she was doing, she teared up and spelled out the words: N-O G-I-F-T. I assured her that I had given her a gift for her birthday, thinking that she didn't remember, but she became even more upset and spelled out the words: H-A-T-E G-I-F-T."

Kevin laughed it off and told his mother not to worry, that he was sorry she didn't like the box. He gave the box to his sister, but she returned it after a week, complaining that the doors wouldn't stay closed. He turned around and handed it off to his brother, but he too brought it back. While the brother smelled fresh jasmine coming from the box, his wife smelled only rancid urine. Kevin eventually sold it to a middle-aged couple who had wandered into his store and, at that point, Kevin was sure that the box nobody wanted finally had a permanent home. But when he returned to his antique shop the next day, the Dybbuk Box was waiting for him on the front step. A note was attached that read: "*This has a bad darkness.*"

Kevin shrugged it off and took the box home with him. He began having a startling nightmare, recurring every night. "I find myself walking with a friend, usually someone I know well and trust and, at some point in the dream, I find myself looking into the eyes of the person that I am with. It is then that I realize that there is something different, something evil looking back at me," writes Kevin. "At that point in my dream, the person I am with changes into what can only be described as the most gruesome, demonic looking hag that I have ever seen. This hag then proceeds

to beat the living tar out of me." Kevin has awakened from this dream several times to find bruises and marks on his body where he'd been hit by the old hag in his dream.

It never dawned on Kevin that his horrible run of bad luck was because of the Dybbuk Box until his brother and sister both related to him, on separate occasions, that they'd had the same exact dream Kevin had, complete with the old hag and the beatings. When his girlfriend told him she too had dreamed of a violent old hag, Kevin finally connected the dots and saw the Dybbuk Box as the common denominator.

For weeks afterward, the activity surrounding the Dybbuk Box intensified. Kevin began seeing shadow figures everywhere, clouding his peripheral vision. The smell of cat urine was constant. Finally, Kevin decided to try and research the box on the Internet, but fell asleep in front of his computer. He had the same nightmare of the old hag. "I woke up at around 4:30 a.m. (when it felt and smelled like someone was breathing on my neck) to find that my house now smelled like jasmine flowers," he says, "and just in time to see a HUGE shadow thing go loping down the hall away from me."

Kevin thought about destroying the box, but wasn't sure if that was the wisest thing to do. Instead, he opted to sell it on eBay®, complete with a very detailed description of his horrid experiences with the box (which was a great find for me when I set out to research the story of this artifact). He found a buyer for the Dybbuk Box in St. Louis, Missouri, by the name of Jason Haxton. Jason was interested in the paranormal and finding the Dybbuk Box on eBay was enough to raise his curiosity about the box, but he researched it much more thoroughly than Kevin had and found some startling facts about it. Eventually, Jason and his roommates took turns sleeping with the box in their rooms, testing what Kevin had said had happened to him. Each one was stricken with burning eyes, a lack of energy, and the sudden onset of nausea. The house they lived in filled with small bugs. He found that his garage alternately smelled of jasmine and urine with no discernible source. All of what Kevin Mannis experienced was now being experienced by Jason and his roommates. They were also suffering through an incredible bout of bad luck, car trouble, sicknesses, and electrical shorts.

A Dybbuk in Hebrew folklore is a displaced spirit who is denied access to both Heaven and Hell, grounding it in Gehenna (Purgatory) instead. If the dybbuk escapes from Gehenna, it is then free to roam the Earth searching for a host, one that will do its bidding. According to the legend, the box is possessed by the spirit of at least one dybbuk and one priest, a "keselim." The spirit of the priest is supposed to manage the demon inside the box, but once the box is opened, the priest no longer has control over the dybbuk and it is free to cause chaos and mayhem. The two locks of hair, one blonde, the other dark brown, was meant to symbolize the two spirits locked together in the box. As for the other items in the box, such as a small statue gilded with the term "Shalom" on it, a red rose, a wine cup, and a candlestick holder, while appearing to be a random array of items, are all considered holy, integral tools in the ceremonies of exorcism. Jason also managed to decode the carving on the back. It was a Hebrew prayer that was often recited at Kaddish, a Jewish ceremony commemorating the dead.

Hear O Israel, the Lord is
our God, the Lord is one.
Blessed is the name of his
honored kingdom forever.

For at least three centuries, the story of the dybbuk was a Jewish folktale told to frighten children and adults alike. It wasn't until Jewish playwright Shloyme Zanvl Rappoport, under the pseudonym S. Ansky, wrote his groundbreaking play, *The Dybbuk*, that the legend became a mainstream fable. The story tells the tale of a Russian Jew who pines for the woman he was meant to be betrothed to, yet in a dramatic twist, she is allowed to marry another. The spurned lover incites evil spirits and begs them to murder him, releasing his soul as a dybbuk. In his angry form, the new dybbuk possesses the body of his lover and proclaims, "I have returned to my predestined bride, and I shall not leave her." In the end, the dybbuk claims his bride's life and the two go off to Heaven together.

But the dybbuk terrorizing Jason, Kevin, and all their friends and loved ones was no spurned lover. While not a demonic entity, it still managed to spread fear, terror, and horror wherever it was allowed to roam. Jason understood the power of the box and has readily, if not somewhat warily, taken on the challenge of being its guardian. Consulting with numerous rabbis and Hasidic clerics, it was determined that the Dybbuk Box would have to be contained in a gold lined ark or box. Jason had such an ark built based on the specifications related to him by the rabbis, which now houses the Dybbuk Box for much of the time in an undisclosed location. He rarely opens it, for he knows that by doing so, it places him and all of his loved ones into incredible danger: if the dybbuk cannot be banished, it must remain imprisoned for the rest of eternity with little to no opportunity to escape into the world.

THE ANCIENT RAM INN

WOTTON-UNDER-EDGE

GLOUCESTERSHIRE, ENGLAND

It is, alas, the evil emotions that are able to leave
their photographs on surrounding scenes and
objects and whoever heard of a place haunted
by a noble deed, or of beautiful and lovely ghosts
revisiting the glimpses of the moon?
–Algernon Blackwood

Driving through the small English market town of Wotten-under-Edge in Gloucestershire is much like driving through any other small English town. The streets are narrow and winding, the houses are pushed together tightly in rows, and exceptional greenery from trees and shrubberies compliment the quiet and cozy town. Most of the homes are modernized and updated. There are cars and trucks on the streets. Modern conveniences abound. But then you pass by a building that doesn't seem like it belongs in the more modernized parts of this town. Rather, it resembles the ghost of a 13th century pub, appearing from the mists of yesteryear to cast its dark and strange shadow across the face of the present. It's mere presence orders you to slow down and admire this incredible piece of history and its tentacles reach out to pull you into its long and winding story.

A Grade II listed building*, the Ancient Ram Inn seems to house a variety of evil and darkened souls, birthed from séances, the property's dark history, and the slight touch of illicit witchcraft. "There's so many ghostly entities in this building that it's impossible to count," owner John Humphries has said. "The evil that's in this building is a power that's almost equal to God himself."

Humphries, though eccentric and dramatic, does speak from experience. He himself claims to have been constantly seduced by the Ram's resident succubus and has been the target of wrath from other entities, including being picked up and thrown across the room.

Writer and historian C.J. Romer believes that the history of the Ram goes back even further than it was originally believed. "The first written record is 1142, which is 350 years before Columbus sailed to the States. The original church (across from the Ram) was built in 940 and we know there was a building there right on the site of the Ram where the masons stayed." Romer also points out that, at one time, the Ram was part of a medieval manor; it would have seen criminal trials, executions, and even murders. "The whole area is soaked in blood," he says.

"The only way I can describe this is as a national treasure," declared historian Richard Felix. "And, of course, a *haunted* national treasure." One obviously feels the love Felix has for the Ancient Ram Inn in his voice, but his ardor for the 13th century building is dwarfed by that of its current owner.

The Ancient Ram Inn is currently owned by Mr. John Humphries, who calls it his home as well. Local legend indicates that the house may have been built upon a 5,000-year-old pagan burial ground. This would very clearly indicate why the Ancient Ram Inn is so haunted, and haunted by incredible evil at that. Whatever evil seeped into the ground so many years ago is still there to this day, a stain on the past, influencing the present, and bound to remain for many years into the future.

The ramshackle building hosted not only rituals of black magic and Satanism, but also human sacrifices, namely the sacrifices of small children to appease their gods. Bones have been found in the earthen floors of the Ancient Ram Inn, dated by archaeologists to have been in the ground since the Middle Ages. The house itself is said to have once housed workers, slaves, and masons constructing the nearby St. Mary's Church, which owned the Ancient Ram Inn during this time. During construction, streams of water had to be diverted around the church so that the church would not become a flooded, muddy mess, leading many to speculate that doing so may have helped to open a portal to the other side. Most paranormal scholars know and understand the importance flowing water has in amplifying a haunting, and this instance is no different. For those who don't know, river and stream waters, because they are constantly flowing, are said to build up a natural energy, something entities and ghosts are known to feed off of. In the case of the Ancient Ram Inn, the constant running water is like a buffet line for spirits and, if there is an open portal nearby, those spirits will come to the source of energy like cattle.

Another interesting geological anomaly that may help explain the unnaturally active haunted house is that it was built on two intersecting ley lines, both originating from the fabled, storied, and incredibly mysterious Stonehenge. Ley lines are a mystery of both earth science and magic. They are a network of prehistoric pathways criss-crossing the country, and most believe them to have some sort of mystical significance. A ley line seems to be a straight line that carries an altered form of the earth's magnetic field. Birds, fish, and land animals use them as compasses to find their way back to mating grounds and to warmer climates during winter months. An article in *New Scientist* magazine, published in 1987, suggested that species as diverse as pigeons, whales, bees, and even bacteria

* Grade II: A distinctive term used to designate particularly important buildings of more than special interest in the United Kingdom. A historical protected building.

107

This Medieval illustration depicts what may have happened on the property prior to the Ram's occupancy: the burning, and unholy burial of, suspected witches and pagans.

can navigate using the earth's magnetic field. So yeah, ley lines, in theory, are pretty powerful and can influence a great many things in the known and unknown world.

Ownership of the Ancient Ram Inn changed hands in 1350 when it was bought by a French expatriate by the name of Maurice de Bathe. Ever since then, the inn and pub has remained private property. The deed of ownership changed numerous times over its long history and it is claimed that the spirits of those former owners have been sighted sitting amongst the tourists and caretakers of the Ram. Tunnels and underground cellars are rumored to run beneath the Ram, holding onto the bones and remains of those thought to be either former owners or curiosity seekers who were swallowed up by the Ram.

In 1968, the home met its newest and most current owner. John Humphries was a man who felt the uncanny need to save the house from destruction. At the time he bought the house, it belonged to a local brewery and was in danger of being torn down due to its advancing age and somewhat lackluster performance as a pub. In order to save the Ancient Ram Inn, John sold off every other thing he owned and bought the old house, making it his new and permanent home. That very first night he spent in the house, the spirits welcomed him by pulling him forcefully from his bed and dragging him across the floor by the arm.

"Something definitely happens here, there's no doubt about it," says Caroline Wallis who, as a child, lived at the Ram with her father, John Humphries. "Pictures fall off the walls, objects always sort of move around, but you don't see them move, you just find things in different places. As children, they didn't even tell us about the ghosts. We only found out because we did a bed and breakfast and people would leave through the windows."

Stepping from the street, across the threshold and into the old house, you immediately feel the heavy air and dense atmosphere. So many people have felt this, but are never quite sure if the heaviness is due to the hauntings and ghosts or the thick fields of electromagnetic energy running underneath the Ram. Mediums, however, are fairly certain that it is the sheer number of spirits treading the grounds of the Ram that thicken the air. What is especially terrifying is the fact that these spirits are all malignant and evil, and they all know how to terrify and torment the living. They do so without impunity or prejudice. A bishop in Gloucestershire by the name of Reverend John Yates set out to exorcise the building in 1993, but the cleansing was hardly successful. The twisted, evil spirit of a former monk delighted in bringing Reverend Yates to his knees, sending him out into the wide world, terrified and most likely emotionally scarred for the rest of his life.

In the adjoining barn lies the Ram's most heartbreaking story. It is here that archaeologists uncovered the shallow graves of children, murdered, the daggers still lodged between their ribs. But one important thing to note is that the daggers had all been broken after the child had been killed, a medieval wives tale that assures the person who's receiving the sacrifice that the blade would never be used again for any other purpose.

These rituals and sacrifices may have ultimately been responsible for conjuring the demon known as the incubus and succubus, an asexual demon who steals sperm from a man as he sleeps. The demon takes the form of a female to do this, then transforms into a male demon in order to impregnate a sleeping human woman. To this day, John Humphries claims that a succubus visits him on a regular basis, effectively raping the old man before disappearing with the old man's semen. The succubus always comes to him at night while he sleeps, leading some skeptics to believe that he may be suffering from some sort of sleep disorder or night terror. But John is firm in his resolve: it is a demon, make no mistake. A photograph of the supposed demon has shown up in English newspapers as a thick white mist, looking almost solid as it glides across the staircase.

John's grandson, Marc Alway, even claims to have seen the supposed incubus. "Me and a friend about three years ago was down here having a drink with John, and we hear some noises. We figured, 'What was that?' We walked up to the stairs, and point blank, on the stairs, there it was. Incubus. That was the most terrifying thing we'd seen."

Another demon, one not wishing to get frisky, but wishing to get violent, also seems to stalk the room known as the Bishop's Room, called that because a bishop had a horrifying encounter with the demon while he was lodging there. It is in this room of the Ram that demonic activity reaches a fever pitch. According to John Humphries, a total of ten people had to be taken across the street and exorcised after staying in the Bishop's Room, an alarming number to be sure. The demon takes hold of those who are even the slightest bit open to it, and violently reacts to those who oppose it. Visiting paranormal investigators have been hurled across the room after reciting prayers of protection and many have caught sight of a deeply black apparition materializing in the room, then slowly disappearing as it advances toward them.

John Humphries believes, and some occult scholars agree, that the Bishop's Room may have been the primary source of devil worship ceremonies and rituals. Satanic artifacts have been found lodged in the chimney stone of this room, one being the iron shoe for a cloven-hoofed animal. The spirit of a priest is also said to haunt the Bishop's Room, but his appearance in a traditional black robe and comforting white collar mask his true intentions; mediums believe he is a man interested more in the dark arts than in religious salvation, a spirit working very well in tandem with the other demonic influences.

The evil, torturous spirit of a witch is also said to wander mercilessly here, shadowed by the nasty spirit of her faithful cat. Local legends and folktales say that sometime between 1200 and 1500 A.D., a witch and her cat holed up in the Ancient Ram Inn before she was apprehended, tried, and burned at the stake along with her black cat—punishment from those who believe that the woman had bedeviled some of their neighbors.

Whether any of this is true or not is speculation, but the specter of a woman has been seen flitting in and out of the rooms. Men have felt women's hands grab them by the throat, and women feel wave-like nausea that usually culminates in vomiting. As for the cat, its spirit has been proven even more so than the witch's has. EVPs collected by nearly every team lucky enough to investigate the Ram include at least one instance of a cat mewing or screeching, and some have even seen the apparition of a cat as well, something of a trick given that John Humphries doesn't own a cat at all.

Paranormal investigators find the Ram to be an incredible adventure, one that rarely disappoints, but also seems to offer a much more dangerous level of spiritual interaction. The ghosts and demons living at the Ram are so powerful, so intelligent, that if you continue on without first casting a spell of protection upon yourself and your group, you can rest assured that they will take full advantage and make your life, literally, Hell.

Medium Chris Fairclough is drawn to the Ram, particularly the evil dwelling within the Bishop's Room. "I felt its energy. And I picked up a lot of names while I was there, that were connected to the property. The Bishop's Room is such a negative room. The incubus and succubus didn't come into the room—we left after 11 p.m., but we did feel as if we were being watched."

John's need to save the Ram has cost him dearly, not only in terms of finances, but also in a more personal sense. His wife and three young daughters left him, unable to cope with not only the hauntings, but with John's fierce determination to save the Ram from destruction at any cost.

Vandalism and thefts from visiting paranormal groups and tourists, as well as those not inclined to treat the elderly with respect, have caused John Humphries to close the Ram to investigations and tours, which ultimately left a bitter taste in the old chap's mouth. Perhaps one day he will reopen the Ram to the public, but maybe it is also better that he keep it closed—not for his benefit, but for the benefit of anyone wishing to foolishly test the mettle of the Ram's ghosts.

THE DORIS BITHER CASE

CULVER CITY, CA

It was like discovering that your innermost fires and
terrors, the things you believed no one else could fathom,
were in fact the basis of a recognized philosophy. Some
part of you felt intimately invaded, threatened; some
other part fell to its knees and sobbed in gratitude that
it was no longer alone.

–Poppy Z. Brite, *Exquisite Corpse*

In the end, the case of Doris Bither would forever change how the paranormal is dealt with on a psychological, spiritual, and emotional level. The turbulent life of this ordinary woman fighting unimaginable demons from the inside out went on to become known as "The Entity" case, after the much lauded book written by Frank De Felitta and the film, based on the book, directed by Sidney J. Furie (De Felitta also wrote the screenplay). Opinions are split over the source of the entities that plagued Doris, but no one can deny the poltergeist-like activity that drew the attention of Dr. Barry Taff, a leading figure in the science of parapsychology.

The first thing Dr. Taff would notice on that warm summer morning, in 1974, was how much of a mess the house was—in a state of shambles would be a fair assessment. Messy home notwithstanding, he had planned on being in and out, case closed almost as quickly as it had been opened. It had been only a week or so since the strange little woman in her thirties had approached his associate, Kerry Gaynor, in the paranormal section of Hunter's Books in Westwood Village. Having heard Kerry discussing the paranormal with a colleague, the little woman approached the two and told them that her house was haunted. The activity began with sightings of one large and two smaller apparitions, usually appearing in Doris's bedroom. But in the summer of 1974, the attacks began. Doris endured unseen slaps, punches, and pushes for weeks.

Up until that point, neighbors and school kids had all thought of the Bither home as being haunted, though there was never a solid reason why. Over a hundred years old, the small L-shaped home had boasted of being incredibly haunted for years, yet the history of the building and the neighborhood itself betrayed that proclamation. No murders, rapes, attacks, or assassinations of any kind had ever taken place in the house. So where was all the paranormal activity coming from?

Kerry Gaynor took the stories he had been told to his colleague, Dr. Barry Taff. It was decided that the two would at least investigate the claims, but neither were confident that it would amount to much of anything.

What they found in Doris Bither's home in Culver City would change the landscape of paranormal investigations, hauntings, and the capabilities of spirits. "On our first visit to Doris's tiny Culver City house," wrote Dr. Taff some time later, "we spent the evening securing detailed information pertaining to the alleged phenomena that had been occurring over the past few months. The family consisted of Doris, a petite, middle-to-late thirty-year-old woman, a six year-old daughter, three sons, aged ten, thirteen, and sixteen. We questioned all members of the family, with the exception of the six year-old daughter, whom we never saw."

According to Dr. Taff, the accounts of the hauntings were all fairly similar in detail, particularly when speaking of an apparition the kids had dubbed "Mr. Whose-It." This apparition, according to the children and Doris, would appear in a semi-solid, darkly cloudy form and stood well over six feet tall. In addition to the large spirit of the man, Doris and her oldest boy claimed to have seen "two dark, solid figures appear from out of nowhere" within Doris's bedroom. The two figures also seemed to be struggling with one another, pushing and shoving each other violently. Doris even claimed to have bumped into one them while walking down the hallway of her small home, taking a hard shouldering from the diminutive specter. To the family, the apparitions were terrifying and incredibly real. "Neither Doris nor her eldest son would accept the possibility that the apparitions might have been imagined," said Dr. Taff, "or simply prowlers or intruders who forcibly entered the house."

Doris believed that these specters were incredibly evil and that her entire family was in danger of being hurt or even killed by these spirits. When pressed by Dr. Taff to explain why she felt that way, Doris related to them a story that changed the face of the investigation and set a new precedent for what spirits could allegedly do to those they haunted.

These three spirits, the two smaller spirits and Mr. Whose-It, were responsible for a vicious series of sexual assaults upon her. The two smaller apparitions would hold her down, while Mr. Whose-It would violently rape her. "According to Doris's testimony," wrote Dr. Taff, "this event took place on several separate occasions, each time leaving behind large and distinct black and blue wounds, especially around the ankles, wrists, breasts and groin area of the inner thighs."

It usually began with her being tossed about, punched, and maimed until her resistance faded. It was then that she had felt hands holding her arms and legs down. She felt the unmistakable girth of a man as he climbed on top of her or pushed up behind her. All of this was perpetrated by violators who she couldn't see, but could feel, hear, and, eerily, smell.

Doris's oldest son had actually heard the scuffle coming from his mother's bedroom and went to investigate. Upon opening the door, he witnessed his mother being thrown about the room, slammed into walls, and dragged across the carpets. When he tried to intervene, he was thrown backwards by one of the invisible entities and suffered a broken arm for his trouble.

All of this came at Dr. Taff and Kerry Gaynor like a ton of bricks, but they took it in stride with remarkable aplomb. In fact, they didn't seem to initially believe Doris and her children's stories. In all honesty, without having witnessed it, who could believe such a thing? As a result, Dr. Taff referred Doris and her family to one of the psychiatrists in their unit at UCLA.

It is a grim possibility that Doris Bither must have felt let down by the eminent Dr. Taff. Whatever was happening to her was real and it was escalating. The attacks and sexual assaults became more violent and more prevalent. When she returned to Dr. Taff and told him that five other people outside of her immediate family had seen the entities, he returned to the squalid home in Culver City and embarked on the most important case of paranormal phenomena of his career and one of the more groundbreaking and important cases in paranormal history.

Research conducted on the home's past prior to their return yielded only two cases of death by natural causes as actually occurring in the home throughout its history. No other violent events, people, or crimes occurred in or around the house at any time. This lack of historical motive led Dr. Taff to two conclusions: either it was a bona fide poltergeist or a completely psychosomatic haunting, bred in the mind to deal with the horrors of reality.

Dr. Taff would soon have proof that it was quite possibly a healthy dose of each.

The background of the woman in question was one of the first things Dr. Taff and his colleagues examined. Born Doris McGowan, she had grown up in an abusive household; her mother and father were both severe alcoholics and it is alleged that her father had sexually molested her as a child. In addition to the sexual abuse, there was rampant physical and emotional abuse as well from both

parents, creating an incredibly fragile woman in Doris. When Doris was ten years-old, the family moved from their Midwest home to California. It is alleged that, sometime during her turbulent teenage years, she had a severe argument with her parents; becoming pregnant with her first son may have predicated the disagreement. This altercation led to her being disowned, not only by her two parents, but also by her aunt and uncle and many extended family members. Their animosity toward Doris was so acrid that they left nothing to her in their wills, leaving all of their money to her brother. Doris McGowan had nothing left but to try and make a decent life for herself and her child on her own.

As she grew older, her behavior leaned more toward the abusive, as she began to take up with men who seemed to be a shade of her father, abusive and alcoholic. A number of failed marriages and courtships yielded four children total, all having a different father. Her own alcoholism got progressively worse and the relationship she had with her three sons and one daughter disintegrated to the point of nothingness. It is speculated, but not proven, that Doris eventually resented the four children, for they were constant reminders of mistakes she had made with her life. This created an environment of extreme stress in the Bither house. Her sons didn't like her and she didn't seem to like them.

Taff and Gaynor had taken into consideration the fact that the home they were living in had a relative feel of incredible hostility and anxiety, generated not by the spirits within, but by Doris's children and how they both treated and felt about her.

"Doris's relationship with her four children was anything but cordial—in fact, it was downright belligerent," says Dr. Taff. "I will refrain from going into all the bizarre stories that were related to us for we cannot substantiate them."

Dr. Taff immediately noticed the comparisons. Doris was being raped by three male spirits, two smaller, weaker ones, and an older, more dominant one, the same dynamics shared by her three hostile and obnoxious sons. Add into that mix one very abusive father and a long line of abusive boyfriends/husbands, and you have the makings of a very disturbed woman who is under so much oppressive male domination that she had to create fictitious ones to lash out at safely. This was Dr. Taff's initial diagnosis.

Until the entities showed up.

They signaled their arrival with a rapid and steady drop in temperature in Doris's bedroom, odd considering it was the middle of August, there was no central air, and all of the windows were closed. These cold spots seemed to move with Dr. Taff and his colleagues, varying in intensity until the cold was replaced by the abhorrent stench of rotting flesh. Mingling together at times, the cold and the smell faded in and out of the senses from time to time, sometimes disappearing altogether. While Doris and Dr. Taff remained in the bedroom, the rest of Taff's colleagues searched the grounds and basement for the source of the coldness and odor, but returned empty handed. It was only the first anomaly in a long series of unexplained occurrences in Doris's house.

Cameras were installed in the tiny house, equipped with high-speed infrared film. Polaroid instant cameras were employed by nearly everyone on hand, so that there was instantaneous documentation of paranormal activity. Then, as if on cue, the show began. Kerry Gaynor had been in the kitchen speaking with the oldest son when one of the lower cabinet doors swung open.

"A frying pan flew out of the cabinet, following a curved path to the floor over 2.5 feet away, hitting with quite a thud," says Dr. Taff. "Now, of course, the immediate thing to surmise is that the pan was leaning against the cabinet door and finally pushed it open as it fell out. But we cannot accept this explanation for the trajectory of the pan as it came out of the cabinet was elliptical. It literally jumped out!"

Doris had been joined that night by Candy, a close friend and psychic, who seemed to have an uncanny knack for tracking the entities. Each time she had pointed to a spot in the bedroom where an entity was, the resulting Polaroid was bleached white. When Candy had told them that they were gone from that area, Dr. Taff and Kerry Gaynor took another photograph, the photograph this time appearing completely normal. Not only was Candy a true psychic who could sense where these things were in the room, there was now mounting evidence that seemed to prove that Doris was not crazy, that this was really happening to her.

"The next picture I took facing the door to the bedroom," says Dr. Taff. "The motivation for shooting at that particular time and in that direction was the sudden onset of a cold current of air accompanied by a pervasive stench flowing in from the direction of the closed bedroom door."

This photograph turned out to be the cornerstone of Dr. Taff's case for paranormal activity. On the floor of the bedroom, just inches from the door was a small sphere of light almost a foot in diameter. No one had seen this ball of light with their own eyes, but here it was, captured on film for eternity. We commonly know these balls of light today as "orbs" or "light anomalies," but in the mid- to late-1970s, these anomalies were still quite rare, especially captured on film.

But while Dr. Taff and his colleagues marveled over the single ball of light in the picture, it paled in comparison to what was about to happen. Several blue balls of light had materialized near the ceiling and were moving quickly back and forth. The resulting photograph looks nothing like the display Taff and the others had witnessed, but it was compelling and incredible nonetheless.

Over the course of several nights, the light show continued to dazzle, even answering questions by blinking on and off a certain number of times to signify yes and no. During the day, however, the entities frequently lashed out at Doris and her oldest son.

One of the more well-known incidents involved Doris and thirty or so investigators crammed into her small bedroom. When asked to provoke and call out to the spirits, Doris responded by swearing and screaming at the entities to appear. With frightening accuracy, the lights appeared. Doris provoked the spirit, daring it to show itself. The balls of light began to take the shape of a man who seemed to be very large and packed with muscle. No one could define its facial details, but all were certain that this hulking apparition was the one who had violently ravaged Doris on numerous occasions. Both she and her sons believed the entity to be the spirit of their grandfather, Doris's father.

But eventually, the lights began to fade and disappear altogether. Even the daytime experiences ground to a slow halt. Doris at this time was not drunk, as she usually had been for the other séances and experiments, and was in good spirits. Perhaps because now her claims had been solidified. She felt vindicated. As her mood lightened and the alcoholism stayed at bay, the entities seemed to dwindle and fade.

But as Doris moved from home to home and state to state, and her sobriety waned, she found the poltergeist was following her, meeting her at each home in each state with new fervor. This entity, simply put, was like an unwelcome guest who constantly and brutally invited itself in whenever it felt like it.

So what exactly was going on in the Doris Bither case?

Doris and her family were the victims of an incredibly powerful poltergeist, an entity capable of channeling the negative energy within the house into kinetic energy. The spirits were real, but their actions and their motivations were spurred on by this negativity in the family, as well as the tortured psyche of Doris herself. These entities acted out the negative thoughts and feelings in Doris Bither's life. Regret, repression, anger, and general hostility. This is classic poltergeist activity, with the attention placed specifically on one person, typically a woman or girl with a lot of repressed anger or sexuality. In Doris Bither's case, she had a lot of both. She also had a very volatile relationship with her three sons. Was the appearance of three separate, very angry spirits that beat her up and raped her a coincidence, or were they the projections of the boys' animosity toward their mother, acted out by a cruel and sadistic spirit?

The case found a new popularity as a best-selling novel by Frank De Felitta. De Felitta had been one of the witnesses at Doris Bither's home, there to photograph the activity, as photography was his main trade. De Felitta was so inspired and terrified by the case that he wrote one of the scariest books based on the subject, 1979's *The Entity*. The ensuing film version came out in 1981 and starred Barbara Hershey and Ron Silver. Despite a few changes and additions, many have declared it to be relatively accurate as far as the details of the investigations are concerned. The most glaring change was the portrayal of Doris Bither, known in the book and film as Carlotta "Carla" Moran. In life, Doris had been a hardcore alcoholic who maintained a toxic relationship with her sons. But in the film, she is portrayed as a sexually repressed straight arrow who also happens to be a stellar mother to her kids.

In May of 2009, Doris's middle son, Brian Harris, granted a rare telephone interview to journalist Javier Ortega of GhostTheory. com. During the course of the interview, Brian confessed that "…

everything about what was reported was true. It did happen. Living in that home was hell…The whole rape thing was real. My room was right next door to my mother's. I would hear the attacks happening. Things being thrown, her screaming. Then she would come out of the bedroom and have all these bruises. On her legs, her inner thighs. Just like in the movie."

Doris Bither never reconciled with her sons and it is understood that she never seemed to shake the demons of her youth. She died in 1999 of pulmonary arrest at the age of 58, a sad end to a sad life, reportedly still plagued by the spirits of her past.

So is it possible that, in the Bell Witch and Doris Bither cases, that the poltergeist or spirits in question could have been manifestations from traumatized women seeking an outlet for self expression? The theories of psychokinesis point to these kinds of examples. The best known example of psychokinesis, by far, is that of Carrie White, the titular heroine of Stephen King's novel *Carrie*. While Carrie can make things move with her mind, she can also manipulate her surroundings and influence fire to engulf her enemies. This isn't as far fetched or as fantastic as it sounds, even though Carrie is a fictional character. According to writer Nannette Rochford, many scientists in the field believe that the manifestation of poltergeist activity is actually recurrent spontaneous psychokinesis, wherein "psychokinetic energy may unconsciously leave the body of an emotionally charged person who is harboring repressed emotions, such as, anger, fear, or rage which manifest themselves as physical disturbances of the immediate surroundings." Others believe that as well, but also believe that spirits of the dead work in alliance with the psychokinesis, reveling in the energy it produces. The dead, like drug addicts, will do anything the person wants them to do in exchange for the ever necessary boost of energy from a living person.

Now, onto some other things. Let's let the noisy spirits rest a while, shall we?

WHISPERS ESTATE

MITCHELL, IN

**Ultimate horror often paralyzes memory
in a merciful way.
–Howard Phillips Lovecraft**

There doesn't seem to be anything remotely otherworldly about the house at 800-898 West Warren Street. Stately and old, it blends into the small Indiana town very nicely—so much so that, if there wasn't a sign up in front of it declaring it to be Whispers Estate, one might just drive on by and not give it a second glance. That's one of the draws of a haunted house: it looks like every other house on the outside, but peel back the skin and a tangled framework of tragedy and superstition lies underneath, kept alive by the wounds, shattered hopes, and unfulfilled dreams.

The town took its name from General Ormsby McKnight Mitchell, a Civil War general and West Point graduate who initially helped survey the land that became Mitchell, Indiana. The town of Mitchell itself was established in the mid-late 19th century as a railroad stop on the old Monon railway that ran from Louisville, Kentucky, all the way up to Chicago, and the Ohio-Mississippi railway that ran from Cincinnati to St. Louis. Smack dab in the middle of these two intersecting railways, the town of Mitchell sprang up. As you can probably imagine, a great number of people from vastly different portions of the country all seemed to come through the small railroad town.

Two of those people were Dr. George White and his wife Sarah. The two had come East to set up a private practice after George had suffered a falling out with one of his partners in California. Intent on making his fortune, George knew that setting up a doctor's office in a small railroad town would provide a constantly revolving door of new patients every week. He set out to make that dream come true.

George and Sarah bought the land on what is now West Warren Street and began to construct an enormous manor house, one that was big enough to house them and their servants, as well as provide an office for George to tend to his patients.

The house was completed and the couple moved in, in 1894. But five years later, for reasons I cannot uncover, George and Sarah sold the house to another doctor and his wife, John and Jessie Gibbons. Neither George nor Sarah are buried in the Mitchell city cemetery, so it is possible that they made their fortune, or floundered due to a lack of it, and moved onto greener pastures.

Dr. Gibbons and his wife were philanthropic people who repeatedly adopted abandoned or orphaned children—children that the railways would bring in on a regular basis. They were good surrogate parents, looked on well by the community, and provided a comfortable life for the children they took under their wing. But as soon as they moved into the house on West Warren, things for the Gibbons family took a dark, tragic turn.

Their adopted ten-year-old daughter Rachael died two days after being badly burned in a fire she set in the front parlor of the house. "The story goes that, in 1910, she was sneaking a peek at Christmas gifts, and she got too close to an open flame," recalls Van Renier, the house's current owner. "Fire ensued, and she died two days later in the upstairs bedroom."

Some say that, shortly after Rachael's death, strange things began to happen in the house. Some servants noticed doors had been opened after having been pulled shut just seconds before. Common household items would disappear, only to reappear in another part of the house. Jessie Gibbons herself and people who came to call on Dr. Gibbons also reported seeing a young girl in different parts of the house at different times, and the little girl's voice could be heard echoing through the hallways.

Not long after the death of Rachael, the Gibbons family suffered another tragedy. Elizabeth, a ten-month-old infant they had adopted when her mother had died during childbirth, died of unknown causes while sleeping in her crib in the master bedroom. She had been found by a servant, but no foul play was suspected. Today, it would be referred to as S.I.D.S. (Sudden Infant Death Syndrome).

After Elizabeth's tragic death, the Gibbons and their servants would often hear the chilling sounds of a baby crying coming from behind the master bedroom door, but the crying would stop when it was investigated, replaced by the even eerier smell of fresh baby powder.

The Gibbons thought they were cursed. And this curse would eventually claim another life. Dr. Gibbons's wife, Jessie, died in the same bedroom only two weeks after Elizabeth's death, as she suffered an agonizing bout of double-pneumonia. And like her adopted children before her, Jessie Gibbons became part of the haunted history of the house that would eventually become Whispers Estate. Dr. Gibbons, up until the day of his death in the house, in 1944, was convinced that his wife and children were still there. Additionally, servants recorded having heard the residual sounds

Old Victorian windows. (Photo by the author.)

of Jessie's deep, throaty coughs as the double-pneumonia took its toll on her. They have even said that, at times, they find it difficult to breathe.

New owners brought new stories to the house on West Warren, including the tragic death of another child, this time a little boy named Gary, in the 1970s. He succumbed to injuries he sustained after falling down the stairs. His favorite game, it seems, was hide and seek; his favorite hiding spot the master bedroom closet, and visitors to the house have seen and heard the closet door handle jiggle, moved by unseen and mischievous hands. I'm certain that

Rachael's fondness for dolls is well known at Whispers Estate, where dolls often disappear from one room and reappear in another. (Photo courtesy of the Library of Congress)

somewhere in the house, a ghostly young boy was probably giggling heartily once he realized just how much he was freaking out the strangers who keep coming to visit.

Owners became hard to come by. It had become the eerie old Gibbons place, a place where teenagers whispered about its ghosts and legends, and dared each other to go inside. The house on West

Warren stood empty and alone for several years, deteriorating slowly as the ghosts within watched the world go by without them.

In 2006, ownership changed once more and a massive renovation began. Almost immediately, the strange and bizarre paranormal activity began to occur once more, but this time, there was a new phenomenon, one that would give the house its famous moniker.

Visitors and paranormal investigators would regularly hear soft whispers in their ears. These voices would be indistinct and the words hard to understand, but they would feel the breath of the speaker and the tiny hairs inside their ears would stand on end as the voices of the dead called out in their eerie whispers.

The new owner dubbed the house Whispers Estate. A very successful bed and breakfast already, it soon became known as one of the most haunted houses in the world, once stories from visitors and guests got out about the scary things that go bump in Whispers Estate.

The third-floor room is a haven for negative energy; guests have reported having horrible nightmares while sleeping there. The doorknob jiggles violently in the middle of the night, startling them awake, and usually keeping them awake. Beds are shaken and picture frames have fallen without impetus. This isn't unusual, as most psychics have stated that a vortex or portal to the other side runs up from the front parlor, through the house and empties out into the attic, allowing god-knows-what access to the house at will and random.

Perhaps most terrifying is the horrific apparition of a Shadow Person that has been dubbed Big Black. It has been seen all over the house, but prefers the doctor's rooms in the old office portion of Whispers Estate. As with all Shadow People, it is something of a misnomer to say that they are harmless and the playful nickname given to this entity is a betrayal of its true purpose.

Shadow People are usually brought forth by death and darkness and are on an otherworldly mission to collect the souls of the living. They will influence and terrorize the living into giving them what they want and their incredible spiritual power usually gives them dominion over weaker spirits, allowing them to be controlled and manipulated. The presence of Shadow People in a haunted house makes it a very dangerous environment for the living and should never be taken lightly.

An investigation of Whispers Estate by the Indiana Ghost Trackers, filmed and produced for Dan T. Hall's documentary, *Ghost Stories 2: Unmasking the Dead*, produced a number of interesting but unintelligible EVPs, as well as a garbled string of incoherent words during a spirit box session. But the most interesting catch seemed to be a series of video clips from two static cameras set up in Rachael's room and just outside it. Suddenly, a small cloud of dust particles was seen being kicked up in the foreground of the shot. With no central air and the heat not being turned on in this empty room, this alone was a strange anomaly. Investigators were startled to see a brilliant flash of light move in front of the camera in Rachael's room, but were even more startled when they saw that the same movement of light could be seen from outside of Rachael's room. The two movements coincided perfectly and from the outside of the room, it looked like someone was walking around.

At a later time in Rachael's room, two investigators both saw the dark outline of a young girl in a white dress walking down the hallway toward them, her steps tentative, as if she were scared. An EVP session being conducted at the time revealed the small, springy voice of a young girl, her words still unintelligible. One of the female investigators who saw this apparition is convinced that it was Rachael. But when Rachael's ghost absconded, it was replaced by a darker, more authoritative spirit. Whether this spirit stepped between Rachael and the IGT investigators in an effort to protect the young girl, or if the darker spirit frightened her away is not known, but it was replacing the lightness Rachael brought with her into the room with an acrid, suffocating energy that nearly drove them all out of the upstairs completely.

But while Rachael is the most sought after spirit at Whispers Estate, there is another spirit that you might come into contact with as she steps up to protect her daughter. Indianapolis psychic intuitive Marilene Isaacs is convinced that it is Jessie Gibbons and not her husband who still holds sway over Whispers Estate. "She is in the light. She's the gatekeeper. When we feel her here, it's not because she's trapped because she died here. It's because she is this place, and she is the gatekeeper, but she's in other places."

ENGLEWOOD POST OFFICE

ENGLEWOOD, IL

Like the man-eating tigers of the tropical jungle,
whose appetites for blood have once been aroused,
I roamed about this world seeking whom I could destroy.
–H.H. Holmes

H.H. Holmes: Businessman, con artist, serial killer. The source of this mugshot is unknown, but it is likely to have originated with the Chicago Metropolitan Police Department.

His main motivation in life was money. It's what drove him to do the things he did, dark things in the inner sanctum of his hotel, that dank and horrible place where he brought those whom he could profit from. Some he'd poisoned, others he would bludgeon. Most times, he would blow carbon monoxide into their airtight bedrooms and asphyxiate them as they slept. Once dead, it was nothing to dismember the corpses of those who'd chosen to be in his employ, tossing them into the crematory as their insurance policies tossed money into his bank accounts. For the man formerly known as Herman W. Mudgett, greed was a good thing, and his love of money turned husbands into widowers and parents into mourners. True, his main motivation was the incredible amounts of ill-gotten cash languishing in his bank books. But the demon within him had a taste for blood and it had infected Mudgett to the point where his lust for it was almost as great as his lust for cash. All of this took place on what was once a busy, high-profile city street in a suburb of Chicago, Illinois, called Englewood. Today,

on the corner of South Wallace Street and West 63rd Street, is a large post office taking up a pretty sizable chunk of the city block it sits upon. To most, it is simply a post office. But to those in the know, and those who seek out the strange and the bizarre, it is a place of suffering, evil, death, and pain, for the post office wasn't always in the spot it is now. Up until 1895, another building sat there. That building belonged to a man named Herman Mudgett, a charismatic doctor and pharmacy owner whose building burned to the ground following a horrific revelation over what was actually taking place behind its closed and bolted doors.

When the terms "bizarre," "depraved," and "horrifically smart" are mentioned, visions of Jack the Ripper or Ed Gein come to mind. Even Hannibal Lecter might get a mention. But they pale in comparison and tremble in the shadow of this man, later known by his most popular moniker, H.H. Holmes. Holmes was a dapper and elegant man, well-manicured and worldly. His charisma shone brightly—as did his ambitions. But Holmes wasn't always a wealthy, charismatic man about town. He'd been born and raised as Herman Webster Mudgett, the middle child of a poor, middle-class family in New Hampshire in 1860. He was the son of a postmaster and an uber-religious mother, and most say that he became the ultimate "mama's boy" very early on, allowing himself to be spoiled by his mother and undisciplined by his otherwise stern father. Mudgett had decided very early on that he was not going to die in what he called the slums of New Hampshire; rather, he devised a plan that would ensure his wealth in the world. He decided to become a doctor, and better yet, he found a rich girl willing to pay his way.

His initial foray into the world of death came at a young age when a group of bullies, discovering his fear of corpses, forced him to touch a skeleton in a school room. But rather than become repulsed and horrified, the young Mudgett was fascinated, and so began a scary and disturbing phase in the life of a burgeoning psychopath. Mudgett soon began to embark on grisly, under-the-table forays into body snatching, selling fresh corpses to medical schools in the area. He became adept at concocting outrageous and complex schemes to collect insurance money on some of the corpses, the plans so well written that very little evidence ever pointed to anyone in particular, neither he nor his accomplices.

Barely graduating college, Mudgett soon found himself in dire financial straits, selling everything he had just so that he could eat. He'd left the wife who had paid for his college education and was staring face first into an uncertain future, one that jeopardized his dreams of wealth and power. In desperation, Herman Webster Mudgett planned his own death, with insurance papers naming his accomplice, Mudgett's new wife, as the beneficiary. But finding a corpse that resembled him enough to replace him was futile and Mudgett sank into a deep depression so deep that he even considered killing himself for real. When his suicidal tendencies were discovered, local authorities had him placed in an insane asylum. But Mudgett wasn't mad, not in the slightest. In retrospect, it can be said that nearly every step Mudgett took in life was a carefully conceived play in a gigantic game of chess. Being in the insane asylum provided Mudgett with both lodging and food as he planned his next move, one that involved Mudgett's best friend from medical school, Dr. Richard Leacock. Following his time spent at the asylum, Mudgett set about to lure his friend to his hotel suite in New York; Mudgett murdered his former best friend by administering a lethal dose of Laudanum. As he stared into the dead eyes of Richard Leacock, Mudgett knew his plan would work. Their features were so close in detail, their heights and body sizes nearly identical. No one would question whether or not the body was that of Herman Webster Mudgett. America's first true serial killer had just committed his first murder, but it would by no means be his last. "I realized that at least $20,000 would come to me after a little further trouble," he told police in his final confession. "Thus, after a great deal of trouble and thrilling escapes, I added the neat little sum of $20,000 to my bank account." In more ways than one, Herman Webster Mudgett was dead, and a man by the name of Dr. Henry Howard Holmes had risen up to take his place.

The year 1889 found Dr. Holmes working in Englewood, an affluent Chicago suburb, as a pharmacist under the tutelage of Dr. and Mrs. Holden. Few people realized that the industrious, hard-working and dapper man named Holmes hid a dark and bony past. After Dr. Holden died of lung cancer, his wife mysteriously disappeared; Holmes said that she'd sold the business to him and headed west. No one questioned him—they were happy to do business with Holmes and the pharmacy's business continued to grow. So when it was announced that the World's Fair would come to Chicago in 1893, Holmes announced his next business venture: a luxury hotel across the street from the pharmacy, built specifically for tourists and participants of the fair. Aptly named the World's Fair Hotel, Holmes claimed the hotel would bring the perfect luxury visitors the fair would require, but in reality, the hotel would be nothing more than a mousetrap, the fates of its visitors sealed when the door slammed shut behind them. This was a building built specifically for the murder of human beings, and the ever-so-patient Holmes spent two years developing and building the World's Fair Hotel, specifically so that he could rob, murder, dismember, and dispose of visitors to the World's Fair. But the people of Chicago would come to call it something else following Holmes's arrest: The Murder Castle.

Sitting at 701 63rd Street, the hotel Holmes built used a revolving door of various artisans, laborers, and construction crews. Holmes deliberately rotated his workers on and off the project so that none of them would know the entire layout, or the purpose, of the gigantic house. Only Holmes was aware of the way in and out of his maze of terror and that is precisely how he wanted it. Over 100 windowless rooms dotted the third and fourth floors. Doors opened into brick walls. Hallways twisted and wound into a labyrinth of confusion, leading people into dead ends and away from any hope of finding their way out. The rooms themselves were lead lined and thick walled, essentially soundproof so that not even the tenants in the adjoining rooms could hear the screams of their neighbors. Some rooms were built with trap doors leading directly to the basement. Other rooms had gas lines built into the walls so that, with the turn of a handle, Holmes could asphyxiate his victims quickly before discarding them to the basement dumping ground and readying them for sale to the medical schools in the Chicago area. The basement was, in and of itself, a house of horrors, filled with dissecting tables, bottles of poison, barrels of quicklime and acid, a gas chamber, coffins filled with female corpses, and an incinerator filled with the charred skeletons of little children.

With his wealth secured and his impeccable standing in the wealthy Englewood community, Holmes no longer needed to carry out the ghastly work of selling bodies and skeletons to the medical schools. But his appetite for blood couldn't be swayed and his

H.H. Holmes's infamous murder castle once occupied the area next to the post office in Chicago's Englewood suburb, at the corner of 63rd and Wallace Streets. Much of the original foundations are still visible by exploring the basement of the post office next door. (Photo by the author.)

murderous intents began to manifest in his sexuality, incorporating the murder of pretty women into his fantasies. A man without boundaries or limits, Holmes had once used his artistry for murder as an extension of his lust for power. But now, with power beyond imagination, he began to use it as an extension of his lust for women. Holmes lured much of his prey to their deaths by offering jobs to small town girls; these girls were sworn to absolute secrecy about their employment plans, because Holmes was afraid his competitors would steal them away from him. As a condition of their employment, they were forced to take out insurance policies naming Holmes as the sole beneficiary. These women were imprisoned, tortured, raped, and finally killed once Holmes had had his fun.

From 1891 to 1894, H.H. Holmes killed untold numbers of women, children, men, and business rivals and comrades, but it wasn't a trail of blood that led to his eventual arrest. It was his trail of paperwork and masterful swindling that proved to be Holmes' undoing. Pinkerton agents were investigating Holmes on a hunch that he was swindling insurance agencies and they were dangerously close to discovering the horrible secret of the hotel dubbed the "Murder Castle." On August 19, 1894, the Castle burned to the ground, deliberately set ablaze by Holmes before he fled Chicago for Philadelphia. It wasn't long after that, some neighbors began to comment about hearing the distant cries of women and children racked by immense pain coming from the darkened shell of a building that had been gutted from fire. Others began to see odd, confused women stumbling around the streets surrounding Holmes's Murder Castle. When people would go to them to aid them in what was obviously a time of need, the mysterious women would vanish into the night. Strange children would be seen walking amongst the ruins of the Castle, disappearing into nothingness when confronted.

Holmes stayed on the run for only a few months before he was arrested in Boston for insurance fraud. The resulting expose of H.H. Holmes became sensational, exploitative news and people clamored for information on this unrepentant con artist. No one knew he was a killer, only a well-educated swindler. His hastily published memoirs became a must-have bestseller as people continued to be seduced and drawn into the killer's charisma. But Pinkerton agent Frank Geyer knew something strange was afoot

with Holmes and set out to dig deeper. While trailing his mail to a Toronto address, the Pinkerton agents discovered the corpses of two children belonging to his now-missing business partner, Ben Pietzel. This gruesome discovery led police back to Chicago, where every aspect of his abominable murder factory was uncovered. Rotting corpses lay all over the basement floors and bloody clothes were piled up in different rooms of the hotel. Holmes eventually confessed to twenty-eight murders, though the actual number is most likely much higher. Because authorities could only positively identify four victims, he was tried and convicted in a Philadelphia courtroom of only four counts of murder and sentenced to hang.

Even as his death came to him, Holmes refused to repent for his crimes. He was given communion in his cell by two Catholic priests prior to his hanging, but refused to ask forgiveness for the blood on his hands. On May 7, 1896, Holmes was led to the gallows. His last request was that he be buried under concrete so that he wouldn't be dissected after his execution. Fittingly, his death by hanging took about fifteen minutes; his neck broke, but his heart refused to stop beating. Following his wishes, Holmes was buried in an unmarked grave in Holy Cross Cemetery in Yeadon, Pennsylvania, under two tons of solid concrete. Today, there are theories as to which plot of land contains his corpse, but no real evidence that he's there. In the end, Holmes ceased to be a real person and became a boogeyman, birthed into the world as a Chicago legend.

Immediately after his death, a so-called "Holmes Curse" was loosed upon the world. A number of the people involved with his trial died under bizarre circumstances, including one of the priests who had visited him prior to his execution, the doctor who certified him as dead, and the coroner who testified against him. Even the warden of the prison where Holmes was executed committed suicide, and several others involved in the life of H.H. Holmes found themselves facing untimely ends. It was so bad that people became convinced that Holmes was continuing his rancorous and depraved behavior from beyond the grave and those who were involved in the case, but survived the curse, spent the rest of their days waiting for it to catch up to them—waiting for H.H. Holmes's specter to claim them.

The ruins of Holmes's Murder Castle were demolished and the empty lot at the corner of 63rd and Wallace Streets became home to a large city post office in 1938. I find this to be somewhat ironic, given that Holmes's stern and unforgiving father was a postmaster himself.

Most believe that the post office was built atop Holmes's old basement and hotel foundation; bricks making up certain sections of the post office basement do not match up with the newer, more contemporary designs of the rest of the post office. But much of the land where Holmes's Murder Castle stood sits unoccupied, save for two trees and some lush grass. Full-bodied apparitions, bloodcurdling screams, and echoing footsteps have been seen and heard all over the basement areas. Poltergeist activity in the form of slamming doors, flickering lights, and faint vintage music being heard in the lonely corridors have the employees of the post office holding their breath each time they have to descend the steps into the basement.

"The basement is a secure place. When we were waiting there to get permission to go inside, three or four of them came up and said, 'Don't go down there, it's a terrible, haunted place!'" says author Jeff Mudgett, the great-great grandson of H.H. Holmes. "They all talk about it, they've been instructed not to." People have been pushed, hair has been pulled, and pinches to their arms and legs seem to come from out of nowhere. Mudgett himself saw a vision of a ghost and heard the disembodied voices of the dead, experiences that convinced him the paranormal was real.

"Before I walked down the steps, I was a non-believer. Absolutely not. I would have walked into any building in the world," proclaims Mudgett. "An hour later when I came out, my whole foundation had changed. I believe."

Employees of the post office warn about going down into the basement alone, knowing full well what lurks around each corner. Some have even claimed to see H.H. Holmes's ghost standing outside, looking on the building as if he were wondering where his sanctuary of pain, torture, and death had gone.

LAKE SHAWNEE AMUSEMENT PARK

LAKE SHAWNEE, WV

The witching hour, somebody had once whispered to her,
was a special moment in the middle of the night when every
child and every grown-up was in a deep deep sleep,
and all the dark things came out from hiding
and had the world all to themselves.
–Roald Dahl, *The BFG*

The little girl would watch them from the swings, blood still matted into her golden hair, her eyes tracking them with interest as they made their way through the dark, overgrown amusement park. "Why did they keep coming back here?" she would think, tilting her head quizzically as they played with their light-up toys. She giggled a bit; it was funny to her that they were surrounded by the ghosts of the past, but couldn't see how really close to them they were—that is until the cold chills raced up their spine and raised the skin and hairs on their necks and arms. Then, they knew. They knew what was around them and all the little girl did was smile and play on her swing set. Eventually, they would come to the swings—they always did—and then she would have fun with them. Like she always did.

From the dark, the rotting iron structures loom, covered in the woods and vines of neglect. The eerie silhouette of an 87-year-old Ferris wheel, cast against a pale, bloodless moon, throws a chilling blanket of dread across the abandoned swimming holes, concession stands, and swing sets. Amusements, their rusting joints creaking and groaning in the wind, mingle with the distant giggles of children, for when the darkness falls, the spirits come out to play, wafting to their favorite playthings that have been sitting there, neglected by all but them, for almost ninety years. Lake Shawnee Amusement Park in West Virginia is closed now, and it has been for some time. But it remains open to a select few who will always play there. Forever.

The tale of how Lake Shawnee Amusement Park came to be is a complex one, with all the trimmings of a great ghost story. And the best part about it? Nearly all the legends that make up its tale are true. It begins in the spring of 1775. A European immigrant by the name of Mitchell Clay brought his wife Phoebe and everything he owned into what is now Mercer County, West Virginia. To most, it was an idiotic move, for the county was known to be a haven for members of the Shawnee tribe. In fact, Mitchell Clay was the first white man to settle that part of the region, setting up house and building his family surrounded by the rough hewn wilderness. But Mitchell Clay was optimistic: he didn't mean any harm to the Shawnee people, and he hoped that his good nature would sway any kind of hostility coming from them. In 1783,

however, that all changed when they discovered where he had placed his new home.

It was a hot day in August when the young boy saw them. Bartley Clay was plucky, blonde, and all smiles as he played in the fields of his father's farm with some friends from neighboring farms, but the sight of four Shawnee Indians on horseback emerging from the woods made him stop. His smile began to fade, and his friends ran. Only Bartley remained left behind by friends who knew better than to tangle with a Shawnee.

The four Shawnee surveyed the farmland before them. This was their old homeland, once a sacred place that held the bodies of some of their dead. Now, there was a barn, a house, and a stockade of cattle and horses, all laid across land that the Shawnee treasured. To the Clay family, it was home, but to the Shawnee, it was a sacrilege. Enraged at the desecration, the Shawnee warriors descended upon the homestead, cleaving the young boy's skull with a tomahawk.

From the front porch, Mr. Clay's middle child, Tabitha, ran to her younger brother's aid, screaming in terror as the Indians began to scalp the child with a long, bone-handled knife. But her help was in vain: an arrow found its way into her heart, fired by a waiting Shawnee as another descended upon her, his own dagger brandished.

A large stone caught one of the Indians in the temple, knocking him from his horse as Mr. Clay's oldest child, Ezekiel, attacked the furious Shawnee. But he was no match for the Indians, who chose not to kill him on sight, but to abduct him and return him to their settlement.

Their mother could do nothing but watch and sob in horror as the Shawnee retreated with her eldest child. Once they had disappeared into the woods, Phoebe Clay dispatched two of Ezekiel's friends on horseback off to find her husband with the news.

Mitchell Clay returned home that day to find his two youngest children dead, brutally killed and scalped, left rotting in the summer sun. Ezekiel was nowhere to be found. Enraged and without a clue where Ezekiel was, Mitchell Clay organized a hunting party with two expert trackers and a slew of men from the farms around him. They took off after the Shawnee warriors, trailing them closely until they reached Ohio. At that point, the Shawnee party split up. Mitchell Clay and his posse followed the group that they thought had Ezekiel. But when they caught up with the Indians, they were horrified to realize that they had tracked the wrong party. After killing the Shawnee, Mitchell and his party turned tail and headed back the way they came, racing to cover lost ground and catch up to the other Shawnee party. But they were too late.

They found Ezekiel Clay's smoldering body, tied to a stake, burned beyond recognition. Defeated, the father retreated to his home in West Virginia and buried his children. He and his wife packed up their things and moved to a different, safer portion of West Virginia near the New River valley. Today, a stone marker stands on the land that once belonged to Mitchell Clay, commemorating the untimely deaths of his three children who are still buried there to this day. This place used to be Mitchell Clay's farm, but today, it's known as Lake Shawnee, and the story of Mitchell Clay's tragedy is only the beginning.

In 1926, an entrepreneur named C.T. Snidow bought the land that used to be Mitchell Clay's farmland, with the intention of creating a posh, entertaining amusement park. Complete with a variety of carnival rides, swimming holes and pools, and cabins that could be rented for the night, Lake Shawnee Amusement Park was a bustling success. But not all of it was amazing. There were some dark times that fell upon the place during its forty years in operation, times that would forever cast a dark light over Lake Shawnee.

There are stories that tell of how a soda truck, backing up from the concession area, had come too close to the mechanical swings. (This is the ride where a hundred swings are spun in a circle, making them lift higher and faster into the air.) As the truck backed up, one of the swings swung around quickly and smashed into the truck, killing the young girl riding it instantly.

Another tragedy befell Lake Shawnee in 1966 when a young boy drowned in one of the swimming holes. His mother had dropped him off at the Fun Park on her way to work, but when she returned in the afternoon to pick him up, he was nowhere to be found. Draining the lake, they found the boy, his arm stuck in a water return pipe. Not only did Snidow shut down the amusement park after that, it is rumored that this incident may have inspired the premise of the original *Friday the 13th* and given birth to the fictional Camp Crystal Lake.

Shawnee warriors, like the one pictured here, were just as protective of their burial grounds as they were of their homelands, responding to perceived insults with vengeful and often brutal attacks.
(Photo by Edward S. Curtis, courtesy of the Library of Congress.)

Lake Shawnee sat empty for twenty years, quickly gaining a reputation for being haunted. Those who dared to tread on the creepy grounds have reported hearing child-like giggles in the breeze. Doors and windows have opened and shut on their own. The rusting swing sets sway back and forth gently on nights where there is no breeze. All of this didn't matter to Gaylord White Sr., who worked at the park in the 1950s. In 1985, Gaylord White bought the old fun park, seeing an opportunity to get the park back up and running. When that fell through, he opted to try his hand at real estate developing.

"When we closed the amusement park down, we were going to turn it into a housing project," he explained. "When we got the equipment out here, we started pushing up a lot of skeletons. When we found out that it was (a burial ground) we just stopped construction." Archaeologists from Marshall College came to the land, sifting through the land and uncovering two skeletons, one of a child, the other, an adult male. In addition, they discovered tools, pots, and other artifacts that pointed not only to the Shawnee, but to tribes earlier than the 1700s. Like, 9,000 years earlier.

So much money and so many dreams have come and gone with the Lake Shawnee Fun Park that some believe that this is part of the Shawnee curse on this land for the disrespect shown to its sacred ground: that this land would never profit or be used for anything other than to harbor the bodies of the dead. Those who would try, would find their endeavors plagued with death or, in the very least, horrifically bad luck.

Ever since the day the Whites bought Lake Shawnee Fun Park, they've been immersed in the legendary tales of ghostly children, especially that of the little girl killed on the swings. Gaylord Sr. remembered a time when he sensed her looking over his shoulder as he mowed his field on his old tractor. "I had about an acre to mow and I was trying to finish. I could feel, like, something on my right side, something on my left side. So after a few seconds, I looked around, and when I did, there was a little girl sitting on the fender of my tractor. Appeared to be about eight years old. She was just smiling, just as cute as could be. So I said, 'Honey if you like this tractor all that well, I'm gonna give it to ya.' So I got off the tractor and walked away." He left the tractor in the field for her that day and it's been there ever since. He won't let anyone move it.

His son Gaylord Jr. has had his own run-in with the dead little girl, but she appeared far less cuter than she had to his father. "She's the most powerful presence we have on the property," he's said. "She's blond-headed, wearing a pink dress. She's got blood matted in her hair. Her dress is covered in blood. And it was probably one of the scariest things I've ever seen in my life."

Even Gaylord Jr.'s daughter, Frankie, has seen the little girl. "One day I was down here sitting under the pavilion and I looked toward the field from the lake. There was a little girl in a red dress. She looked like a sweet little girl. She was in the distance, I really couldn't make her out, but I knew it was a little girl in a red dress. I just picked up my guitar and ran home."

Everyday Paranormal, headed by brothers Brad and Barry Klinge, investigated Lake Shawnee Fun Park in 2010 for their show, *Ghost Lab.* "They didn't call this 'the Theme Park of Death' for nothing," says Brad, as he motioned toward the decrepit swing set. "Kids have died on these rides, supposedly died on this swing, this was the original swing that was in this amusement park."

Gaylord White Jr. agrees, saying that ghostly activity seems to swirl around one seat in particular of the massive swing set. "Sometime the seat will start to move underneath your hand until you feel cold air blowing through the seat and into the palm of your hand. When you get to the middle, you'll feel something warm, and we believe that that's her spirit."

The Klinges' investigation was daunting: covering over 100 acres of land and dealing with a huge multitude of very loud bullfrogs made it tough to make out phantom voices on their digital audio. But one EVP they caught was unmistakable. Rising above the sounds of the frogs was the crystal clear voice of what sounded like a Native American, chanting in the distance. They also were fortunate enough to capture what sounded like a battle cry.

These are not isolated cases, by any means. Numerous people have reported hearing the chants and whoops of Shawnee Indians, feeling the touch of a little girl's hand as she tugged on a shirt tail or sleeve, and seeing the eerily swaying swing set on nights where the wind is still. Shadows and dark apparitions move about the forest like black clouds wafting through trees. "This is like an amusement park for the spirits and, sometimes, they're nice enough to show you what they can do," says Gaylord. Truer words were never spoken, for when you're at Lake Shawnee, there is little doubt that you are ever truly alone.

CHEESMAN PARK

DENVER, CO

**Maybe all the schemes of the devil were nothing
compared to what man could think up.
–Joe Hill, *Horns***

Daniel and Theresa had just finished their meal at Table 6 at a high-end restaurant on Corona Street in Denver, Colorado. To cap off their evening, the two decided to take a moonlit stroll through Denver's picturesque Cheesman Park. They were new in town and hadn't had a chance to check out the sprawling park filled with plush grass and protective trees. As the couple walked arm-in-arm through the marble pavilion in the center of the park, Daniel could swear they were being followed. He'd heard muted footsteps and the slight murmurs of two men somewhere behind them. They quickened their walk, but the footsteps behind them kept pace. Both of them kept stealing glances over their shoulders, only to find that no one was there. They stopped and the sounds of the ghostly footsteps ceased as well. Had they asked around about Cheesman Park, they would have heard the stories of how haunted it was, especially at night. What Daniel and Theresa experienced was but a trifle compared to what has been reported at Cheesman Park after dark.

It all started in 1858 when a man named William Larimer bought up over 300 acres of land for a graveyard in the burgeoning metropolis of Denver. His dream was to create a sprawling, lush, beautiful place of peace and rest for the dead, where the rich and influential would pay buckets of cash for the opportunity to lay their bones amongst the most prestigious of Denver's society. Of course, the paupers and the criminals would have their place too, on the farthest edges of the land itself. He dubbed it Mount Prospect, an ironic name considering his dream of becoming wealthy in the business of death was about to go belly up, so to speak. Victims of crime, executed criminals, and the poor were the first to fill up graves in this land, which made the wealthy and the affluent avoid the place, now commonly referred to as "The Old Boneyard" or "Boot Hill." They chose to bury their dead at the Riverside Cemetery and Fairlawn Graveyards, Larimer's competition in Denver. Add to that the shoddy caretaking and handling of the graves, and you have a place most people don't even want to look at when they pass by. It seemed as if William Larimer had the dream and the cash, but lacked elbow grease and a good work ethic to maintain that dream.

By 1873, the city opted to rename the graveyard, picking the much more generic name of City Cemetery. But the graveyard was still an eyesore. Tombstones had been cracked and had fallen over, groundhogs had turned the once flat and plush grounds into a lumpy mess, and local farmers allowed their herds of cattle to graze amongst the dead.

Larimer gave up fairly easily, selling off the land to a cabinet maker-turned-undertaker named John J. Walley. Walley didn't do much to help the image of City Cemetery either, and he found himself on the business end of public pressure to do something about it. City lawmakers wanted to try and get Walley and his toxic little graveyard cleaned up and used for something useful, but couldn't figure out a way to do it—legally, that is.

Someone in the United States Government had done some homework on the land and discovered that it was originally part of a treaty with local Indians that dated back to 1860, making the land technically the property of the government. John Walley was out and the Denver lawmakers were in, buying up the land from the federal government for $200.

During Walley's ownership, the cemetery had been divided into three sections: one for the city, one for the Catholic burials, and a third for Jewish burials. The Catholic and Jewish portions were well maintained and clean, but the city's portion? Ghastly, unkempt. Pretty rough to look at. Soon after Denver took over the cemetery, the Jewish churches removed their dead from the graveyard and leased the land to the Water Department. The Catholic Church purchased their own land for a graveyard and kept their portion of the cemetery in superb condition until about 1950.

A mandate went out the following summer, wherein City Hall announced that anyone who wants to should remove their dead and relocate their graves elsewhere. They gave a ninety-day period in which to do this. The immediate plans for the land weren't made known right away, but those with loved ones buried in the City Cemetery rushed out and had the bodies exhumed and reburied across town.

More than 5,000 bodies went unclaimed, which meant another big job for the local government. Mayor Platt Rogers questioned the safety of opening thousands of coffins and exposing the possibly hazardous remains to the air of Denver.

So what did they do? The same thing government does now when a dirty job needs to get done and they don't want to do it

It may look serene, but beneath the plush green grass and beaming sun lie thousands of corpses, remnants of Denver's worst cemetery relocation process ever. (Photo by Harry Mellon Rhoads, courtesy of the Library of Congress.)

themselves: they waited until Mayor Rogers went out of town on business, then contracted out the job to the lowest bidder, an unscrupulous undertaker by the name of E.F. McGovern. The Denver City Council offered McGovern $1.90 for every corpse he exhumed and removed, a pretty good deal considering there were still almost 4,000 bodies to be removed. According to

McGovern, each body would be dug up and the body removed, placed into a new casket, and moved to Riverside Cemetery. The only problem? The caskets were only 3½ feet long and a foot wide, roughly half the size of a normal-sized coffin. Bodies still in relatively good condition were broken in half or dismembered so that they could fit into the small boxes. McGovern also divvied up the remains into multiple coffins, effectively doubling or tripling the number of coffins and padding up his paycheck. Workmen and day laborers would loot the gravesites, stealing the brass nameplates from coffins and the jewelry left on the bodies at the time of their funeral.

The line of desecrated graves at the southern boundary of the cemetery sickened and horrified everybody by the appearance they presented. Around their edges were piled broken coffins, rent and tattered shrouds and fragments of clothing that had been torn from the dead bodies...All were trampled into the ground by the footsteps of the gravediggers like rejected junk.

—The Denver Republican, March 19, 1893

Around the time of this uncouth removal of bodies, nearby residents and neighbors of the cemetery reported seeing dazed and confused spirits that would look in their windows and bang on their doors at all hours of the day and night. When darkness fell over City Cemetery and the workers returned to their homes for the night, it is said that the agonized groans of the dead could be heard all over the cemetery grounds. Locals claim to still hear these eerie groaning sounds to this day.

One of the workers, a man named Jim Astor, was allegedly attacked by a ghost, the spectral fellow jumping onto his shoulders. Astor became so frightened that he threw aside a stack of the brass nameplates he had been looting from the coffins and ran from the cemetery in terror. He never returned for work the next day, or any other day.

When Mayor Rogers returned from his trip abroad, he was shocked by what he read in the local papers about the desecration of City Cemetery and the workers' haphazard way of dealing with the corpses. Mayor Rogers launched an immediate investigation, putting the body relocation project on hold until a more humane and civilized way of exhuming and re-burying the dead of City Cemetery.

Of course, the investigation went nowhere and the work never resumed at City Cemetery. The people of Denver forgot about the multitude of bodies still under the soil when developers began planning Cheesman Park in 1907, named after wealthy Denverite, Walter S. Cheesman. Eventually, even the Catholic church sold off their cemetery and had the bodies removed neatly and respectfully.

But thousands of bodies still lie under the plush green grass of Cheesman Park, where children play and where families have their picnics. Trees and flowers that grow there are fed from the corpses of people that have been lying under six feet of dirt since 1858. But anthropologist Larry Conyers of the University Of Denver says the presence of human remains numbering in the thousands doesn't seem to bother most people. Using ground penetrating radar, Conyers and his students once found the small coffin of a child near the pavilion. "People play Frisbee® on top of that little boy or little girl, and they have picnics here in Cheesman Park... and it doesn't seem to affect the spirits of these people as far as I know. This was their final resting place and I'm apt to believe that they should just remain here. I'm not a big believer in exhumation."

But the spirits *are* restless at Cheesman Park, and they come out to play with frightening regularity. It begins with innate feelings of sadness, depression, or an unknown heaviness weighing upon their souls. These eerie feelings are often followed by the sight of willowy, semi-transparent figures in the dark, their misty forms gliding in the moonlight. Strange shadows and apparitions dance along the walls of the Cheesman pavilion.

While stories and personal experiences of ghosts at Cheesman Park are plentiful, true scientific evidence of the paranormal is scarce, leading many investigators to conclude that Cheesman isn't haunted at all. But not all paranormal groups dismiss Cheesman so quickly. Some point to the fact that, because the cemetery was treated with such disrespect, the opportunities for paranormal activity can escalate.

"Our outlook on this is that cemeteries normally aren't haunted; there is no reason for them to be," said Bryan Bonner, an investigator for the Rocky Mountain Paranormal Research Society. "At Cheesman, there was desecration."

THE BLACK HOPE HORROR

CROSBY, TEXAS

Revenge is a confession of pain.
–Latin proverb

In 1979, in a small suburb of Houston, Texas, a new housing development was being planned for a small tract of land known as Section 12 on the developer's blueprints. The Purcell Corporation had bought the desolate piece of land, rife with overgrowth and century-old pepper trees. The houses that were built on this land were snatched up quickly by middle-class families in the suburb that was called Newport.

It wasn't too long after that Sam and Judith Haney, owners of a home on Hilltop Drive, got a most interesting visitor. The old man who had shown up on their doorstep was old, his dark skin weathered with age and the sun. He was an African-American man, pushing perhaps 80 years old. Dressed in overalls and a striped, button-up shirt, he held his straw hat at his side and spoke plainly to the new homeowners.

"There's something in the backyard you need to know about."

The Haney's had just begun preparations for a new in-ground swimming pool, so what the man had said piqued their interest intensely.

"I followed him around to my backyard and he pointed at the ground and said that there are some graves right here," recalls Sam. "And he marked a spot on the ground where they were. And I really didn't know how to react to that. I didn't know if he was just joking. I couldn't understand why anyone would want to joke about something like that."

The old man's direction as well as his conviction were convincing and ominous—so ominous that Sam had to know for certain if what the old man said was true. Making good use of the backhoe already on the property for the pool construction, Sam Haney began to dig. Only a few feet down, the backhoe hit what sounded like hollowed out wood.

"We stopped with the backhoe and we got down into the hole and continued digging by hand. There were pine boards. When we lifted up the first board, we could see an indentation of a skeleton form. It didn't take long to figure out that it was actual human remains."

The bodies were those of Betty and Charlie Thomas, sharecroppers who had died in the 1930s. In fact, fifty or so years earlier, much of the community of Newport went by a different name: the town of Black Hope. The Haney and Williams's homes sat in section 12, which covered the small town's graveyard, known as the Black Hope Cemetery. The old man who accurately pointed out the graves of Betty and Charlie Thomas would eventually be revealed to be Jasper Norton, a man who buried many of the sixty or so bodies located in the former Black Hope Cemetery.

"I was horrified that I had desecrated these two graves," said Judith Haney.

Feeling a sense of guilt for having disrupted their four decade long rest, Sam and Judith opted to rebury the bodies in a proper grave outfitted with bright flowers. One might think that this would be enough to placate the dead, but it was not.

Not long after, Judith Haney woke in her bed to see the alarm clock on the bureau across from her bed glowing an ominous blue light with showers of sparks radiating out of it. Curiously, the alarm clock was found to have been unplugged the entire time. Sometime later, Sam began working the third shift, leaving Judith home alone at night. One night, Judith was getting ready for bed when she heard the sliding glass door open in the kitchen. Alarmed, Judith's ears perked up when she heard a male voice say, "Hey, whatcha doing?" In a panic, Judith went to investigate, thinking it might have been her husband. But no one but her was in the house and the sliding glass door was now closed.

Sam and his wife eventually sued the developer of the suburb, but lost their case when a minor loophole in the building contract exonerated the irresponsible developers. Sadly, the Haneys lost much of their savings to massive court and legal fees and were forced to file for bankruptcy.

THE BLACK HOPE HORROR

The properties that eventually made up the community of Newport in Crosby, Texas, were originally owned by a wealthy slave master and property owner by the name of Mercer McKinney. Following the abolition of slavery and Mercer's death from exposure in 1863, the McKinney family gave the former slaves several parcels of land, so that they might build their own community. The town of Black

Hope flourished initially, with a church, school, and a small general store. The McKinneys also gave them permission to bury their dead on some of the land. They called this burial ground the Black Hope Cemetery.

These same former slaves returned to the McKinney's to sharecrop the land year after year and brought many other workers with them. A good number of these workers were buried in the Black Hope Cemetery. But as the small town flourished, a massive fire wiped it out, leaving behind shattered hopes and dreams for a new life. The residents fanned out into the surrounding communities and the town of Black Hope was eventually forgotten. Forty years of silence and tranquility fell over Black Hope as the dead remained at peace in their graves.

Eventually, William McKinney Jr. sold the land Black Hope sat on to the Purcell Corporation, who developed the land into a new suburb for middle-class families. The first purchase of a home in the new suburb was made by Ben and Jean Williams, who chose a parcel of land with an enormous, very old pepper tree. Something about the tree intrigued Jean, who noticed it was adorned with the carving of an arrow pointing down toward the ground. Two deep slash marks ran underneath the arrow point. Ben Williams wanted the tree cut down and the house built over the top of it. Jean argued against cutting it down, and eventually, the couple agreed to build the house around the tree. Ironically, had they opted to cut the tree down, chances are they would have come across a body or two, as the upside down arrow indicated the location of the dead. This discovery early on in the development process, had the Purcell Corporation known about the Black Hope Cemetery, would have prevented the continued development of Newport and the old pauper's graveyard would have been spared—even memorialized as a historic site.

But there are many that believe that the Purcell Corporation not only knew about the Black Hope Cemetery, they tried to cover it up as best they could by removing the headstones and leaving the bodies behind. Descendants of the McKinney slaves live in nearby Barrett Station, and more than a few knew that there were graves in what is now known as the Newport subdivision. "The place was owned by Will McKinney," says Barrett Station resident, John Armstrong. "And he let our folks bury up in here for a long

Following the end of the Civil War, most slave cemeteries were abandoned when newly freed slaves would leave the area and embark upon their own. They were easily forgotten and sold off to land barons, who had no trouble selling sacred grounds to business, homeowners, and financiers. (Photo by Jack Delano, courtesy of the Library of Congress.)

time." Jasper Norton and Barrett Station resident Freddie Eagleton also claim that the Purcell Corporation exhumed no bodies and no reburials ever took place prior to development. Either they had no idea that there were bodies buried in their planned housing project, or they didn't care. No one seemed to do any research into the area either, for if they had, local legends and stories would have pointed to the old settlement and its lonely graveyard.

The Haneys were so traumatized over the fact that they had desecrated two sacred burial plots that they sued the Purcell Corporation for not disclosing that their home had been built over a former graveyard. Initially, they were awarded $142,000 by way of a jury trial, but a judge took it upon himself to declare that the developers were not liable, nor were they required to pay the Haneys a dime. Instead of being vindicated, the Haneys lost their judgment, and instead were instructed to pay almost $50,000 in court costs to boot.

Almost immediately, paranormal activity began to swell, not just in the Haney household, but in the homes of their neighbors as well. The disturbance of the pauper graves seemed to unlock an incredible amount of unexplained happenings, benign at first, but becoming darker and more sinister as time passed. Across the street, Ben and Jean Williams began to experience things they couldn't comprehend or explain. Table lamps, televisions, and faucets seemed to turn on and off at random, and toilets flushed on their own at all hours of the day and night. Thousands of ants and swarms of black snakes began to invade their property and home. Flowers and plants refused to grow or flourish. These instances were quickly joined by the ominous appearance of sinkholes in the Williams's back yard, large indentations that took on the shape of coffins in their desolate flowerbeds, and the horrifying appearance of human-like shadows that would cast upon the walls in the bedrooms and hallways of their home.

The Williams's granddaughter, Carli, was staying with them while her mother was out of the country. A child of ten at the time, she vividly remembers many of the traumatizing incidents inside the home. "It would be very, very chilly and you'd have this feeling of foreboding, or just, you know, like something wasn't right. Anywhere in the house you'd have a feeling that you were not alone. Somebody was watching you. It terrified me to be in the house by myself. You could hear people murmuring to themselves. It was a presence or spirit or something there. Something that wanted to be heard. Wanted me to know that it was there."

This is generally the case for spirits, especially those that feel as though they had been forgotten. Former slaves buried in pauper graves is bad enough, but to have rich white people pave over your final resting place and put houses on top of it, well—some might think that whoever did it and whoever lived in those houses were asking to be haunted. It is a perfect storm of coincidences that bred a powerful haunting whose legacy still remains to this day.

"I absolutely believe that all of these things happened to us because we were on the graveyard," says Jean Williams, "and that we were simply going to be tormented until we left there."

The most tragic part of the Black Hope Curse began when six of the Williams's relatives were diagnosed with rare forms of cancer. Three of them died from it. "You just don't have that much sickness and death in that short a period of time," Ben Williams later said. "The spirits of the dead wanted me and my family to get off of their graveyard."

The Williamses had planned on suing the developers as well, but news of the Haney's outcome made them a tad gun shy. Essentially, if the Williamses wanted to prove to the state that there was a graveyard beneath their feet, they would have to produce a body. Buried at the base of that pepper tree were supposedly a pair of sisters whose graves were marked by their brother forty years before. He had marked the tree trunk with an arrow and two slash marks underneath so that he might easily find the graves of his sisters again with ease.

Jean Williams knew there were bodies under her feet and she began digging furiously with a shovel at the base of the tree. She dug for a few hours before she began to fall ill, overcome with flu-like symptoms. Her daughter, Tina, took over for her as her mother recuperated, but after only a half an hour of digging, Tina herself collapsed, deep in the throes of a massive heart attack. Two days after she had been rushed to the hospital, Tina succumbed to her injury and died. She was only 30 years old. At that point, Jean and Ben Williams conceded defeat and left their home in the Newport community. "We paid the price. The price was so heavy," Jean later recalled. "We paid with our family, we paid with our health, and we paid with our savings. Everything was gone. If we had not left the cemetery, we would not be here today. I believe that."

It has been reported by the current homeowners that no paranormal activity ever occurred once the Haneys and the Williamses moved out. No excavations have taken place in the parcel of land built over Black Hope Cemetery and probably never will.

If the story of the Williamses and the Haneys sounds familiar, you're correct. It is alleged that Steven Spielberg, having read about the families in the newspaper, modeled the basic story of 1983's *Poltergeist* around the happenings on Poppet's Way Drive.

WAS THERE A BLACK HOPE CURSE?

But it is important to note that not all of the popular Newport subdivision homes reside over an old slave burial ground. Section 12 ran for roughly one square block, encompassing much of Poppet's Way, all of Poppet's Court, and a good deal of undeveloped, forested land. It is also imperative to note that not all of the homes have a body buried in the back yard, nor have all of the homes been a haven for paranormal activity.

But was it all true, or was the idea of a curse merely a search for meaning in a continuing series of unfortunate and tragic events? What is true is that Black Hope Cemetery certainly existed and maps from the assessor's office in Crosby place the Newport homes directly over the location of the old graveyard, last mapped out in the late 1930s. We also know that Betty and Charlie Thomas's bodies were real enough, documented by the county coroner's office when the bodies were reported to the authorities. And, sadly, the death of the Williams's daughter Tina is a grim and sad fact as well.

In between those concrete truths is a chilling ghost story that must be taken on faith, for in this line of work, personal experiences and the integrity of others is tantamount to the Holy Grail to some. If the person telling the story has a strong moral compass, their story grows a spine and strong legs.

Ben and Jean Williams, by all accounts, were friendly, hardworking, and caring parents and grandparents. Their passion for community was matched and exceeded by their passion for their family and, in the eyes of their family and neighbors, they stood on solid ground built on integrity.

As an investigator and a sensitive, I have little doubt that what happened to the Williams family actually happened. We've all felt the cold spots, heard the whispers. Some of us have even been lucky enough to have witnessed the Shadow People flicker in and out of our lives. But it is my belief that this was not a haunting of epic proportion, but a classic example of a true, Hoodoo curse.

Hoodoo was a powerful conjuring form of magic popular amongst African tribes and Americanized slaves. Essentially, the use of Hoodoo was meant to enrich their daily lives using magic rituals to improve luck, financial prosperity, and love. But whereas Hoodoo was used mainly for positive purposes, it could also be used to practice revenge and necromancy, a form of magic that summons the dead to reveal the future or influence the present. This is generally perceived as making contact with the spirits of your ancestors so that they may help accomplish the goal of the conjurer. It is my guess that this form of conjuring was very popular amongst the residents of Black Hope and it is all too possible that a curse was laid over the graves of the dead to protect them during their rest. Given the climate of strife between blacks and whites of the late 19th to the very early 20th century, it is not just a possibility, but a verifiable certainty that a curse may have been placed on the African graveyard.

In the event of a true curse, only those directly responsible for desecrating the final resting places of the dead are targeted and once the curse is fulfilled, it withers away back to where it came from until the time comes for it to begin again. In this case, the two families who ended up fleeing their homes were the ones who desecrated the graves. The Haneys literally had dug up Betty and Charlie Thomas, and The Williams' were in the process of doing the same to the graves of the sisters.

While the other neighbors may have experienced inconveniences like lights turning off and on, whispering voices, and the occasional shadow figure darkening their doorstep, the Haneys and the Williamses experienced financial, personal, and traumatic hardships that nearly led them to ruin. The fact that no other paranormal activity has ever been reported in these homes only solidifies my theory that it was they who were haunted, not their homes. But despite my hypothesis, to this day, the community of Newport is sharply divided between those who believe the hauntings persist and those that think it's all a bunch of bunk. Amateur investigators have claimed to have caught EVPs of voices in the surrounding woods, capturing the voice of a black man or boy saying, "Get out da woods" and a small child drawling, "Daddy, I want to see my mommy." They have posted their findings Online and, if genuine, they are quite compelling.

In the end, the spirits got what they wanted. The defilers of their graves were gone and they could return to their peaceful sleep once more. And as long as no one else decides to go digging for graves in their backyards, they will continue to sleep. To the Williamses, the memory of living at Poppet's Way Drive is a torturous one. "It should have been a lovely place to live," remarked Ben Williams in an interview with the *Houston Chronicle*. "But we had nothing but Hell there."

PROSPECT PLACE

TRINWAY, OH

Turn to the light. Don't fear the shadow it creates.
–Ted Dekker

1988

It is entirely possible that Dave Longaberger knew what kind of work lay ahead for him when he purchased the old house in Trinway, Ohio, a brick mansion that had stood there since 1856. Time had had its way with the old place, as had the handful of malicious and disrespectful vandals that sprayed paint across the walls and stolen the ornate staircases and light fixtures. The leaking roof would be the first thing Dave replaced; the rain that had run through the building had turned the floors to mush and the plaster was beginning to mold and rot away. Somewhere from within the walls of Prospect Place, eyes watched with hope that this man would restore the building that had sat empty and vulnerable since 1977.

Unfortunately, this was not to be. The roof was the only thing that Dave Longaberger restored before his untimely passing in the 1990s.

How did this stately mansion, once ripe with joy and hope, become so lonely atop its hill? How, also, did it become known as one of the new "princes" of the paranormal world, a haunt so popular with investigators and tourists alike that, after nearly forty years of sitting empty and alone, became alive again with a renewed energy? And how did it become such a terrifying place in the American cultural landscape?

1856

It all began in the spring of 1856, when George Willison Adams, a known abolitionist and railroad man, had the home built for his new bride. Adams was a fairly wealthy man who specialized in contracting and would become the President of the Steubenville and Indiana Railroad. His business savvy and charismatic nature won him both friends and clients with ease. It is entirely possible that no one in Dresden, Ohio, had a bad word to say about Adams, and those who did got themselves corrected very quickly. He had been born in 1800, one of thirteen children, to former plantation owners-turned-abolitionists, George Beal Adams and Mary Turner Adams. George, at age 45, had married before, to 21 year-old Clarissa Hopkins Shaff in 1845, who gave him four children before

yellow fever took her life in 1853. He married his second wife, 22-year-old Mary Jane Robinson, in 1855, and it was for her that Prospect Place was built, a home of such comfort and safety that nothing could harm her. In return, Mary Jane loved her husband deeply and brought six more of his children into the world.

The only other thing that George W. Adams felt more passionately about than his family was the scourge of slavery, and he fought valiantly as an abolitionist, like his father and mother had, to end this abomination of human nature. It was his untarnished reputation and steadfast loyalty to his fellow man that eventually helped get Prospect Place listed on the National Register of Historic Places.

When Prospect Place was completed in the fall of 1856, Mr. and Mrs. Adams were well pleased, for the house was a beauty and provided a warm, safe environment in which to raise a family. Copper roofs, ornate woodwork, plenty of places for the children to play and rest. George W. Adams was living the dream.

A fire, starting mysteriously in the basement, decimated and destroyed the house one night, making George Adams vow to rebuild quickly and make it bigger, better, plusher, and more luxurious. He spared no expense, even implementing the very new innovation known as indoor plumbing and hot water. He even fire-proofed the house by making the interior walls out of solid brick instead of wood and plaster, and he laid a two-inch thick layer of mortar between the first floor and the second floor, effectively keeping any fire that might break out from spreading. The man, dear readers, was a dedicated and loyal genius. Prospect Place also featured a unique refrigeration system to cool milk, cheese, and butter. "Air conditioning" was created by pulling in cool air from the basement into the living quarters during the summer months via ducts in the outside walls.

By the time the new Prospect Place had been built and the Adamses had moved in, there were rumors floating around about who might have started the fire. The more popular tale was that an old Native American woman, warmly referred to as "Satan" by the townspeople, had started the fire as a punishment for building the house on top of ancient burial grounds. These tales are unfounded and most likely the product of imaginative and somewhat idle minds. The rumors became fact when a local mason and alcoholic named George Blackburn openly bragged about setting the Adams's house on fire. Adams was not only wealthy and popular, but also loved in the nearby town of Dresden, so it didn't take long for friends and neighbors to go to George Adams and tell them what they'd heard. Adams had Blackburn arrested: he was tried and convicted for arson, and sent to the penitentiary in Columbus. In an interesting and head-shaking twist of fate, the penitentiary in Columbus happened to be a building Blackburn knew well: he'd helped lay the bricks for it, and in doing so, knew his way around the prison. Of course, he escaped, but was killed while breaking into a farmer's house. The farmer, not taking too kindly to Blackburn's insistence that he rob them, cleaved his skull with an axe.

With his dream home complete and his family safe and happy, George Adams set out to make his other dream a reality: the freeing of all slaves and equality for every man. To do this, Adams became a major player in the Underground Railroad, an intricate network of tunnels, homes, safe houses, and hiding places designed to conceal and smuggle out escaped slaves from the South seeking freedom in the North. Prospect Place became one of those stops on the Underground Railroad, hiding refugee slaves in the barn areas and in the house itself. Though he was certain no one would turn on him, he still kept it as secret as possible, for if word got out that he was helping runaway slaves, then other stops on the Underground Railroad would have been in just as much peril.

It was because of this that one of the more haunting and enduring legends of Prospect Place and, more specifically, the three-story barn out back, began. It had been built using the surviving timber and bricks from the first incarnation of Prospect Place and served as a home for the family's horses and carriage, as well as their loyal farm hands. In the present day, visitors to Prospect Place have reported feeling anxious and cold and fearful of the barn during certain parts of the night, and some have even seen a tall, ominous figure dressed in a long black coat. For some time, no one had a clue as to who or what it might be. But sightings of the tall man in black clicked when the story of a runaway slave-collecting bounty hunter came to light. It is a documented fact that yes, a bounty hunter had tracked some runaway slaves from Louisiana all the way back to Ohio. The bounty hunter was certain that their trail led right to George W. Adams front porch at Prospect Place, and when he confronted George Adams about it, he was met by the homeowner's pistol and four heavily armed farmhands. Needless to say, the bounty hunter saw the predicament he was in and retreated, empty handed. According to the Prospect Place website, this is "where the oral-tradition story ends. The story picks back up with modern psychics who have filled in the blanks from that point on."

According to psychics and mediums, the farmhands tracked the bounty hunter to his camp, kidnapped him, and held a trial in the barn, where he was convicted of crimes against God and hanged from the third-floor hay loft. The farmhands quickly buried the body of the bounty hunter and swore each other to secrecy. Today, it is said that the spirit of this man roams the barn, looking to exact his own revenge on those who murdered him. Many have seen him in the pale lantern lights of the third-floor windows, some have seen him pacing about the grounds, and still others have been grabbed or touched by rough hands from behind. Whether the tale woven by psychics is true or not, there is something lurking in the dark of that barn, a presence not welcoming of visitors, especially those of African-American descent, which may lend credence to the psychic's tales of the vengeful bounty hunter.

Relatively speaking, much of the time at Prospect Place was peaceful and calm. George Adams lived there with his wife until his death in 1879, and Mary Jane Adams until her death in 1915. For a long time, the house went through owner after owner, finally becoming completely vacant, rundown, and condemned in 1976. It sat crumbling and moldering along the Ohio countryside, until Dave Longaberger, who lived near Prospect Place, bought it to save it from demolition. He'd lived alongside Prospect Place all his life and couldn't bear to see the old place torn to the ground. It was his dream that attracted George W. Adams's descendants back to Prospect Place, who took over the restoration and the running of it following Longaberger's death from cancer.

The tale of the bounty hunter had been around for some time and was a well established legend at Prospect Place. But as restoration commenced on the building, historians and other keepers of Prospect Place's legacy came forward with several tales of their own. Some local historians have said that, while holed up in the Adams's basement, runaway slaves suffering from sickness or wounds may have died in the house, then were most likely buried secretly on the property. There's no proof of any covert burials, but there have been sightings of a black slave woman wandering about the basement areas, a deep head wound making her loll back and forth slowly before she evaporates into the cool, dense air.

But the basement holds many ghosts for reasons other than the death of slaves. In the late 1800s, there was apparently a nasty train wreck involving two passenger trains. One train had stopped on the tracks, while another rammed it from behind, causing both passenger trains to derail and crash. Most of the passengers were killed instantly when the boilers of both trains exploded, and those who didn't die suffered tremendous burns over most of their bodies. With no hospital anywhere close to the wreckage, the surviving victims of the crash were taken to the house nearest the site of the devastation: Prospect Place. Once there, anguished moans filled the air and falling skin littered the lawns of Prospect Place, as a makeshift triage and field hospital were set up to aid the wounded. The cool basement, in particular, was used to house the more mangled of the victims. Some survived their ordeal, but most succumbed to it, and the basements of Prospect Place became their new home, a subterranean tomb that they wander through endlessly, still moaning in pain, still looking for help that never seems to come. Late at night, when everything is still and the quiet is all you hear, a distant groan or creaking sigh can be heard coming from somewhere in the dark basement, filtering up the stairs and into the rest of the house. The moans of the dying have woken people out their sleep and caused others to run from the house in terror.

The most widely-known tale involves a young servant girl who died after falling from the house during the winter sometime in the 1860s. Because the bitter cold had frozen the ground, it was impossible to bury the poor girl until the spring thaw loosened the soil. Until that time, her body was kept cold in the basement until farmhands could finally dig her a proper grave. It was said that her mother visited the girl's body every day until she was finally buried in a Christian funeral. But until then, and periodically to this day, people would hear the young girl's laughter and see her ghost flitting through the hallways, often appearing translucent beside one of the old servant's fireplaces. In a creepy twist, people have also heard the wailing sobs of her grieving mother, echoing through Prospect Place's dark and hollow chambers. "There have been many instances of people encountering the ghost," writes author Troy Taylor, "or hearing her voice and identifying it as that of a little girl, who have no idea that the spirit of a little girl allegedly haunts the place—or even that the house is regarded as haunted at all!"

But of major hope to all that all is well within Prospect Place is the appearance of a well dressed man in fine clothing of the period in which he died, the late 1800s. It is believed by some that he may be the spirit of a servant, or that of William Cox, one of the home's later owners who mysteriously vanished without a trace some years ago. Whoever the man may be, it is obvious that he is a sort of sentinel, watching over Prospect Place with an eagle's eye, keeping out the darkness that lurks in the barn. The spirit of the man has been seen most often on the staircase, looking down at those walking in through the front door for the first time. But his appearance is rare; the glimpses, fleeting. If he were here to protect Prospect Place, he probably knows he can rest assured. It really is in good hands and, hopefully, it will be for years to come.

LEMP MANSION

ST. LOUIS, MO

**No bird soars too high if
he soars with his own wings.
–William Blake**

You've gotta love the wealthy, jet-setting socialites of turn-of-the-century America. Without them, there would be no horrifically tragic stories for middle- and lower-class families to enjoy. This would be a shocking and audacious statement had I said it about such philanthropic money titans as Andrew Carnegie or Benjamin Guggenheim. But to say such a thing about the Lemp family? Not as bad. To be honest, the Lemp family of St. Louis, Missouri, was wealthy, snotty, and proud of it, flaunting their excesses in the face of the world. They didn't start out that way—not at all. The patriarch of the Lemp family, Johann Lemp, was a German immigrant who began a small, modest business selling groceries and his own home-brewed beer from a storefront in downtown St. Louis in 1838. As his business took off, so did his dreams for making a dollar and a cent in America. His brewery quickly began to expand into one that rivaled other, bigger companies, and he and his wife found themselves seated at the upper echelon of St. Louis society. But wealth and fame couldn't save Johann Lemp from his own death, which came for him in 1862. Taking up where his father left off, William Lemp expanded the brewery further, eventually taking up a massive five blocks.

One thing the wealthy had in those days was an overpowering sense of entitlement, prestige, and immortality. Coupled together, it created an attitude not unlike that of a psychopath: I can do what I want, whenever I want, and no one would ever dare to correct me. This was the attitude William Lemp harbored as Lemp Brewery flourished and his bank accounts got larger. In the midst of all of this success, the Lemp family experienced the first of many tragedies, when Frederick Lemp, William's favorite son and heir apparent, died in 1901 at the age of 28 of an apparent heart attack. Devastated, William Lemp retreated to Lemp Mansion and was rarely ever seen outside again. Reclusive, depressed, and possibly losing his mind, William Lemp eventually killed himself, firing a .38 caliber bullet into his head.

His other son, William Jr., took control of the brewery from his father at that time and, when you hear about this guy, you'll understand why William Lemp laid the success of the brewery at his son Frederick's feet.

William Jr. was, for lack of a better word, a brat, raised with the same sense of entitlement and vanity that his father had. But whereas William Sr. had used those senses to build and grow the family brewery, William Jr. used those same senses to womanize, drink, burn through cash, and live the life of a carefree millionaire who had not done a lick of work to deserve it. To William Jr., inheriting his family's business meant not helping the business to flourish, but reaping the benefits and profits gained from it.

William took a wife, Lillian, in 1899 who sired him a son, William III. Coming from a wealthy family herself, Lillian settled into William's spend-crazy ways rather easily. It is said that William gave her $1,000 a day and told her that if she didn't spend every cent of it that day, then she would receive no more allowances. Lillian was known by most of society as the "lavender lady," for she always wore lavender gowns and dresses, accessorized with lavender, and chose the color for many of her favorite places in the mansion. For all intents and purposes, Lillian Lemp was a happy lady.

With his wife taken care of, William turned his focus first to sustaining the brewery, then to sustaining his playboy lifestyle. He held parties regularly for himself and his friends, complete with free beer, a lavish swimming pool, and the finest prostitutes St. Louis had to offer. All of these parties took place under his wife's nose in the caves and caverns running underneath the sprawling house. In fact, the most enduring legend of Lemp Mansion was born of those hedonistic parties, that of the so-called "monkey-faced boy."

Today, there is no official documentation that this child existed, which is precisely what William Lemp Jr. wanted. Not only was the child a bastard, but he was also mentally and physically handicapped. Born of a prostitute and given the name Zeke, William's illegitimate son was born with Down's Syndrome and became an embarrassment for upper crust curmudgeon William Lemp. Rumors persisted for years afterward that William Lemp had this unfortunate boy locked up in an attic room of Lemp Mansion, kept away from public view. Former employees of Lemp Mansion have testified to St. Louis historian Joe Gibbons that a child was raised in the attic rooms amongst the servants who lived there and that there had been strict instructions that he never be allowed out of the attic.

Occasionally, Zeke would poke his head out of the attic window to take in the sights of the city around him. That was when rumors of a deformed boy that hides out in Lemp Mansion began to circulate. It was yet another scandal that would forever plague the Lemp family—yet another reminder of their poor life choices.

In 1908, William grew bored with Lillian and filed for divorce. In this day and age, with William's philandering and party-boy lifestyle, it would seem odd that Lillian herself didn't file for divorce. But in 1908, divorcing the father of your child and essentially your benefactor was as scandalous as fathering a child out of wedlock. The divorce trial that followed became all the news in St. Louis as tales of William's violence, cruelty, drunken parties, and cavorting with prostitutes came to light. But despite all of these proven acts perpetrated by William, Lillian still almost lost custody of their son because of a photograph showing her smoking a cigarette.

Lillian was able to retain custody of their son and she immediately retired from public view, withdrawing into a quiet life with her son and praying for people to forget she was ever named Lillian Lemp. But today, Lillian Lemp is looked on as a true ribbon of light in the Lemp family story. An elegant painting of her still hangs in the Lemp Mansion to this day.

William eventually remarried, but when prohibition came along in 1919, things in the family changed, obviously. He closed down the brewery without notice and his workers only learned of it when they showed up for work and saw the gates locked up. A year later, William's sister, a wealthy heiress herself, shot herself in the same manner as her father had years before.

Eventually, prohibition was repealed, but it was too late for the Lemp dynasty. They were forced to liquidate much of the family's holdings for a mere fraction of what it was worth. Not surprisingly, William slipped into a massive depression and shot himself in the heart with a .38 caliber revolver, ending his life in the very same building his father had died in only eighteen years before. With no other heirs willing to take up the brewery business, the Lemp empire had come to a dismal and devastating end. But that's not the end of the story, by any stretch.

Remember Zeke, the so-called "monkey-faced boy"? William's brother, Charles, moved into the house and renovated it, also taking Zeke under his wing and caring for him. Following the death of Zeke, Charles himself seemed to go a little mad. He shot himself as well, this time in the basement. The last Lemp son, Edwin, never returned to the house and died in his sleep at the age of 90. Per his wishes, following his death, all Lemp family histories, documents, paintings and memorabilia were destroyed in a huge bonfire. The Lemp family line, as well as their history, was officially at an end.

Eventually, the neighborhood surrounding Lemp Mansion began to deteriorate, as did the mansion itself. But with the crumbling of the buildings came stories of odd sounds, phantom lights, and sightings of a deformed young man peeking out the windows of the old Lemp Mansion. The house served as a boarding house at one time, but remained a decaying shell of its former self until around 1975, when it was bought up and renovated to its original grandeur. Lemp Mansion re-opened as a restaurant, art gallery, and museum.

That's when the tales of hauntings began to spread throughout the community, and the name Lemp would soon become synonymous with tragedy and ghostly horror. Sounds of screams, gun shots, hideous laughter, sobbing, and eerie voices calling the workers out by name had been heard throughout the renovation process and led to the early resignation of several tradesmen until the renovation was complete.

Interestingly, some have witnessed the ghost of Lillian Lemp, the lavender lady and William Jr.'s former wife, gliding about the plush carpets on the second floor, choosing the aptly named Lavender Room as her official grounds of residence.

Xenia Williams, a self-proclaimed photographic medium, visited the mansion in 2005 with her husband, where she claims to have had an experience with Lillian Lemp. "While sitting at a table in the bar, I had my husband snap a photo of me at the bar and another by the Lemp mirror on the right side of the bar," she wrote on the Lemp Mansion page of the Legends of America webpage. "I then took a picture of the doorway near where the Lemp mirror hung. When these photos came back from developing we discovered some rather unusual images. The photo of the doorway had a strange foggy type smoke that spread from the bar to the doorway along the wall until it formed a full silhouette of a woman. I believe it to be the lavender lady." Other visitors have claimed to smell the lavender perfume Lillian was fond of wearing, as well as catching sight of a willowy type woman, her head cast downward as if in despair. They notice this almost as quickly as they notice the lavender gown this spirit always seems to be wearing.

The basement and cave areas underneath Lemp Mansion have always been a hotbed of activity, whether it be for William Jr.'s parties, or, much later on, the flurry of paranormal activity that is said to remain here, albeit on a mostly residual level. The sounds of merriment have been heard mingling with the sounds of despairing cries. These caves and tunnels were, in fact, where Charles Lemp committed suicide, the last Lemp to have done so. It comes as little surprise that visitors to the caves and tunnels enter with what they feel are hundreds of eyes watching them. Sinister, deep whispers have been heard echoing throughout the caverns, and pieces of limestone have been tossed at those people searching for ghosts in the darkened passageways.

Perhaps the most active portion of the house, the attic was said to have been the hiding place/prison for Zeke. Those visiting the attic have found it to be an odd mixture of both heavy sadness and relative happiness, almost as if the spirit of Zeke is sad that he's still stuck in his prison, but happy that others have come to see him. On more than one occasion, tourists have reported hearing the voice of a child, calling out in the darkness, "Come play with me" over and over again. EVPs have been captured in the attic bedrooms as well. St. Louis's Paranormal Task Force investigated Lemp Mansion in November of 2005.

At the time of analysis, investigators thought they were hearing the voice of a woman. When I played back these same EVPs from their website, I found the voice to be eerily reminiscent of a Down's Syndrome child's pattern of speech. This same phrase of "Come play with me" has been heard by others as well, making one wonder if it is an intelligent response to the teams' presence or a residual one.

Though people go to find Zeke or the lavender lady, the spirits of William Sr., William Jr., and Charles Lemp all tend to make themselves known whether you want them to or not. Oddly, the presence of William Jr. is marked by the odor of sewage, an odor that seems to grow and grow until it becomes incredibly pervasive before dissipating quickly. When he does manifest, it is to fondle women and push men out of his study. Witnesses have also heard the residual sound of William Jr. running up the stairs to his father's room after hearing the gunshot. William Jr. has also made lecherous appearances in the ladies' restrooms, watching them do their business before vanishing into the air.

Charles Lemp has been known to open and close doors and cabinets in his old bedroom. While not doing anything as unnerving as what William Jr. has done, his presence is therefore a welcome, sometimes playful addition to the experience of staying at Lemp Mansion. Charles has also been seen walking through the hallways, ignoring those calling out to him, then disappearing as quickly as he had appeared.

Current owner Paul Pointer just shrugs his shoulders and smiles. "People come here expecting to experience weird things," he told author Troy Taylor, "and fortunately for us, they are rarely disappointed."

SEDAMSVILLE RECTORY

CINCINNATI, OH

And the most terrifying question of all may be
just how much horror the human mind can stand
and still maintain a wakeful, staring, unrelenting sanity.
–Stephen King

The demonic is a rare and interesting breed of haunting. Opportunistic, arrogant, and full of loathing for all things good, it seems as if demonic entities revel in being given a chance to plague a home or place that was once Holy and reverent, almost as if they want to show the world how hollow they think the Christian religion is. But when evil is met at the door of a holy place by evil, it becomes a battle of wills to see who will win out in the end. Such is the case of the Sedamsville Rectory, a former home to presiding priests in the Cincinnati suburb of Sedamsville.

Dedicated on May 5, 1889, the church known as Our Lady Of Perpetual Help was a worship and meeting place for mostly German immigrants in the Cincinnati area. The church itself is a stunning work of art, a Gothic monolith that casts a long shadow over the rather average suburban Ohio town. But within the church, evil began to proliferate, bred from holiness, and the door would soon be opened to the demonic influence that still hangs over this place to this day.

According to affidavits filed in both Ohio and Florida courts, two young men charged that a former priest at the church had sexually molested them while they were serving as altar boys. This occurred several times during the 1950s and 1960s by a priest named Father John Berning. Criminal charges could not be brought up because the statute of limitations had expired, but the two men were now free to file a civil lawsuit against the church. Berning retired in 1970 and moved to Florida, but when questioned by the Archdiocese of Cincinnati, Berning did not shirk responsibility. In a letter to the archdiocese, he rather shockingly admitted to his indiscretion.

"As I remember there is only one day that I molested the boy. I do not remember the day," he wrote, in October of 2002. In a chilling and creepy turn, he ended the letter on a secular note: "With best wishes and kindest regard, I am sincerely yours in Christ."

However, the archdiocese chose not to pursue punishing the priest, citing his age (96 years old) and waning health as chief motivators. Father Berning died in 2004 and was never held accountable, either by the church or by law enforcement authorities.

Zak Bagans said it perfectly during the October 19, 2012 episode of *Ghost Adventures*: if you're a man of God "and you're doing that, that turns you into a man of Satan." It is speculated by psychics and investigators that the spirit of Father Berning may be serving out a sentence imposed by God, living in limbo in the place where he committed his greatest atrocities against children who trusted him. It is thought that he serves time with a demonic spirit that his actions helped summon.

THE CRUELEST EVIL

In 1976, the church closed and merged with another church in East Price Hill, known as Holy Family Church. The church and all of its adjoining properties, including the rectory, were sold to private buyers. But the rectory didn't sell right away. In fact, it stayed empty for some time and became a favorite place for squatters to set up camp. That is, until the underground dog fighters came along. In the mid- to late-1980s, and even a few times early in 2007, the federal government and local law enforcement broke up a massive ring of underground dog fighting camps in the Cincinnati area. What they found when they stormed the Sedamsville Rectory horrified, angered, and saddened even the most hardened policeman.

Police found the corpses of several dogs stacked in the basement and in shallow graves within the earthen floor. Several pit-bull terriers were seized from the rectory, kept there behind closed doors in the basement and lower levels of the rectory until fights could be arranged with rival syndicates. They suffered wounds to the face and body, infections that had become gangrenous, and severe malnutrition. Some had even worn their claws and paws down to bloody nubs as they scratched and clawed at doors that had been closed and locked for days on end. The overpowering stench of feces and rot permeated the entire basement and lower levels of the house. Police even found dog teeth in the drain of the basement floor. There's no telling how much blood was washed down that drain and how much pain it hid from the world. The members of the syndicate were gone, but the gory evidence of their practices were left behind.

The Sedamsville Rectory. (Photo by the author.)

Eventually, the rectory did find buyers in Tim Brazeal and Terri Scott. With help from the Midwest Preservation Society, the couple began a complete restoration of the rectory in March of 2011. Almost immediately, the Scott's realized that they had probably bitten off more than they could chew, for all the horrid things that occurred there had expunged all that was holy from the rectory, opening a doorway for something dark and violent to step through.

Since taking over the rectory, Tim and Terri have been scratched, pushed, and a thick blanket of darkness and oppression seems to settle over them as soon as they enter. But of all the odd and frightening things that have happened, it is the time when the demon of Sedamsville Rectory made itself known through a disturbing and haunting growl. It happened the week following a planned investigation by a local paranormal group. Upon leaving, the group was supposed to lock up when they were done. But when Tim and Terri arrived at the rectory to clean up and get the place ready for another team to investigate, they discovered that the front door was wide open and all the lights were turned off. As Tim went to investigate and make certain the place was empty, Terri was left in the front room facing a swathe of blackness. Suddenly, out of the darkness came a deep, disturbing growl that chilled Terri to the bone. This demonic warning from the darkness haunts her to this day. A cleansing performed on the house by a local Byzantine priest succeeded only in riling up the evil shades that stalk the house. It is thought that Tim and Terri brought part of the evil home with them after they left: Tim found himself struggling to get past the partial possession he experienced and Terri began having vivid nightmares on a regular basis that have yet to cease.

While Tim and Terri aren't as chummy with Sedamsville Rectory as they used to be, they have no problem letting in other teams to investigate for a fee. It is an effort to further figure out what exactly is going on in the house. Several teams have visited, and very few have gone away disappointed. But make no mistake: this is not a Halloween attraction or thrill ride that you can laugh off later on the car ride home. There is a very real and very scary chance that true evil lurks in Sedamsville Rectory, and it may just like you enough to want to follow you home.

Hailing from Illinois, the Chicago Paranormal Nights group investigated Sedamsville Rectory in 2011. Lead investigator Edward Shanahan is also a self-described Spirit Feeler or intuitive and this gift of his seemed to come in handy early on in the investigation. During a twelve-minute EVP session in one of the bedrooms, Shanahan began to pick up the image of a child being whipped with a belt. During playback and analysis of the session, Shanahan was shocked to hear not only the whimper of a dog, but also the screams of a small child right after he'd had the vision of a child being beaten.

Resident Undead, a paranormal group specializing in independent documentaries about haunted places, profiled and investigated the Sedamsville Rectory for one of their very popular YouTube episodes. Investigator Adam Kimmel had a very active night, but by far the most chilling moment in the evening came after the investigation had come to a close. Kimmel had chosen one of the old bedrooms on the second floor to crash in. "Not even an hour into sleeping, I was woken up by this cold chill, and as my eyes started to adjust to the room, I was looking up to what looked like a dark shadow figure looking over me. I remember shaking my head a little to wake up and as I sat up I could see in the corner of the room this shadow, about five and a half feet, fly towards the closet extremely quick. I sat there for a moment and I was about to write it off as me seeing things...but then I remembered...I was sleeping inside the Sedamsville Rectory."

Tim and Terri welcome the other teams and have a voracious curiosity of what really lives inside the rectory, and while they have allowed other teams into the building to investigate, they still keep a healthy distance from Sedamsville Rectory. They do not stay inside the building any longer than they have to and Terri won't go in alone anymore at all. But her resolve to withstand this oppressive and demonic influence is evident in the October 13, 2012, entry of her blog. "I think the Rectory holds onto pain like a sponge, feeding off despair," she wrote. "I know I am at my breaking point...it is hard to function on a daily basis. If this nightmare inside the rectory truly is a battle for our souls? Then I know what side I am standing on. I can't give up. I REFUSE to give up. If the Sedamsville Rectory has a problem with that? Then GAME ON."

THE MANSION OF MADAME LALAURIE

NEW ORLEANS, LA

There was something in her, something that was...pure horror.
Everything you were supposed to watch out for.
Heights, fire, shards of glass, snakes,
everything that his mom tried so hard
to keep him safe from."
–John Ajvide Lindqvist, *Let The Right One In*

The cook had counted the days.

Forty-six days had passed since she was able to sleep in the slave quarters with her husband and daughter. Normally, the madame would have released her by now, and she'd surely learnt her lesson. It was almost as if the madame had forgotten her. She looked to the chains, thick and rusty, that held her captive to the hot iron stove. The metal had begun to eat into the flesh of her ankle and the heat of the stove, mingling with the heat of a very warm April, was about to drive her mad. Sweat stung the red raw wounds of her ankle, and the metal rubbed it in deeper.

As the cook turned and saw the other slaves milling about the kitchen, their misery was evident not only in the open wounds the madame had inflicted upon them, but also in their eyes. Somewhere, deep inside those eyes, a spark still shone in the darkness, a spark of hope, and as the cook stood wearily to begin preparing the madame's lunch, she happened upon an idea, one that would bring to light the pain and torture she and the others were forced to endure. Almost as if in a trance, the cook took off her apron, held it to the open flame of the oven, and watched it slowly begin to burn.

Somewhere in the house, the madame was screaming at one of the other slaves, probably David this time, followed by the all too familiar "thwacks!" of the madame's whip, the same one that had driven poor little Lia to her death. But she couldn't be bothered with that now. She'd had enough. The others in the kitchen stood and watched her, some worried, others knowing full well what the cook was plotting. They slowly filed out of the room, quietly rustling up the others, moving silently so that the madame didn't get wise.

When the cook was satisfied that the fire had taken properly, she tossed the flaming fabric into the linen closet, watching the fire spread quickly, almost as quickly as the smile spread across her face.

Others would come, she thought. Others will come and then they'll know what she did. Even as the flames grew and began to devour the mansion, she didn't care that she was still chained to the stove. Death would be a release after all that the slaves had been through and the fire, which would roar throughout the house, would rip down the walls and show the world what Madame LaLaurie was hiding from it.

The home of the brutal and deviant Madame Delphine LaLaurie and her equally demented husband, Louis. (Photo by Reading Tom CCL.)

The city of New Orleans is swarming with the ghosts and ghouls of its past, clogging the streets with both positive and negative energies. From inspiring the elegant creatures of Anne Rice's vampire novels to the real life voodoo magic of Marie LaVeau to the devastating floods created by Hurricane Katrina, the city of New Orleans has seen its share of horrors.

But there is one place that stands above the others, a true monument to the suffering inflicted upon an already downtrodden people by a cruel mistress. Sitting on the corner of Royal Street is a luxurious mansion, standing three stories tall. It sits in the center of town, the pinnacle of the New Orleans elite, the mansion of Madame Delphine LaLaurie.

Born Delphine McCarty in 1775, the future Madame LaLaurie was the youngest of five children. Her parents, Barthelme Louis MaCarty and Marie Jeanne Lovable, were crown jewels in the white Creole sector of New Orleans, known for their wealth, opulent tastes, and political influence. Delphine herself was always complimented and revered for her beauty; many coveted her raven tresses, flawless alabaster skin, and beautiful face that some claimed she inherited from her mother.

What's more is that Delphine knew she was beautiful, privileged, and untouchable. It was this brattiness that showcased the almost immediate division between herself and others, namely the slaves working in the house. It was not uncommon for Delphine, even as a young child, to berate and yell at her servants, mostly adult women slaves who could do nothing when it was obvious that Delphine needed a spanking. Instead, Delphine's sense of entitlement and power went unchallenged and the treatment of her slaves and servants would eventually worsen to the point where her diva-like behavior would become legendary in the slave quarters.

When Delphine was 25, she married a high-ranking officer in the Spanish army by the name of Don Ramon de Lopez y Angullo, exchanging their vows at New Orleans's plush Saint Louis Cathedral. Four years later, while Delphine was pregnant with her first child, the two traveled back to Don Ramon's homeland of Spain; some say it was to receive a commendation from the Queen, and rumors floated back to the States that the Queen of Spain was taken by Delphine's beauty. But in truth, the happy couple never made it past Cuba. Don Ramon died in Havana, en route to Madrid.

Delphine returned home to New Orleans with her newborn daughter, Marie. In June of 1808, Delphine took up with a prominent financier named Jean Blanque and married him. That marriage, before his death in 1816, provided Delphine with four more children and the family home at 409 Royal Street.

It is unclear how Delphine's actions toward her slaves became in the years since her marriage to Don Ramon, but most sociologists and psychologists would assume that, giving her ultimate propensity for violence, intimidation, torture, and murder, that the slaves would have been treated incredibly bad, enduring beatings and punishments for the most minor of infractions. Though the pinnacle of her life as a psychopathic person had not yet been reached, she would have most definitely been well on her way toward that goal. Some say it was her third marriage that may have forever cemented her legend as a cruel and ruthless madame of the house. On June 25, 1825, Delphine married her third and final husband, the renown physician Leonard Louis Nicolas LaLaurie, a man much younger than she. Having already been very wealthy, the newly christened Madame LaLaurie purchased a spot of land at 1140 Royal Street, and by the end of the year, had built a luxurious three-story mansion for her family to live and thrive in. With her five children and a respected doctor as her husband, Madame LaLaurie knew that her name and reputation would excel and last well into the next century—and it would, but for all the wrong reasons.

By this time, many people's accounts of how Delphine LaLaurie treated her slaves were sort of mixed. British writer and abolitionist, Harriet Martineau, wrote in 1838 that Delphine's slaves were seen to be "singularly haggard and wretched," while those in the public saw Delphine to be fairly polite toward blacks and interested in their well being. There are records on file with the courts that even state that Madame Delphine LaLaurie freed two of her own slaves.

But as the years passed, the rumors of Delphine's treatment of her servants became too much to ignore and a representative of the courts was sent to investigate. This lawyer found that many of the rumors were unfounded, which perplexed most of her accusers, considering many callers to Delphine's home were met by the same haggard and wretched slaves that Harriet Martineau observed. Sadly, it would take the tragic death of a child to finally bring some hope to the oppressed and maimed slaves under Madame and Doctor LaLaurie's care.

One of the LaLaurie's neighbors had witnessed a young slave girl named Lia fall to her death from the roof of the mansion, trying vainly to avoid punishment by Madame LaLaurie, who had chased Lia to the top of her home, brandishing a whip. Lia was buried on the property near the slave quarters, and another investigation into the LaLauries was launched. This time, the two did not come out as squeaky clean as they had before.

The LaLauries were caught, red-handed this time, exhibiting cruel and unnecessary punishments toward their slaves, and were forced to forfeit nine of the most brutalized of their servants. But because the slaves were property of the LaLaurie family, the nine were given to relatives of Delphine and Louis, who promptly returned them to the place of their torturous servitude. One can only imagine the sense of relief that must have swarmed over the nine, only to be replaced by sheer terror when they were unceremoniously, and illegally, returned to their cruel owners.

By this time, the LaLaurie slaves had had enough. Nothing they could do would bring their terrible situation to light, but one woman had a grim idea, one that would be dangerous but ultimately rewarding for most of her people being tortured and beaten by the LaLauries. It is thought that the a cook, chained to the stove in the kitchen, started a massive fire in the LaLaurie Mansion on April 10, 1834, one that quickly enveloped the entire house. People just walking by the house attempted to go in and help those still trapped inside, but both Delphine and Louis LaLaurie refused to allow them in, keeping the front door keys securely wedged in their pockets. Instead, the growing mob of bystanders knocked the doors down to the slave quarters and found a grisly sight before them.

Seven slaves were found dead, hanging from the neck, their bodies torn, mutilated, and horribly decomposed, indicating that they had been there for some time, possibly even months. Ropes had been tied to their wrists and ankles, pulled tight to stretch out the limbs at impossible angles.

One of those attempting to help extinguish the fire was a local magistrate by the name of Judge Jean-Francois Canonge, who witnessed seeing two black women in the house, one wearing an iron collar, and the other with an incredibly deep head wound that kept her too weak to walk. According to the *New Orleans Bee* newspaper released the day after the fire, when Canonge angrily confronted Louis LaLaurie about the treatment of their slaves, LaLaurie reportedly replied: "Some people had better stay at home rather than come to others' houses to dictate laws and meddle with other people's business."

But the dead slaves in the Slaves Quarters and the injured servants in the house were nothing compared to what fire fighters found in the uppermost rooms of the LaLaurie Mansion. Tucked away in the attic was a vision straight from the depths of Hell.

As firefighters were working their way through the decimated house on Royal Street, ensuring the fire was out everywhere, they happened upon a locked door in the attic. Hearing the slight gasps and murmurs of human voices, the firemen knocked down the door and were immediately overcome by the stench of death, rot, and fecal matter.

Slaves of every age and sex were chained in the attic, bound to the walls. Their bodies had endured countless tortures such as amputations, eviscerations, and the disturbing practice of skull drilling, an ancient technique used by Native Americans to release demonic spirits. In this case, the LaLauries had drilled into the skulls of some of their slaves and jammed a stick into the hole in an effort to stir their brains while still in the skull. Women and children had been stuffed into small animal cages and were left to die. Some had their arms and legs broken, then reset at odd angles so that they seemed to resemble crabs. Buckets of blood, organs, and skulls were found all over the attic space and there was an incredible array of torture instruments such as spiked paddles, whips, and knives hanging on the wall. The LaLauries, both Delphine and Louis, had been torturing, murdering, and experimenting on their slaves, possibly for years before they had been found out.

When news of this latest development hit the streets, an angry mob rushed the LaLaurie Mansion and began to destroy everything in sight that hadn't already been touched by the fire. Soon, the mansion stood as empty as a shell could be, dark, laden with shadows, and destroyed. The tortured slaves were taken to a local jail, where they were put up for public viewing. It was said that up to 4,000 people had viewed the tortured slaves over the course of only two days in an attempt "to convince themselves of their sufferings," according to the *New Orleans Bee*.

By this time, the LaLaurie's had already fled New Orleans, instinctively knowing that their secret life as murderous socialites would finally be revealed and that it was possible, though they were white, that they would hang for what they had done. Some say they fled to Paris, France, and lived out the rest of their days there. But others weren't so sure. It was rumored that, while the LaLaurie's *said* they were going to France, they actually stayed in Louisiana, shacking up in a plantation house in nearby St. Francisville. Proof of this is hard to confirm, but a caretaker working in the Lafayette

New Orleans's old St. Louis Cemetery, where Madame LaLaurie's forgotten grave was rediscovered. It was quite a shock to the citizens of New Orleans; most believed she'd died in Paris, and very few were aware that her body had been returned to the States at all. (Photo courtesy of the Library of Congress.)

Cemetery in New Orleans stumbled upon a grave that had been overrun with weeds and neglect. The brass nameplate on the monument read: "Madame LaLaurie, née Marie Delphine Macarty, décédée à Paris, le 7 Décembre, 1842, à l'âge de 6--." This is verily the only proof of Delphine's death in Paris, her body returned in secret to New Orleans and buried quietly with no fanfare or public awareness. The fate of her husband, Louis, is completely unknown; as all blame seemed to be placed on the shoulders of his wife, Louis was able to retreat into the world anonymously, following an obvious change of his last name. It is possible that he was the one who arranged the burial for his wife in New Orleans, but again, that is pure hearsay.

Shortly after the destruction of the house, it was remodeled and rebuilt to its original architecture and grandeur. But like all renovations in a home with a storied and violent past, the ghosts that slept there awoke and decided to take a look around. The former LaLaurie house became an integrated school for girls of every color, but black children were eventually forced to leave the school by the so-called "White League." The house then became known as a popular music conservatory and dance academy, but closed down quickly when rumors of a teacher's sexual dalliances with several of his female students reached the public.

In the 1880s, a wealthy New Orleans businessman named Jules Vignie lived secretly in the house until his death in 1892. Oddly, he died in squalor, his body found on a beaten-up, old cot while thousands of dollars and numerous valuable antiques lay strewn around the house. After Vignie's death, it was bought up by greedy landlords, offering up cheap housing to a huge wave of immigrating Italian artisans and laborers. One very scary story that arose from that incarnation of the LaLaurie house was that of an Italian renter who was attacked in one of the upstairs hallways by naked black man, his hands and feet chained together. The renter fell to the floor under the weight of the attack, but found that no one was there. The attacking black man had disappeared. His story isn't unique. Children have claimed to have been chased by an angry woman in a green dress with a whip, and a young mother awoke to find a woman matching Delphine's description bending over her baby's crib, only to vanish from sight moments later.

Once word of the strange happenings got out, the place was even harder to rent out to tenants, eventually forcing the owners to sell the house. It soon became a furniture store, though the business faltered and failed quickly. The owner of the store found his products ruined on numerous occasions by the appearance of a black, stinking liquid coating the sofas and settees. Convinced vandals had perpetrated the act, the owner sat inside the store all night, a shotgun at his side. No vandals or intruders broke into the store

that night, but when morning came, the owner noticed that the furniture had been streaked with the black liquid once more.

He quickly closed the business and moved.

Stories began to circulate around the Creole communities that the LaLaurie Mansion was haunted. People walking by the house have claimed to hear the horrific screams of dying men and women, echoing from the inside of the house and pouring out onto Royal Street. Ominous figures have been seen walking through the empty house, their profiles dense and dark, yet otherworldly and chilling. Some have even heard the small, terrified cries of a young girl, possibly Lia, who fell from the roof of Delphine's house and was buried near the slave quarters.

New owners bought up the property and uncovered a mass grave where the slave quarters used to be, bringing to light once more the evil deeds of Madame LaLaurie and her villainous husband, Louis. The bodies were removed and given proper burial, but this did not stop the activity at all. Strange sounds and apparitions were still being reported, and the ghostly goings-on attracted the attention of the most famous owner of the LaLaurie Mansion: actor Nicolas Cage, who felt protective of the spirits within his new home, turning away paranormal teams repeatedly who wished to investigate the house because he felt as if allowing them in would somehow exploit the spirits. But Cage found little prosperity in the house. He would eventually put the house into foreclosure following a near-crippling bout of tax evasion. It seems that anyone who tries to make a good, decent home or business out of the LaLaurie Mansion finds failure around each corner.

Today, the LaLaurie Mansion has been converted into upscale apartments and the activity seems to have died down somewhat. But will it ever truly go away? Perhaps its best that it doesn't go away, for if we forget the horrors of the past, we will always, invariably, be condemned to repeat it. In the case of the LaLaurie Mansion, this past should never be forgotten.

THE TRAGEDY OF BILL AND MARLES HOOD

PORTLAND, OR

The tragedy is not that love doesn't last.
The tragedy is the love that lasts.
–Shirley Hazzard

DECEMBER 23, 1973
2:50 A.M.

The gun was leveled in her face. The long tunnel known as the barrel stared deep into her right eye: she saw the infinity of darkness before her and trembled even more when she saw nothing but the abyss. She had been pushed into a sitting position on the sofa before him, sobbing, begging, and pleading. He had found her there after she'd left their home next door. This house, belonging to the Bellenger's, was supposed to be safe for her and their five kids. Mrs. Bellenger had given them all safe haven in her home when the beatings got to be too much for her to take. The woman was thankful that they were all at the movies with Mr. and Mrs. Bellenger. They were safe. But there was still a part of her that couldn't believe he'd pulled his gun on her, that their marital strife had come to this ugly end. He couldn't pull the trigger, she thought. What of our children? He can't do—

A flash of light and the agonizing pause of confusion overtook her and, as the blinding white began to clear from her eyes, Marles Ann Vater-Hood found herself standing next to her husband, her assassin, as white smoke rose from the barrel of the pistol. The bullet had passed through her skull and shattered the glass doors behind her. She saw her body on the couch, but never winced once when she saw the growing pool of dark blood ooze out from under her shattered face. Instead, she looked to her husband, Bill. He stood as still as a statue, the gun rattling from the tremor racing through his hands, as he fired off two more shots. Finally, his arm dropped to his side. Marles thought of her children and was immediately wrought with sadness, for when they returned home the next day, this was what they would see: their mother, dead on the sofa, drenched in blood.

Bill was filled now with an incredible urge to undo what he had done. The anger and resentment had subsided and he now realized the horror of his actions. But it was too late. Too late, and he knew it. *What have I done?* he thought. As the thought left his mind, he turned to see his wife now standing beside him, eyes full of sadness and heavy with disappointment. As Bill stared into her spectral eyes, he reached out a hand to her. His fingers moved through her, not slowed by her ghost in the least. Still, Marles stepped back in disgust and shook her head. She saw inside him and knew that he was afraid, not of her, but of what would happen to him when the law came for him. In scarcely a moment, Bill had raised the gun to his temple and squeezed the trigger.

THE 1980S

The old Victorian house in suburban North Portland, Oregon, was an anomaly of the neighborhood. Situated on Watts Street, most of the homes in the area were mass-produced single-story homes, manufactured for employees of the local meat processing plant. While nice homes, their ages and sophistication paled in comparison to the regal shadow cast by the house known popularly throughout the neighborhood as "the old Hood residence." To the Brown family, it was exactly what they had been searching for, especially when the already low price tag of $58,000 was lowered to an astonishing $49,000.

Carolyn Brown, her husband Michael, and their two children, three-year-old Cassie and eight-year-old Gennie, were amazed at the low price of the house. Had it needed work, one might understand the low cost. But the previous owner had gone to great lengths to restore and remodel the old house, complete with new floors, light fixtures, fresh paint, and resurfaced woodwork. The house shone like a new, bright penny.

Michael and Carolyn offered $42,000 and were amazed when their offer was accepted without hesitation. However, neither one knew about the murder and suicide of Bill and Marles Hood, which had taken place in the front room of the house they'd just bought. The former owner, stopping by to see the house, only casually mentioned that it had taken place there, but a neighbor confirmed the story.

"What was really strange is that we both had a strange feeling about the house," Michael told writers Michael Norman and Beth Scott. "We didn't really discuss it between us, but we both felt that something was there."

Although they were aware of the house's past, it wasn't until almost two years later that anything remotely paranormal occurred.

This anonymous house bears a striking resemblance to the Hood's former home, where a sad life led to a tragic end for Bill and Marles Hood. (Photo by the author.)

It began as creaks and groans in the darkness, sounds that Carolyn and Michael chalked up to the woodwork shifting or swelling. Eventually, the creaks began to sound like footsteps, and with the sounds came a sense of chilly dread, something both of them kept to themselves until the night their then five-year-old daughter saw one of them.

"She would tell me that a lady was tucking her in bed at night," says Carolyn. "She said she was a very nice lady, and there would be a man off to the side. The man scared her. He would never smile, just watch. He never did anything mean, just watched."

At first Carolyn dismissed it as a child's imagination, but while checking on little Cassie one night, it became clear just how truthful her youngest child was being. "I have a bad habit of not tucking the blankets under the mattress," related Carolyn. "I just pull them up so the kids can get out of bed if they need to."

Before long, when Carolyn would check on Cassie, she would find that the blankets were tucked under the mattress and had been pulled tightly up to the girls' chins. Carolyn had figured it was Michael who had done it, but later conversations with her husband revealed that neither one had tucked the blankets.

"Cassie wasn't afraid at all. She was just curious about why the lady was tucking her in," says Carolyn. Cassie insisted the lady who visited her at night was a nice lady, tall and willowy with long, straight brown hair. The woman barely spoke a word to Cassie, only flashing a warm smile and the occasional "shhhh" sound to calm the little girl.

Once Carolyn and Michael had accepted the fact that their daughter was being visited by a spectral woman, interest then shifted to the disturbed-looking man that always seemed to accompany her, standing slightly behind her at all times, never smiling and always giving off a thoroughly negative vibe. It was so strong that Cassie found it difficult to even look at the man, instead concentrating on the "nice lady" who kept tucking her into bed at night.

Over time, the sounds of footsteps in the hallways at all hours of the night, strange, insistent knockings on the bedroom doors, and the odd occurrence of the downstairs TV and the upstairs radio turning on became commonplace. Yet while paranormal activity was happening on a regular basis, none of it was malicious or negative. In fact, the ghosts were practically family by now. The Browns even gave their ghosts a name: Mr. and Mrs. G. Cassie became so used to seeing Mrs. G that the spirit was looked on almost as if she were a nanny. And Gennie, who never had seen much of the two ghosts, finally saw Mr. G Christmas night of 1989, standing silently by the Christmas tree, admiring the ornaments and gifts for the two girls. While initially frightening to Gennie, she found solace and understanding in her mother, who soothed

and convinced her that Mr. G was just lost and looking for some sort of closure. Once she was satisfied that Mr. G wasn't there to harm or frighten her, Gennie settled easier into the routine of coexisting with the family's ghosts.

Though the spirits were very benign, their constant wanderings about the house made it difficult for the Browns sometimes. Their very pronounced footsteps on the upstairs floors and the clear-as-crystal knockings became a nuisance during bedtime. In almost humorous fashion, Carolyn took to vocally "exorcising" Mr. and Mrs. G. When their constantly moving footsteps on the wood floors would keep the girls awake, Carolyn would merely walk to the stairway and ask them to stop walking around because it was keeping them awake. The footsteps would stop immediately. Such practices became so frequent that Carolyn's daughters began to see it as funny that their mother was constantly telling Mr. and Mrs. G to quiet down.

But not all of the incidents involving Mr. and Mrs. G were innocuous, warm, or nurturing. Visitors to the house, unaware of the presence of spirits, were the ones most likely to see the more frightening aspects of Bill and Marles Hood. Carolyn's nephew, Jonah, had come to visit with his aunt and uncle once in 1988. After falling asleep on the couch, young Jonah was wakened by the sound of intense arguing coming from a man and a woman not six feet from his bed on the sofa. He had thought it was his Aunt Carolyn and Uncle Mike, but unbeknownst to Jonah, Carolyn was asleep upstairs and Michael was still at work.

Jonah pulled the blankets over his head, trying to ignore the argument, but when he finally got up the nerve to peek toward the two squabblers, he was horrified to see Mr. and Mrs. G in the midst of a screaming match. Suddenly, the two phantoms quieted and turned to the young boy huddled under a blanket.

"They stopped and looked at him and it scared the wits out of Jonah," says Carolyn. "He covered his face and told them to go away."

When he finally was able to take another look, he was relieved to see that the two were gone, yet Jonah never returned to his Aunt's house to sleep over. Later, it would be revealed that Jonah had witnessed the spirits arguing in the exact same spot where Bill had killed his wife, then himself.

While the Browns held dominion over much of the house, the third floor seemed to be the one exception. Lights would go on and off at all hours of the night. Doors and windows slammed shut and whipped open at random. Bursts of cold air would appear from nowhere and dissipate just as quickly. The heated sounds of arguing would echo throughout the entire floor and the family dog refused to go up there, always cowering away fearfully. It was quietly decided that, while the first two floors of the house belonged to the Browns, the third floor belonged to the ghosts of Bill and Marles.

Today, the Brown's still own their old Victorian home in Portland and they still share it with Bill and Marles Hood, aka Mr. and Mrs. G. After a while, as the children grew older, Marles Hood stopped coming to them so much at night, tucking them in and such. Carolyn and Michael have accepted the two spirits as part of their own family, living together in a way unthought-of in most haunted houses.

This case is perfect evidence that not all hauntings are textbook examples of negativity and despair. In the case of Bill and Marles Hood, just by the sheer number of similar cases, it would be almost a certainty that such violence and madness would spill over from one lifetime and into another. But it hasn't in this case. Rather, it seems to have been the opposite. In death, perhaps the Hoods are finally working on getting along, if not with each other, then with their new houseguests. This haunting, when put beside every other story that it is similar to, is a welcome anomaly that more people need to hear about when theorizing about the behavioral patterns of ghosts. It seems that ghosts, like their fleshy counterparts, are indeed capable of growing emotionally and spiritually. Bill, who brought so much negativity into the house while alive, seems to have grown and accepted his past behaviors—if not just a little tenuously—in the years since his death. Despite all the mistakes they made in life, in death Bill and Marles seem to have renewed their love and seem to see new hope in each other.

UNIT 731

PINGFANG DISTRICT OF HARBIN, CHINA

It is my conviction that killing under the cloak of war
is nothing more than an act of murder.

–Albert Einstein

In my first book, *Lost in the Darkness*, I profiled the horrors of Auschwitz and the sad hauntings of those souls left behind there in that desolate place. But the horrors of mankind's inhumanity to itself wasn't reserved for the bloodthirsty Nazis and their "beloved Reich" alone. While it is generally accepted that World War II brought out the courage and bravery in most men and women, it is also an accepted fact that the Great War brought out the worst in others, most notably the infamous Nazi regime of Adolph Hitler. Hitler's war on the Jews and undesirables of Eastern Europe still remains as an open wound on the neck of humanity. But Hitler wasn't the only psychotic butcher at large during World War II.

A slightly lesser known, but no less inhuman, atrocity was being committed in the Pingfang district of Harbin, China while the Japanese Imperial Army waged its war on the Chinese. Because the Japanese were largely forgiven their brutality, not much thought has ever gone into how they treated their prisoners of war. But ask any surviving WWII Allied soldier what they thought of the Japanese and their treatment of POWs and you'll most likely get one or more of the same answer. They treated their prisoners with extreme hostility and went out of their way to be barbarous, torturous, and cruel. Those who were beheaded got off easy. Death came for them quickly. Brutally, but quickly. But like Auschwitz in Poland and the countless other Nazi death camps scattered across Europe, other prisoners faced a fate worse than death when they were transported to Unit 731.

THE RAPE OF NANKING

The year 1937 saw the Japanese at their most brutal as the Imperial Army succeeded in sacking and taking over the Chinese capital of Nanking. Hundreds of thousands of men, women, and children were executed, beheaded, raped, mutilated, and buried alive. Contests were held to see which commanding officer could reach 100 kills with a samurai sword first.

John Rabe, a Nazi party member and the organizer and leader of the Safety Zone in Nanking, wrote about the Rape of Nanking in his diary: "17 December. Last night up to 1,000 women and girls are said to have been raped, about 100 girls at Ginling Girl's College alone. You hear nothing but rape. If husbands or brothers intervene, they're shot. What you hear and see on all sides is the brutality and bestiality of the Japanese soldiers."

Fathers were forced to rape their daughters and sons were forced to rape their mothers. Random executions and beheadings became commonplace. Blood and fire seeped through the streets and soaked into the ground, squelched only by the sounds of screams and the dying. It was as if the gates of Hell had opened and spat forth every atrocity imaginable onto the Nanking streets.

This massacre, which lasted an agonizing six weeks, became known as The Rape of Nanking, and those who didn't perish in the streets and forests of Nanking were sent to experimentation camps. The stories of brutal Japanese tactics became legend and when America was brought into the war in 1941, American soldiers feared being captured by the Japanese based solely on the stories rising from the ashes of Nanking.

Around this same time frame, the Army Epidemic Prevention Research Laboratory was founded. This was a year after the Japanese began its conflict with China and the Imperial Army had already gotten quite a foothold on China's lands. General Shiro Ishii, chief medical officer of the Japanese Army, was placed in command of the AEPRL, which he renamed Togo Unit. Ishii was allowed to work with relatively few restraints, having convinced the Imperial Army that the Americans and the British were already working on developing their own chemical weapons. The Nazis had already had much success with German-developed chlorine gas at the second battle of Ypres and that was enough to convince the hierarchy of Japanese military leaders that it was a necessary science to be studied. General Ishii's main goal—straight from the beginning—was to become world famous pioneering chemical and biological weapons, and to do that, he envisioned a pristine complex of laboratories and holding cells where doctors could work unencumbered by ethics or moral codes.

Ishii chose Manchuria simply because there would be a near limitless supply of enemy Chinese and Russian citizens, people who could be arrested at random by the Japanese secret police for virtually any reason. Jails and prisons would offer up their prisoners to Ishii and his butchers as well, supplying them with men, women, and even children.

JAP. TROOPS AT HARBIN

Japanese troops arriving in Harbin outside of Manchuria, China. Within hours, they would all be engaging in what many consider to be one of the most horrific massacres of World War II, the Rape of Nanking province.

"To characterize Ishii as a monster would be appropriate," says author Sheldon H. Harris, "because the man had no sense of humanity whatsoever. He loved his children, he was a good father, and he was a good husband, by the culture's standards of the time. But one can say that Adolph Hitler liked children too."

For two years, the Japanese camp opened and closed, located and relocated, numerous times before finally settling in Pingfang in a larger and more structurally sound facility. From August of 1940 on, the camp was officially referred to as the Epidemic Prevention and Water Purification Department of the Kwantung Army. Insiders called it "Unit 731" for short. In order to maintain an air of secrecy, the people of Harbin were told that Unit 731 was nothing more than a lumber mill, an ironic lie considering that the doctors and scientists often referred to their test subjects as "logs."

Ishii's "death factory" found very prominent backing from Emperor Hirohito himself, who saw the experimentation of disease and biological weaponry as essential to the Japanese war effort. He also made clear that Ishii answered only to him and no other, keeping the purpose of Unit 731 secret from much of the outside world. That was the initial purpose: the study and creation of deadly diseases to be used in times of war. But when it was finally shut down in August of 1945, stories of incredible atrocities and gruesome experiments began to filter out of the very private laboratory, stories that rivaled those told by the Jews of Hitler's concentration camps.

Unit 731 was divided into eight divisions, with each one focusing on different maladies, their treatments, and how such sicknesses could be transformed into usable weapons. Division 1 focused on research of the Bubonic Plague, Cholera, Anthrax, Typhoid and Tuberculosis using live human subjects. For this purpose, a prison was constructed to contain around three to four hundred people. Division 2 focused on research for biological weapons and how to spread them evenly upon populations. Division 3 saw the production of bullets and artillery shells that contained biological agents. Division 4 oversaw the production of other miscellaneous agents. Division 5 was used to oversee the training of workers and soldiers at the Unit. Divisions 6, 7, and 8 held equipment, medical and administrative units.

Most any kind of Prisoner of War was eligible for Unit 731, including Russian, Chinese, and, following the attack on Pearl Harbor in 1941, Philippine and Allied soldiers captured during the battles in the Pacific. All were known to have been sent to Unit 731, never to be seen or heard from again. Behind the stone walls of the camp, hundreds of thousands of men, women, and children were gruesomely executed in bizarre medical experiments that included live vivisection, injection of deadly diseases, and outright execution by beheading. Test subjects were kept alive generally for about four weeks before being executed and being sent to one of two massive crematories onsite. It is rumored that upwards of 2,000 bodies a day were incinerated in these two ovens that mirrored the ones being used in death camps across Europe by the Nazis.

Ishii knew no boundaries, and when a prototype of a weapon was developed successfully, he had no trouble using the Manchurian countryside and cities around him to test them out. The Japanese Air Force once spread the Bubonic Plague across China by air-dropping parcels of infected fleas onto the cities from above, eventually infecting over 100,000 Chinese citizens, and 1,600 of their own soldiers. They even spiked the local water supply with the deadly disease, all in the name of finding the perfect delivery system. Ishii and his scientists even handed out sweets and chocolates laced with anthrax to children of the neighboring villages.

Vivisections were performed on prisoners after infecting them with various diseases. Scientists performed invasive surgery, removing organs to study the effects of disease on the human body. These were conducted while the patients were alive because it was feared that the decomposition process would affect the results. The infected and vivisected prisoners included men, women, children, and infants.

Limbs were amputated so scientists could study the loss of blood and its effect on the human body. These same limbs would be reattached to the opposite side of the body; the left arm would be sewn onto the right-hand side. Still, other experiments dealt with frozen and amputated limbs. Stomachs were removed and the esophagus reattached to the intestines.

Japanese surgeon Ken Yuasa confessed to the *Japan Times* in 2007 about his role in the vivisections of Chinese dissidents and POWs: "I was afraid during my first vivisection, but the second time around, it was much easier. By the third time, I was willing to do it." He went on to testify that he believes at least 1,000 surgeons, veterinarians, scientists, and dentists were involved in vivisections and other forms of experimentation on live human subjects at Unit 731.

Human targets were used to test grenades exploded at various distances and different positions. Prisoners were engulfed in the fires of flame throwers and others were used as targets in tests noting the accuracy of chemical and explosive bombs. Prisoners were hung upside down to see how long it would take for them to choke to death. In some other cases, subjects were starved in efforts to determine how long one could go without eating or drinking before finally dying. They were spun in centrifuges until death found them. Lethal doses of X-Rays were administered to prisoners. The list of atrocities goes on and on, and it is a list that the Nazis' infamous "Angel of Death," Dr. Josef Mengele, would be especially proud of.

THE END OF UNIT 731

As the Russian Army invaded China and attempted to oust the Japanese from their Asian ally, Unit 731 was ordered closed and all documents destroyed. Most of the buildings that made up Unit 731 were blown up following the desertion of the Japanese, but because they were so solid and well-built, much of the buildings remained intact.

Ishii ordered each and every one of his subordinates to take the secrets of Unit 731 to their graves. To compound that statement, he issued them all vials of potassium cyanide, poison to be ingested should they be captured by Russian hands. Most of the doctors and staff fled back to Japan, where they enjoyed security and protection for a time.

When the Japanese surrendered to Allied troops in 1945, all bets were off. The Russians held many of the surgeons accountable at war crime tribunals for the indiscriminate executions of many Russian prisoners, sentencing them to up to twenty-five years in a Siberian prison camp.

But the Americans were far more accommodating. General Douglas MacArthur, the Supreme Commander of the Allied Army, promised immunity to the Japanese in exchange for the exclusive rights to their research on biological weapons. It was thought of as a way to keep potentially dangerous research out of the hands of America's enemies, particularly the Russians, but others saw it as an underhanded desecration of the lives lost at Unit 731, a devaluation of the brutal murders committed by a brutal Empire. It was a pretty hollow deal: the Russians eventually built their own biological research lab based on physical materials confiscated from Unit 731.

Still, despite all of the evidence and eyewitnesses, many Japanese refuse to acknowledge that Unit 731 and even the Nanking Massacre ever happened.

THE HAUNTINGS BEGIN

Eventually, the Chinese government sanctioned Unit 731 and the surrounding area as a learning center for future generations of Chinese in much the same way the Jews reclaimed Auschwitz from the Nazis. Recently visitors from the West have been allowed access to the killing fields at Harbin where mass executions and live burials took place.

Earlier in this book, I told you about the thick sadness and mournful ghosts of Aokigahara Forest in Japan, and like Aokigahara, personal experiences of hauntings and paranormal events at Unit 731 are few and far between. Stories mainly from tourists and Chinese citizens have seeped out of the death camp at a slow trickle, but have luckily been accepted into the legend of Unit 731 nonetheless. Like Aokigahara, I chalk up the tight-lipped stories to the superstitions of the Asian peoples. To speak of the dead would be to invite them into your homes and lives.

But with all of the murders and deaths dealt out at Unit 731, it should come as no surprise that paranormal activity around the camp is both plentiful and outgoing. The ghosts that walk at Unit 731 rise and walk the earth, unashamedly searching for justice. White, mist-like apparitions have mingled with full-bodied, solid-looking spirits. Shadow People dart about the peripheral vision of those touring the old buildings and ghostly whispers break the reverent silence from time to time.

Reports of paranormal activity have flourished here almost as soon as 731 was closed. It is said that ghost lights and apparitions are seen on a fairly frequent basis. A ghostly figure has been spotted walking through the hallways surrounding the frostbite units. Phantom voices speaking in Chinese and Russian have been heard and eerie light anomalies frequently appear in photographs that have been taken in Unit 731. Electronic equipment, flashlights, and cell phones fail and die, their batteries drained of life.

Ghosts are everywhere here, walking and wandering through the buildings and surrounding fields, blindly searching for justice that will never come, and if justice chooses to remain blind, the spirits of Unit 731 may just have to get a bit more forceful.

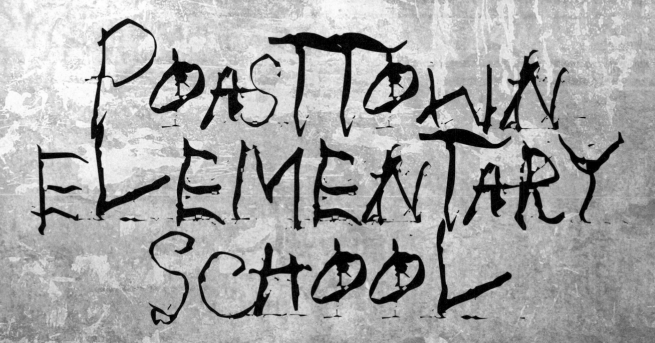

POASTTOWN ELEMENTARY SCHOOL

MIDDLETON, OH

We can easily forgive a child who is afraid of the dark;
the real tragedy of life is when men are afraid of the light.

–Plato

As we end our journey on this road of shadowy tales and tragic times, of melancholy ghosts and haunted lives, we find ourselves in a place that one would never picture as being scary or haunted. True, to a young child, an elementary school can be a frightening place, full of new entanglements and changes, stern teachers, and vicious playground bullies. But in the end, most all of us hold onto a certain affection for our elementary school years.

But don't we also hold onto a memory of someone we lost during those years, a tragedy that stained an otherwise uneventful childhood? For me, that tragedy involved two young boys killed in a single-engine plane crash piloted by their father. One day, Chad Montfort and his little brother were playing on the playground equipment at recess, and the next, their seats were empty and remained so for the rest of the year. For the hundreds of people who flock to the haunted Poasttown Elementary School in Middleton, Ohio, it is an opportunity to connect with spirits of those lost long ago as well, though not all died at the school. In fact, there are no records of anyone ever dying at the school at all. So why is it so haunted?

Let's take a look at that, shall we?

First off, archaeologists have excavated portions of the older parts of Madison Township, uncovering evidence of ancient campfires and human bones that predate the American Indian tribes known to have lived in the area, indicating people once used the hilltop overlooking Poasttown for religious ceremonies and eventual burial of the dead. These ancient rituals seem to have included the act of human sacrifice, followed by the dead being summarily burnt and then buried.

Poasttown Elementary School sits within Madison Township in what is now known as Middleton, Ohio. Before that, it was an unincorporated little town by the name of Poasttown, named after the first man who settled that area in the 1790s. Peter Poast had traveled to the area from the Northwest Territory in search of viable farmland, which he found in abundance. But the land, while rich for farming, was overgrown with forest and foliage. Clearing it would be an incredible, backbreaking job, but in the end it was worth it: a small town had begun to develop from the clearing of the Poast Farm to the north of town and the Banker Farm to the south. A tavern sprang up along the new road separating the two farms, as well as a general store, all owned and run by cousins of

Peter P. Poast. Over the next 100 years or so, and well after the original Peter P. Poast had died, a hundred or so homes had been built within the town, as had a steel mill and a railroad station.

It was during this industrial renaissance in the early 1900s that Poasttown acquired its first ghostly folktale: the chilling story of a young maid who worked for industrialist Paul Sorg and his family. The area of Mount Pleasant, Middletown, and Poasttown were about to become very rife with spirits of all ages and intentions, each with their own tale to tell.

While the hauntings at Sorg Mansion have little to do with the hauntings at Poasttown Elementary, I point them out merely to paint a much larger picture. There is an abundance of ghosts in the Poasttown/Middleton area and for Poasttown, it was about to get a lot worse.

One of Poasttown's biggest resources was its train station and service. For years, the train brought supplies, work, residents, and opportunities to the small town. Still, the train service was not immune to tragedy. Poasttown would see no less than four major train wrecks in its history before the service was discontinued. The first accident occurred on July 25th, 1891, when a passenger train collided with a freight train, resulting in fifty injuries and four deaths. Two more wrecks followed on July 4th, 1895, and January 2nd, 1905. But the wreck that brought the most controversy and notoriety happened on July 4th, 1910, when a passenger train—again—slammed into a freight train, mirroring the accident that took place nineteen years earlier. In this instance, the blame was placed directly on the head of the dispatcher, who had forgotten to relay the news that a freight train was sitting on the same tracks being used by a passenger train. The dispatcher's failure to alert either train that they were on a collision course with each other resulted in a devastating accident. Most all of Poasttown's residents flocked to the scene, both to gawk and offer help, and were met by the most horrific visage of Hell they'd ever seen. Black smoke, twisted metal, and cries of survivors littered the tracks and surrounding fields. The bodies of the dead ranged from twisted and mangled to unrecognizably charred by fire. It would be days before all of the dead bodies would be accounted for, as most were scattered in the tall grasses surrounding the wreck, having been thrown from the train with such force. Because there were no local hospitals in

Poasttown, all of the injured and dying passengers were taken to a makeshift triage and morgue station set up on some old farmland less than a mile away. It was there that doctors would determine who was sent off in the trucks and ambulances first to hospitals in the next town over. In the end, the train wreck of July 4th, 1910, claimed the lives of thirty-six people, twenty-one of whom were killed instantly.

And that triage station, the open field where so many people suffered and died in states of delirious shock following the most terrifying experience of their lives? That was where the village of Poasttown decided to build what would become known as the Poasttown Heights Baby Farm in the 1930s. This "baby farm" is a matter of factual record in the Poasttown archives, and its purpose was to act, at first, as a home for unwed mothers. Women carrying children out of wedlock would come to these homes, have their babies, and return to their lives elsewhere, all the while leaving behind their baby to be raised by wet nurses, caretakers, and other employees of the property. As the children grew, they were used to farm fields, milk cows, and perform all manner of work that most people would get paid for in those days. Often, the children would be adopted out by families or sold to farmers to help out with the backbreaking work a farm life entailed. But when the child was born sickly, underdeveloped, or deformed, it was quickly put to death and usually buried in an unmarked grave or cremated. While it was illegal to do so, and those who were caught were hanged, it was a practice that was quietly common amongst baby farms of Victorian-era Britain, Australia, and the United States, especially when the devastating Great Depression took hold of the world in 1929.

About a quarter of a mile from the train tracks, with only a small patch of woods separating them, where the deadly train crash took place and near where the old Poasttown Baby Farm had lain its foundations...well, that was where the residents of Poasttown, in 1936, decided to build their new elementary school. For sixty-three years, life was perfectly normal at Poasttown Elementary School. It was a fond memory for thousands of children who attended classes there, and no one can recall any instances of tragedy occurring on the grounds themselves. But two cases of tragic ends may have their connections to Poasttown Elementary School nonetheless.

It was said that at one point, a young girl had tripped on the stairway, tumbling down a long flight of steps and severely injuring herself. This little girl apparently died of her wounds while recovering at home. In addition, tales of Poasttown's sentient janitor meeting his end began to circulate around the community in the late 1990s. This janitor, who was known as a fiercely loyal employee of the school, met a grisly end when his mobile home caught fire with him trapped inside. The mobile home had been parked close to the school so that the janitor could easily walk to and from work, and many investigators, residents, and tourists believe that it is the janitor's fierce work ethic that keeps him returning to Poasttown Elementary, intent on protecting the place that brought him so much pride.

Then, because renovations would have been astronomical, the city council decided that they would close down Poasttown Elementary School in 1999. All of the students were bussed to schools in Middletown and a new high school was commissioned instead. The building would eventually house many different groups, including a community afterschool children's center, but Poasttown could not sustain it for long. Interest in the old rundown school waned until Poasttown Elementary graduate Darrell Whisman and his wife Brenda happened upon it. They bought it up for a very good price in 2004 and moved in, intending on living on the property as they renovated it slowly.

But once they were inside the school, and the lights went down, and the hallways were quiet, the Whisman's realized that in the darkness of the school, they weren't alone.

"We started hearing things, seeing shadows and things here. Noises and things happening that we couldn't explain," says Whisman. "So we had a group come in and check the place out. They said there was a lot of paranormal activity in the building and it just keeps getting bigger and better as far as the paranormal world goes."

Whisman began allowing groups into the old school, allowing them to document the thoroughly bizarre activity. As more groups investigated and probed the old school, more instances of activity began to occur. People have felt breaths on the back of their necks. Some investigators would suddenly find themselves holding hands with invisible children, and in one instance, found that a door in

A train wreck, like the one captured above on July 4, 1910, claimed the lives of at least thirty-six men, women, and children in the Poasttown/Middletown area, with the future site of Poasttown Elementary serving as a triage station for the dead and dying.

the basement was being guarded by an overly protective child. It is said that this door will not budge and will not open until you ask nicely to be let in. Once you do that, the door seems to swing open with ease, allowing you entry. Some investigators have captured the sounds of a young girl speaking from behind the door as well.

In the boiler room portion of the basement, it is said that a very territorial and very vocal spirit resides, possibly the spirit of the janitor himself. 765 Paranormal co-founder Justin Arnett was called a "bitch" three times in the same series of EVPs captured during an early 2013 investigation.

Poasttown's reputation as one of the more strangely and actively haunted buildings in America came under fire around 2012, when professional debunker Aron Houdini (a great-great-grandson to Harry Houdini, who spent much of his life debunking spiritualists and the paranormal community) accused owner Darrell Whisman and Jay Lynch of Hindsight Paranormal of staging many of the instances in which paranormal activity was caught by other investigators.

Houdini's claims were outrageous, to be sure, but they were without merit and without proof. While he claimed the two were staging the hauntings, he offered no proof of their actions or intents outside of his own solemn word. Most saw through Houdini, seeing an embittered man lashing out at a world that had—in his mind—forsaken him. In the end, Houdini managed to polarize the entire paranormal community before back-pedaling slightly, saying that it was just his opinion that Poasttown was not haunted.

But according to most every paranormal team that has investigated Poasttown Elementary School before the hoax accusations and after, the hauntings not only continue, but increase steadily in intensity as the years go by. As the slogan for Poasttown Elementary goes, "When You Leave, You Believe."

THE POASTTOWN INVESTIGATION

In September of 2013, I had the pleasure of accompanying 765 Paranormal to Poasttown Elementary to perform a very laid-back, very casual investigation of the old place. My immediate impression of Poasttown Elementary School was that yes, it was haunted. Poasttown felt like a huge receptacle for the residual energies of children and teachers. Paranormal investigators who have been touched by the other side know it when they feel it touch them again. Poasttown was no different than the spirit I felt in my room when I was 15, nor was it any different when I encountered Ruthie's screams at the Trans-Allegheny Lunatic Asylum when I was 40. And yes, I believe Poasttown had something otherworldly about it, a different kind of energy.

The first area to garner my attention was the staircase leading up to the second floor. I first saw this staircase as I came in the front door with the rest of 765 Paranormal. Almost immediately, I knew I wanted to climb those stairs. Even before the investigation began, while co-founder Denny Jones and tech manager Zack Schuette were setting up cameras around the building, the rest of the group headed over to a nearby Dollar General store to stock up on energy drinks and snacks. As I walked them out the front doors and watched them leave, I was immediately compelled to turn and look to the staircase to my left. It led up into a very dark second floor and all I could see was the glowing red EXIT sign hanging from the ceiling. But what I *felt* made me want to climb the steps. I was so drawn to this area that I began taking pictures with my phone. All of them came out blurry or washed out. No matter how steady I held the camera, every shot came out looking as if I either had one hell of a tremor, or the flash of the camera was reflecting off of something that wasn't there. I would find out later, while hearing the backstory of all the hauntings at Poasttown, that this area was popularly known to house a vortex, a doorway that allows spirits of any kind to come and go as they please. This vortex is believed to have been on the land where Poasttown sits for thousands of years. Investigators Ryan Herbert and Justin Arnett were investigating the room known as the "mean teacher's room." In life, this room belonged to a very stern teacher who apparently liked to throw chalkboard erasers at her students. It was in this room that Ryan and Justin were able to capture the sound of a woman's voice saying, "Open the door please." This voice was heard with the naked ear and captured on their digital voice recorders.

Though not much happened to anyone else that night (aside from some bumps, bangs, and footsteps in the old gymnasium) in the end, if you spend six hours in the dark and capture one piece of evidence you cannot debunk, that's a successful investigation.

LIONS IN THE HALLS:

OTHER POINTS OF MACABRE INTEREST

PIERCE CEMETERY

WEST LAFAYETTE, IN

Located near the outer rim of Northeast Tippecanoe County in West Lafayette lies a graveyard, abandoned by all except the spirits that still haunt it and the paranormal teams who visit to capture evidence of the unexplained.

Pierce Cemetery sits near the epicenter of Tippecanoe County's oldest link to the peoples who once lived there, namely the Miami and Wea Indians. The heavily forested areas surrounding the plush, fertile farmlands were ideal for both hunters and farmers of the tribes, and provided plenty of sustenance throughout the entire year, whether it be bitter cold or blazing hot. The farmlands always yielded amazing amounts of corn, and the forest always yielded the heartiest deer and fowl.

The area eventually became a hotly contested prize in the 1811 battle between General William Henry Harrison's army and the Native American alliance under the command of Shawnee warrior Tecumseh and his half-blind brother, Tenskwatawa, also known as "the prophet." Called the Battle of Tippecanoe, it was a humiliating defeat for the Natives, who fled the area immediately. Harrison, in turn, burned and destroyed the villages, crops, and supplies that were left behind.

Most of the research tends to point to the Pierce family as having first owned the land, selling off plots to other families in the region. The earliest known burial at Pierce Cemetery took place in 1803— a woman by the name of Lizzie Ida Bryan. From 1803 to 1943, area farmers and their families used Pierce Cemetery to bury their dead: 296 bodies in all. Most were adults, but many of the dead laid to rest were children and infants taken by illnesses, such as cholera, typhus, and influenza. Less than a mile from Pierce Cemetery lay what used to be known as the County Home, a "poor farm" for vagrants, orphans, and unwed mothers. It is a great possibility that those who died at the County Home also found their place at Pierce Cemetery.

Over the years, the cemetery began to wither from neglect. Headstones broke and shifted, never to be replaced or repaired. The woods surrounding the place began to flourish into schools, golf courses, and housing developments, yet Pierce remained untouched and unsullied, like a secret hidden in the woods.

The first grumblings of something not-quite-right at Pierce Cemetery came in the late 1960s when the burgeoning Tippecanoe School Corporation bought up land from area farmers to build what would become William Henry Harrison High School, named for the 9th President of the United States. He was also a legendary figure in the 1811 Battle Of Tippecanoe, a horrendous and humiliating defeat for the local Indians, who retreated to their homes in Prophetstown before fleeing the area completely. Once the school was completed and opened in 1967, it is theorized that area teens discovered Pierce Cemetery once again and it became a notorious haunt for teen boys wanting to freak out their girlfriends. But Pierce Cemetery's oldest residents weren't having any of that. Almost immediately, tales of the hauntings within Pierce Cemetery began to circulate, first through the school, and then throughout the entire community.

But what began as playful paranormal occurrences turned darker around 2008 and 2009. The manifestations became more aggressive and disturbing. The air turned colder and denser, the unsettling sensation of being watched intensified. People reported the movement of tombstones; monuments that were laying on their side when you walked in are seen as upright when you leave. Rocks and acorns were thrown at visitors by unseen hands, and the chilling sound of giggling children tended to waft through the graveyard. Most ominous, however, is the appearance of two very bright red eyes, looking neither human nor animalistic. They stare out from the forest surrounding the cemetery, visible to the naked eye and sending a chill through whoever catches sight of them.

One of the more terrifying experiences at Pierce Cemetery happened during an investigation held by the Wabash Paranormal Research Society, a local paranormal investigation unit. Former WPRS member and current 765 Paranormal co-founder Justin Arnett walked into Pierce a skeptic, but walked out a believer. Placing a digital voice recorder in the crook of a tree, Justin asked whoever was present with him to knock the recorder off.

The spirit, whoever it was, complied. The recorder flew out of the crook as if it had been tossed, landing on the ground at Justin's feet. Astounded by this feat and curious as to what else was possible,

Pierce Cemetery, in West Lafayette, Indiana. (Photo by the author.)

Justin left Pierce Cemetery with a new mission in life: to seek out the other side. But the spirit of Pierce wasn't content with making Justin a believer. When he returned home that night, his house became a haven for disembodied footsteps, slamming doors, and other unexplained noises. Whatever Justin had interacted with at Pierce Cemetery had followed him home and it was several days before it decided to return from whence it came.

THE CHAMBERS MANSION

SAN FRANCISCO, CA

Richard Chambers built his house in 1887 after making a fortune in the silver mining industry. Some say Chambers went on to become a state senator for Utah some ten years after building the home, but there is no evidence that he went into politics at all. Being a silver baron, he probably had political ties, but no official title in politics.

Chambers lived at the mansion with his two nieces—sisters who apparently hated each other with a passion—and when Chambers died, he left the house to them. One sister, Clarice, built a house next door, while the other, Claudia, remained in the Chambers Mansion. In 1901, Claudia suffered a grim and mysterious end to her life. She had been found in the house, cut almost in half. Relatives of the two girls maintain that she suffered an accident with some sort of farming equipment, while others suspected that she was murdered by an insane family member who'd escaped confinement from an attic room. Still others believe she was murdered by her sister.

Now known as the Mansions Hotel, the house is still believed to be haunted by Claudia's murdered ghost. Visitors and clients have reported hearing strange, otherworldly sounds, flashing balls of light, and phantom footsteps throughout the hallways.

JANE ADDAMS'S HULL HOUSE

CHICAGO, IL

Here's one that would have gotten its own chapter had the house's most haunting tale been proven true. Built in 1856 by real estate investor Charles J. Hull, in what was then the most fashionable end of town, the Hull House sits at the corner of Polk and Halstead Streets near downtown Chicago. It was spared during the devastating Great Chicago Fire of 1871, but when rebuilding of the city began, the elite surrounding Hull's mansion packed up and moved into plusher lodgings, paving the way for industrial and warehousing ventures to take root. The once-posh section of town was now a hub for drug abuse, prostitution, and pretty much every kind of vice imaginable. Criminals banished from the east side found refuge here, on the west side of Chicago. Amid all of this crime was a constant influx of destitute Irish, Polish, and Italian immigrants and refugees, blue collar workers struggling to make ends meet for their families. By 1898, the problems of crime in the west end was out of control and a philanthropist and good Samaritan by the name of Jane Addams happened upon a plan to help the people. Jane set out to establish a settlement house in the neighborhood, one that would help the poor of Chicago's west end with social, medical, and housing issues. She appealed to Charles Hull's lawyers and descendants, who readily agreed to lease the house to her, rent free, so that she could bring some sort of hope and care to the people of the west end.

Hull House quickly became known as a place where help could be sought, and help would be given freely. Catering mostly to women and homeless people, Jane Addams orchestrated what was essentially both a women's shelter and a homeless shelter. Her cause gained incredible momentum, and Hull House became a staple topic of conversation in philanthropic circles, successfully staying open and running on the monetary donations of the wealthy.

What Mrs. Addams hadn't counted on when she took possession of the building were the hauntings of its resident spirits. On her first night sleeping in Hull House, she was awakened by phantom footsteps circling her bed and echoing through the empty halls. While unnerving, it didn't spook her in the slightest. She slept in that room, which was Mrs. Hull's original bedroom, for a few nights, each time being wakened by ominous footsteps in the dark. She later switched rooms and no longer heard the footsteps. Tenants in some of the rooms reported seeing a woman in their quarters, watching them sleep before vanishing before their eyes. The same spectral footsteps were now being heard by nearly everyone on the second floor, in and around Mrs. Hull's bedroom.

The tales of Hull House being haunted started almost immediately after the death of Charles Hull's wife from natural causes, and they haven't stopped since. In fact, the stories got more bizarre. Case in point: the 1915 "Devil Baby" story. The legend goes that supposedly a "devil baby" was born to a devoutly Catholic woman and her atheist husband. According to more popular versions of the story, the husband had told his wife that he would rather have the Devil in his house than a picture of the virgin Mary. *Blammo!* Nine months later, the husband and wife are blessed with a devil baby, complete with hooves and horns. The child was taken immediately to Jane Addams's settlement house, where a baptism by a visiting priest was attempted. But the devil baby rebelled, escaped the priest's clutches, and mocked him by dancing and laughing at him. Appalled, Jane Addams allegedly had the baby locked in the attic, where it later died.

How this story got started is anyone's guess, but the arrival of a legitimately deformed child at Hull House may have gotten the ball rolling. Jane Addams herself turned people away from her doors, trying vainly to convince them that it was all just a story, a tall tale. No one wanted to believe her and finally, she just stopped trying, even after spending forty pages in her memoirs trying to dispel the awful rumor. It is said that this devil baby story even inspired Chicago writer Ira Levin to write his most terrifying novel, *Rosemary's Baby*.

THE RIDDLE HOUSE
WEST PALM BEACH, FL

When you think of Palm Beach, Florida, the notion of a terrifying haunted experience isn't exactly the first thing that comes to mind. But travel west a bit and that is most certainly what you will find, especially if you are male.

Florida's Riddle House was built in 1905 as a model of classic Victorian-style architecture. But it wasn't a house for a family. It was built out of necessity. Back around the turn of the century, looting graves was big business. Wealthy matriarchs, businessmen, politicians, and anybody else who had more than a little bit of cash were buried with the family jewels, silver, and gold. Grave robbers and other ghoulish opportunists exhumed graves on the property and broke into the funeral home, intent on relieving the corpses of their expensive rings, watches, and jewels. The city built a house next door to the funeral parlor as a place for guards to keep a closer eye on the parlor's security. This is the home that would eventually become known as the Riddle House.

It didn't take long for the house to collect its first spirit. Locals rumored his name to be "Buck" and he was an employee at the guard house. Buck was killed in the heat of the moment while in the midst of an argument with another man in the city. Following Buck's death, locals would see him wandering around the graveyard and throughout the halls and rooms of the house. He never seemed to be a hostile or mean presence, yet his sudden appearance still came across as overwhelming to those fortunate enough to see him.

Twenty years passed before the house's namesake came into the picture. Karl Riddle was named City Manager and was subsequently offered the house to live in, so that he could tend to and oversee maintenance of the graveyard. Riddle loved being in the house, but the sudden suicide of a colleague and employee in the house's attic seemed to taint the pleasure of living there. The suicide seemed to trigger an awful lot of negative energy and attention. Visitors to the house would see black shadows from the corners of their eyes, and hear strange murmurs coming from the attic and phantom footfalls in the empty corridors. The spectral image of a man in a black suit with a noose around his neck had been seen by a few employees, perhaps even Karl himself. As a result, Riddle lost many employees because of that house, all of them rightfully terrified of the activity they were surrounded by. Karl himself also seemed to suffer from a debilitating depression, possibly brought on by the dark power inside his home.

Over the years, the Riddle House tried to serve as a front for a number of businesses, including a girl's dorm for the local college, but nothing panned out. By 1980, the city of West Palm Beach had tired of trying to find a use for the old place and decided to level it. It was Karl Riddle's nephew, John, who stepped up and took over the ownership and care of his uncle's old home. He split the house up into three pieces and had it moved to Yesteryear Village, a rustic period themed park nearby. It was at this point that the Riddle House started to become known for its rather prolific hauntings and paranormal activity, mostly directed at men. Steve Carr, a local carpenter, was the first to feel the wrath of the entity at the Riddle House. While working in the attic, the lid from an iron pot lifted up and flew across the room, slamming Steve in the back of the head. Not surprisingly, Steve left and vowed never to return. Following this attack, men were no longer allowed access to the attic. The entity of the man in the black suit who'd hung himself had made himself known and it was obvious that he didn't care for visitors. His dour face has been seen in the darkened attic windows, looking out into the world with his cold, empty stare, and anyone foolhardy enough to enter his domain will soon understand why Steve Carr, and the rest of the Riddle House staff, refuse to enter the attic room alone.

THE SORG MANSION
MOUNT PLEASANT, OHIO

Near the town of Mount Pleasant, Ohio, just north of Poasttown and its infamous Elementary school, there was an enormous, beautifully built mansion, commissioned by millionaire tobacco baron Paul Sorg for his son's new wife, Grayce, in 1887. Intricately detailed woodwork, tall ceilings, sprawling and winding staircases, and rich oak were used to create the ultimate in luxury for his son and his new wife. Because of the harsh winters in midwest Ohio, the Sorg mansion was used primarily during the spring and summer months only, attended and maintained during the winter months by a skeleton crew of servants and caretakers. One of those maids, a young girl by the name of Sara, had tripped on the servants' stairwell, a steep set of stairs near the back of the house. By the time she was discovered, Sara had passed away from her injuries. But Sara was so enamored with the house in which she worked that she remained behind in spirit. She seems to be skittish and shy during the warmer months, but once fall and winter arrive, and the owners of the Sorg Mansion stay at their homes in the city, Sara takes possession of the house once more and looks out for it with a watchful eye.

Some say that during the day, she has been heard in the cavernous basements tossing pebbles into the cavernous cisterns that supplied the house with water. The splashing of these rocks and pebbles have been heard by those walking around upstairs, but when they go on to investigate the cisterns, they find nothing amiss. At night, Sara seems to wander the house aimlessly, admiring the gold and brass fixtures. It is said by many residents of Poasttown and Mount Pleasant that it is only during these twilight hours that Sara's spectral image can be seen, peering through the curtains and blinds of the house. Some who pass by the Sorg Mansion have reported seeing her ghost in the upstairs window, her face illuminated by a candle. Other stories emanating from the Sorg Mansion include those of a deceased actress. This actress, whose name escapes history but whose tale lives on as a gorgeous folktale, was said to have mysteriously disappeared one night while staying at the Sorg Mansion, never to be seen again. She left behind a single red dress,

The Sorg House of Middletown, Ohio. (Photo by the author.)

and it is claimed that this woman is occasionally seen putting on makeup and singing in the back rooms that used to stand in for the ladies' dressing rooms. Those who have seen her testify that she is wearing the red dress she'd left behind. Even more interesting is the fact that she is easily startled by the living and will disappear quickly once she realizes she's been seen.

Today, the Sorg Mansion has fallen on some harder times: the thirty-five room house has been partitioned off into apartments, and maintenance of the old place isn't what it used to be. Still, stories of ghostly footsteps in the tunnels near the underground cisterns and the haunting caroling of a missing actress continue to flow forth from Sorg Mansion and its likely they always will.

HICKORY HILL
GALLATIN COUNTY, IL

Hickory Hill, also known as the Old Slave House, is one of those homes where whispers course through the darkness, where shadows fall and rise again, where the ghosts of the past remind those in the present of the horrors endured there in the name of greed and industry.

Built by John Hart Crenshaw from the fortune left to him by the passing of his father, Hickory Hill became the hub for Crenshaw's burgeoning salt mine interests. At a time when salt was more important than oil, Crenshaw's business began to boom. He eventually became so wealthy that he was responsible for paying nearly 40% of all the taxes collected in Illinois.

Sadly, Crenshaw's business acumen would become something of a footnote to his life story as charges of kidnapping and the illegal trafficking of slaves in an otherwise free state began to quickly surface. John Hart Crenshaw oversaw the abduction of free blacks and pushed them into service in his mines and on his property, chaining them to their workstations. He even bought and sold freed and runaway slaves, all abducted by men he paid to watch the Ohio River at night. Essentially, Crenshaw became so wealthy because he got to keep every single cent of profit, benefiting from illegal slave trades instead of employing and paying honest working men.

But while all of this was going on, no one had a clue what Crenshaw was up to. Visitors to his home at Hickory Hill would have been horrified to learn that his vast number of slaves were being hidden away in the barred prison of the attic two stories above them. "Crenshaw had something unusual in mind when he contracted the house to be built," wrote author Troy Taylor. "There are about a dozen cell-like rooms (in the attic) with barred windows and flat, wooden bunks facing the corridor. Originally, the cells were even smaller, and there were more of them, but some were removed in the past. One can only imagine how small and cramped they must have been because even an average-sized visitor to the attic can scarcely turn around in the ones that remain." In the basement, it was said that there was once a tunnel that led out to

the Saline River, making the loading and unloading of the kidnapped blacks easier and less noticeable.

In 1842, however, Crenshaw's luck took a downturn as he was arrested for kidnapping a free black woman and her three children. News about town began to spread about Crenshaw and his "labor force" and public opinion began to turn against him. His businesses began to fail. According to legend, Crenshaw's fate was sealed when a slave attacked him with an axe, severing the man's leg, for beating a fellow slave woman nearly to death in the fields where he was working. John Hart Crenshaw's life as a cruel overseer to an illegal slave plantation was over. He would never quite recover from the attack, neither physically nor financially. When his "slaves" were set loose, he was forced to sell Hickory Hill. He moved into a farmhouse, began businesses in lumber and railroads, and finally died on December 4, 1871.

And now, many lifetimes after Crenshaw's death, his victims—those unfortunate men, women, and children who were kidnapped off the streets, plucked from the clutches of hard-fought freedom, or bought illegally from unscrupulous slave traders—still walk the empty corridors of the house on Hickory Hill, better known to the public now by its ominous moniker: "The Old Slave House." Voices filtering down the stairs from the attic, moans and groans of pain and exhaustion, and the familiar "slap-slap" of bare feet on wooden floors have all been reported by those who have been fearless enough to step inside. During the 1920s, the Sisk family, who bought the house from Crenshaw, began to publicize the house, charging admission to tourists. A healthy number of people reported feeling uncomfortable, anxious even, while wandering through the old slave quarters. Fear, sadness, and ripples of intense paranoia spilled through them all as invisible hands grabbed at them.

There has been kind of a long-running challenge to the foolhardy ghost hunters out there. In all the years it was open for tours and investigations, no one was ever, *ever*, able to spend the entire night alone in the Hickory Hill house's attic. Some left early into their challenge, others fled long before daybreak. Overnight investigations were ended, however, when a small fire broke out because of an oil lamp that had spilled over. But the challenge Hickory Hill had made to those who dared to tread upon its attic floorboards remained open, and it was a TV reporter who eventually accepted.

According to author Troy Taylor, the Sisk family relented only once on their "overnights embargo." In 1978, Harrisburg TV reporter David Rodgers spent the entire night in the attic as a publicity stunt, becoming the first and only person to spend the entire night in the attic. "Rodgers later admitted that he was 'queasy' going into the house and also said that his experience in the attic was anything but mundane," wrote Taylor on his website, prairie-hauntings.com. "He heard many sounds that he could not identify and later, he would discover that his recorder picked up voices that he himself could not hear."

THE BENTON COUNTY JAIL

FOWLER, IN

The small farming town of Fowler, Indiana, is a classically small, sleepy town. But even this reputation for simple living isn't an antidote for the foul and heinous. The Benton County Jail sits directly in the center of town—and does it have some stories. The one that gets the most recognition, and the most haunts, is the story of a man who was lynched by a posse of vigilantes back in 1876.

It began in the town of Oxford, roughly four miles from Fowler, with an attack on young Ada Heckerson. Ada had been left home alone while her parents visited the nearby hamlet of Templeton and, while they chatted with friends and ran errands for their home, the unthinkable happened. The Heckersons returned home to find their young daughter dead, lying motionless in a darkening pool of blood. The motives were unclear; nothing was touched but the girl, and nothing was missing. A man by the name of Jacob Nelly, who worked on the Heckerson's farm, was accused and, via the harsh and intense questioning of a Pinkerton agent, Jacob Nelly eventually confessed to brutally stabbing Ada Heckerson to death.

He was arrested, and sent to jail until trial. End of story? Not quite. Later that night, a few hours after he'd been brought in, a

The former Benton County Jail in Fowler, Indiana. (Photo by the author.)

lynch mob showed up at the Benton County Jail, hauled the man out of his cell and dragged him back to Oxford. The lynch mob then proceeded to hang the man outside of the Heckerson's home, his body hanging from a tree until it was cut down early the next morning. But not before it was seen by nearly everyone in Benton County, who all flocked to Oxford to view the body swaying in the breeze. Local grade schools even let their classes out early, to walk the mile and a half into Oxford to see Jacob Nelly's corpse. But even though his hanging satisfied many of those thirsting for Jacob Nelly's blood, it did little to satisfy the nagging question of *why* he had murdered the 14-year-old Ada Heckerson. Jacob Nelly went to his grave with the answer to that one, though speculation ran rampant that Ada's murder was the result of a courtship gone horribly wrong.

Today, it is said that some workers and visitors to the old Benton County Jail dungeons in Fowler have heard the struggling commotion in the cells. They have heard sobbing pleas for mercy. Paranormal filmmaker and investigator Dan T. Hall and his film crew were fortunate enough to capture the sounds on digital audio, coming across as a residual remnant from a dark chapter in Benton County's past. One voice was captured begging, the words, "No, oh my God!" coming out in terrified sputters. A second, distinctively different and more southern sounding voice responded to the first man with a resounding, "Shut up," spoken in a way that was so seething and hate filled that you could almost feel the words smacking your cheeks in the dark.

EPILOGUE

Alas, to the end we've come and the candlelight is fading
But the journey is far from over and new horrors are awaiting.
Until next time, dear readers, take comfort in the bright day
When we'll meet again, if I haven't already scared you away.
For in due time, we shall travel where angels fear to tread,
Where there is much more to fear than the living or the dead.
—BSJ 2014

BIBLIOGRAPHY

BOOKS/MAGAZINE RESOURCES

Belanger, Jeff. *The World's Most Haunted Places*, Revised Edition. New Page Books. September 2011.

Hensley, Doug. *Hells Gate: Terror at Bobby Mackey's*. Outskirts Press. 2005.

Price, Charles Edwin. *The Infamous Bell Witch of Tennessee*. Overmountain Press. 1994.

Sankowsky, Lorri, and Young, Keri. *Ghost Hunter's Guide to Indianapolis*. Pelican Publishing. 2008.

Taylor, Troy. *Murder by Gaslight: A True Story*. Whitechapel Productions. July 2013.

Taylor, Troy. *Murdered in Their Beds: The History and Hauntings of the Villisca Ax Murder House*. Whitechapel Productions. February 2012.

Weinstein, Fannie and Wilson, Melinda. *Where The Bodies Are Buried*. St. Martin's Press. 1998.

Williams, Ben and Jean, and Shoemaker, John Bruce. *The Black Hope Horror: The True Story of a Haunting*. William Morrow & Co. Books. 1991.

FILM/TELEVISION/ RADIO RESOURCES

Darkness Radio interview with Josh Gates of *Destination Truth*.

Geringer, Joseph. "The Dark Side". Court TV's *Crime Library*. 2005 Courtroom Television Network LLC.

Ghost Adventures (TV series). Episode 16. "Ancient Ram Inn." July 24, 2009.

Ghost Adventures (TV series) Episode 39. "Villisca Ax Murder House."

Ghost Adventures (TV Series) Episode 75. "Black Moon Manor." October 12, 2012.

Ghost Adventures (TV Series). Episode 76. "Sedamsville Rectory." October 19, 2012.

Ghost Lab (TV Series). Episode 2.05. "Theme Park Of Death." November 27, 2010.

Hall, Dan T. "The Haunting Of Fox Hollow Farm." Gravitas Ventures.

History Channel presents: *Unit 731: Nightmare In Manchuria*. A World Justice documentary.

Kurtis B., Stack J., Garbus L., and Manhardt M., (1997). *The Secret Life of a Serial Killer*. Produced by Gabriel Films, for A & E Network. New York, NY. Distributed by New Video Group, 1997.

Most Haunted. (TV series). Episode 64. "The Ancient Ram Inn." Antix Productions. January 29, 2005.

Paranormal Witness. (TV Series). Episode 2.04. "The Dybbuk Box." SyFy Original Series. August 29, 2012.

Paranormal Witness. "Fox Hollow Farm." SyFy Channel Original Series. September 26, 2012.

Patrick MacNee's Ghost Stories. Wilderness Films. Distributed by Madacy Entertainment. 1997.

Rundle, Kelly (director/writer). *Villisca: Living With A Mystery.* Fourth Wall Films. 2006.

The Hauntings Of Chicago. (TV Series). Episode 1. WYCC Channel 20. October 29, 2011.

INTERNET SOURCES OF RESEARCH MATERIALS

http://barrytaff.net
http://blackmoonmanor.net
http://paranormal.about.com
http://paranormal.about.com
http://paranormalworlds.com
http://questparanormalresearch.com
http://savannahnow.com
http://terrifyingtales.blogspot.com
http://theresashauntedhistoryofthetri-state.blogspot.com
http://voices.yahoo.com
http://whaleyhouse.org
http://whispersestate.net/
www.bellwitch.org
www.borleyrectory.co.uk/
www.crimelibrary.com
www.dibbukbox.com/
www.examiner.com
www.friendslittlebighorn.com
www.ghost-story.co.uk
www.guardian.co.uk
www.harryprice.co.uk/

www.hauntedamericatours.com
www.hauntedhouses.com
www.hauntedhouses.com
www.hauntedhovel.com/hannahhouse.html
www.haunted-places-to-go.com
www.legendsofamerica.com
www.lizzie-borden.com
www.lostdestinations.com
www.mostlyghosts.com
www.mysteriousbritain.co.uk
www.prairieghosts.com
www.rockymountainparanormal.com
www.sedamsvillerectory.com
www.seekjapan.jp
www.strangeusa.com
www.thehannahmansion.org/
www.travelchannel.com
www.trutv.com
www.villiscaiowa.com
www.wiccantradition.org.uk

Fox Hollow Farm, Westfield, IN (photo by author)

"EVIL, HOWEVER POWERFUL IT SEEMED,
COULD BE UNDONE BY ITS OWN APPETITE."
-CLIVE BARKER, THE THIEF OF ALWAYS

Hannah House, Indianapolis, IN (photo by author)

"YOU REALIZE THAT
OUR MISTRUST OF
THE FUTURE MAKES
IT HARD TO GIVE UP
THE PAST."
-CHUCK PALAHNIUK,
SURVIVOR

Our Lady Of Perpetual Help and its Rectory, Sedamsville, OH. (Photo by author)

"SOMETIMES HUMAN PLACES CREATE INHUMAN MONSTERS."
—STEPHEN KING,
THE SHINING

"DEATH MAKES ANGELS OF US ALL AND GIVES US WINGS WHERE
WE HAD SHOULDERS SMOOTH AS RAVENS CLAWS."
—JIM MORRISON, A FEAST OF FRIENDS

Sorg Mansion, Middletown, OH. (photo by author)

"LIFE IS ONLY A BEDTIME STORY
BEFORE A LONG, LONG SLEEP."
-ROBERT BLOCH, LORI